Deaths on Pleasant Street

Without doubt, the public generally refuses to believe, in the absence of positive proof, that a murder has been committed. It is too awful to be credible. If murder there was, it rivals the most grewsome [sic] tales of French fiction in its diabolical conception and boldness of execution. Every feature of the veiled hypothesis is a ghastly enigma of human depravity.

—*The Kansas City Journal,* Jan. 21, 1910

What a Gaborieau or a Conan Doyle might have done with such material may be left to the imagination. Here was a plot, the elaboration of which, in fictional form, might have produced the world's greatest detective story, though it would have taken a Poe to do full justice to a mind that could conceive the use of germ cultures to commit murder.

—*The New York World,* May 16, 1910

DEATHS
ON PLEASANT
STREET

The Ghastly Enigma
of Colonel Swope
and Doctor Hyde

Giles Fowler

Truman State University Press

Copyright © 2009 Truman State University Press, Kirksville, Missouri USA
All rights reserved
tsup.truman.edu

Cover art: Swope Residence, Independence, Mo., ca. 1892. Courtesy of Missouri Valley Special Collections, Kansas City Public Library, Kansas City, Missouri. Used by permission.

Cover design: Teresa Wheeler
Type: MinionPro © Adobe Systems Inc.; Raphael © Adobe Systems Inc.
Printed by: Edwards Brothers Inc., Ann Arbor, Michigan USA

Library of Congress Cataloging-in-Publication Data

Fowler, Giles, 1934–
Deaths on Pleasant Street : the ghastly enigma of Colonel Swope and Doctor Hyde / Giles Fowler.
    p. cm.
ISBN 978-1-931112-91-8 (pbk. : alk. paper)
1. Murder—Missouri—Case studies. 2. Swope family. I. Title.
HV6533.M8F69 2009
364.152'3092—dc22

                                                                        2009010471

To my children, and in memory of Helen and Jonathan.

Contents and Illustrations

Preface

There is probably a useful history to be done on the legal controversies of the century-old Hyde-Swope murder case, especially the question of whether justice was served in the long, grueling prosecution of the accused doctor. Such a project would require the labors of a historian or a law scholar, neither of which I am. Certainly my book is no such ambitious work. Its aim is simply to recount the story, as fully and accurately as I can, of one of the darkest, most baffling mysteries of the last century in the place where I grew up. Until now, the tale has never been the subject of a full-length book, although it has produced innumerable articles and other writings since 1909, the year it all began. Like every account before it, this one will raise more questions than it answers, and perhaps for that reason it will dissatisfy. But the object, really, wasn't to solve the mystery but to reproduce it, concretely, in scenes that would have the textures and immediacy of real experience.

I wish I could say every word of the book is true. But it is only true insofar as the source materials and my interpretations are true. And as every reporter knows, there are many "truths," too many of them pocked with errors, memory failures, lies, contradictions, and self-serving hype. However, I can say that nothing on these pages was made up out of whole cloth. When it was necessary to fall back on conjecture, I tried to make sure the assumptions were justified logically by the documented facts. Where the facts were unknown or blurred by conflicting versions, I tried to make that clear.

What amazed me at first, and then delighted me, was how rich in humanizing details the old records were. Again and again I came upon patches of action, interaction, high emotion, and dialogue that gave voice and personality to these beings from another time. Suddenly they were sentient, fallible, free-willed people. One such moment of discovery—out of hundreds—came while reading the statement of a young doctor, who feared he might inadvertently have aided in a horrible crime. Home from his office, he takes his small son sledding, undresses the child for bed, struggles to focus on his evening paper, and at last rouses his sleepy wife to share with her his anxieties.

From the first, I planned to use reconstructed scenes as the main building blocks of the narrative. Here again, the individual statements and court testimony were amazing treasuries of detailed information. Equally so were the memoirs and other non-official accounts by the players, not to mention the lavish files of contemporary newspapers. But the reliability of all these sources, even the sternest court documents, obviously varied in degree. Trial transcripts tell us what a witness said, not whether a word of it was true.

Newspaper accounts were approached with caution, with allowances for the general quality of the paper's coverage. Overall, the *Star*'s reporting was more complete, sober, and responsible than that of the flamboyant *Post*. At the same time, certain *Post* writers showed impressive gifts for colorful observation and narrative where a *Star* or *Times* reporter might offer only workaday accounts.

With all the pitfalls regarding accuracy, it fell to this writer to cross-check and double-check as much as possible, down to the floor plan of the mansion (never fully established), the placement of a telephone on the wall, and the final score of a college football game. One depiction of a shocking medical crisis in the Swope home had to be assembled from the memories of seven individuals drawn to the scene from various parts of the house. Fortunately they were able to validate each other's accounts.

Then there was the matter of what characters said. Every quotation in the book, direct or indirect, was taken from official documents, memoirs, letters, and newspaper stories. The challenge was to sort out the more accurate spoken passages from the less convincing and the obviously false. Direct witness testimony in court or in sworn statements was safe to quote, of course. Most quotations in the press were considered fairly reliable, especially if two or more papers agreed on what was said. But any speech recalled secondhand or allegedly overheard by chance or circulated as rumor had to be handled with care, if not extreme skepticism. Which quotes made their way into the book, and which didn't, sometimes depended on this reporter's ear for the clunk of a bogus comment. For this I make no apologies. Instinct, when all else fails, may serve the truth, too.

And still, it would take a naïve leap of faith to assume that this book is accurate in all respects. Factual errors and false assumptions will get through—they always do. The experienced journalist knows that the complete truth can be as elusive as fairy dust, but that doesn't excuse him from looking for it.

The research would not have been remotely possible without the help of skilled, knowledgeable professionals who took an interest in the project. For their generous sharing of time and expertise, I am deeply grateful to David Boutros of the Western Historical Manuscript Collection–Kansas City (holder of the James A. Reed papers); David W. Jackson of the Jackson County Historical Society (whose archives include the full transcript of the first trial); Mary Beveridge of the Missouri Valley Special Collections department of the Kansas City Public Library; and Derek Donovan and Janelle Hopkins of the *Kansas City Star* Library. Together, they provided access to the most essential information at the roots of my research.

If this project had a spiritual parent, so to say, it was the late Patrick D. Kelly, Dean Emeritus of the University of Missouri–Kansas City School of Law and a devoted student of the case. Besides sharing key legal insights, Dean Kelly donated useful documents and supported the author as a mentor and friend. Wherever he resides, I pray that he reads the book and approves of my handling of it.

I am equally indebted to Doctor Edward M. Bottei, Medical Director of the Iowa Statewide Poison Control Center, for a most unusual contribution. A toxicologist whose knowledge of poisons is nothing short of alarming, Doctor Bottei came up with a new and fascinating hypothesis of how Doctor Hyde may have ... well, read it for yourself.

Other bits of the narrative puzzle were furnished by assistant archivist Barbara Bernauer of the Community of Christ World Headquarters; Peggy Glover of Ozark National Life Insurance, headquartered in the former library where Colonel Swope lay in state; Ann McFerrin, archivist for Kansas City Parks; landscape architect Mike Ashley, who welcomed me into Colonel Swope's former office; Helen West, secretary of the First Presbyterian Church of Independence; and Bill Crick, former carpenter in the Swope mansion.

For guiding me to gravesites—the final settings of this somber tale—I am much obliged to T. J. Cochran of Mount Washington Cemetery; John Weilert, Bruce Mathews, and Richard Stewart of Elmwood Cemetery; and Kenneth Payne of Machpelah Cemetery in Lexington, Missouri.

Although most of the fact-gathering involved slogging through archival stacks, I was aided, too, by recently published works. Excellent books by Harry Haskell and Richard P. Coleman (see Sources) filled in social and physical details of the old Kansas City I attempted to sketch.

I must likewise salute former newsroom colleagues Charles Gusewelle, Steve Paul, and Brian Burnes for their advice and encouragements; my editor, Barbara Smith-Mandell, who nurtured the project with skill and care; and my family, who forgave me my many absences while I was off mining for the facts.

Finally, a nod of appreciation to another old *Kansas City Star* hand, Joseph A. Lastelic. It was he, forty-nine years ago, who wrote the fine article about the Hyde-Swope case that fired my interest in the misanthropic millionaire, the shadowy doctor, and the great, doomed house on the hill.

Chapter 1

I t was a Friday of all Fridays on the first of October in the best of all years. An almost palpable optimism, born of prosperity and civic promise, must have sparkled like harvest dust in the golden light. The weather was living up to the morning forecast in the *Kansas City Times*: yet another cloudless day, high in the 70s, in one of the milder months in these parts, a region still known to many, in 1909, as the American "Southwest." An engraving on that same front page showed drivers in open cars—"machines" was the fancy word for them—cruising down an electric-lighted avenue on a sweet, early autumn evening.

A headline in the right-hand column undoubtedly caught the satisfied eye of local boosters: "Business Goes on Growing." The story cited evidence that 1909 would show the greatest business expansion ever for Kansas City, Missouri, the get-up-and-grow metropolis that dwarfed every other town between the Missouri River and the West Coast. With its 248,000 citizens, indeed, it had lately become the twentieth most populous city in the United States, and was on the move toward nineteenth. And if it could have merged into a single city with Kansas City, Kansas, its neighbor of 82,000 souls across the state line, the total population would have outstripped that of Los Angeles and equaled the citizenry of Washington, DC.

All around, even in the sweet aroma of grain milling and the funky effluvia from the stockyards, swirled confirmations of wealth. To find them in abundance, you had only to climb into your motor car or buggy—most townsfolk still drove horse-drawn vehicles or relied on trolley and cable cars—and drive up the bluffs from the Missouri River into the jostling, clattering thoroughfares of downtown. The business district boasted skyscrapers with ornate entrances of red granite, marble, and terra cotta, a proud hall built to house the 1900 Democratic National Convention, a new public library of Renaissance Revival design with a grand baronial lobby, and suitably imposing temples of government and justice. Nor were the pleasures neglected. Theaters as gilded and filigreed as any in New York City offered productions both "legit" and vaudeville. Luxury hotels had their swell dining establishments with names like the Pompeian Room and the Savoy Grill, while citizens of less refined appetites could choose among the plentiful chophouses and free-lunch saloons. (The total number of taverns, "wine houses," and cafés serving strong drink in the city reportedly came to six hundred.) Shops and department stores along Eleventh Street, fancifully nicknamed Petticoat Lane, equaled in opulence those of K.C.'s much larger, snootier rival city, St. Louis.

———————

Signs of good times, civic pride, and capitalistic hubris did not end at the edges of downtown or nearby Quality Hill, the mansion-topped citadel of the town's old rich. With Kansas City's growing ownership of cars—its influx of Maxwells and Marmons, Mitchells and Hupmobiles, Stevens-Duryeas and coachlike Woods Electrics—city fathers were extending a boulevard system that not only served motorists but was also creating mile after mile of new subdivisions.

In a fanlike sweep from southeast to southwest of downtown, just beyond blocks of genteel apartments, whole neighborhoods of spanking new houses, many built of the locally quarried limestone, were sprouting over recent fields and newly tamed hills. Typical of the better-type middle-class home was the residence on a quiet side street of an up-and-coming 38-year-old surgeon, Doctor Bennett Clark Hyde, and his lovely, 30-year-old wife, the former Frances Swope of Independence, Missouri. The two-and-a-half-story stone and shingle house at 3516 Forest Avenue was as blocky and solid as a German dairy barn, though its overhanging eaves, broad porch, and big front windows were pure, post-Victorian Kansas City. It was convenient, too. A five-minute walk from the front door would take Doctor Hyde to his Troost Line trolley stop and thence on a three-and-a-half-mile ride to his office suite in the Keith and Perry Building downtown. For the Hydes it was domestic living at its coziest … and all of it made possible through the beneficence of Frances Hyde's extremely rich uncle, who had given the couple their home mortgage-free.

Forest Avenue, however, while pleasant in all respects, was far from the pinnacle of the good life in Kansas City. If you headed west and then south along Gillham and Rockhill Roads, Oak Street, Warwick Boulevard, and Wornall Road, you'd encounter the Olympian homes of lumber lords, meatpacking moguls, wheat speculators, and captains of real estate, insurance, banking, and newspaper publishing. An already established midtown neighborhood known as Hyde Park was rich with redbrick Queen Annes, Italianate villas, and stone manor houses of vaguely Tudor or Cotswolds design.

A newer district of upscale homes, still in the development process, was starting to blossom a couple of miles farther southwest, only blocks from the Kansas City Country Club, the city's foremost bastion of wealth and exclusivity. The club's very name lent cachet to the sprinkling of mini-mansions, maxi-cottages and top-dollar vacant home lots now known as the Country Club District. Those fortunate elect who actually *made* The Country Club could enjoy, as well as golf, the game of the British Raj: polo.

Only fifty-nine years after its incorporation as a rude trading and mercantile outpost on a mud-slimed riverbank, Kansas City had attained huge wealth as well as a measure of urbanity and … well … culture. For those with a taste for the finer things, there was first-rate theater at the Shubert and the Grand, the Gillis and the Willis Wood, where top road companies offered long seasons of comedy, modern drama (one play startlingly titled *The Nigger*), and the classics, of which Shakespeare was the runaway favorite. In a gorgeous, high-ceilinged room of the downtown library, the Western Gallery of Art displayed a collection of Old Masters reproduced in oil by the most skilled of European copyists.

Some of the power elite were pushing for a grand, freestanding art museum that would benefit "the industrial classes" as well as the bourgeoisie, and other culture mavens were raising funds to found a symphony orchestra.

If any single public amenity stood alone, however—stood above every possession and source of municipal pride—it was the gift that gave pleasure and recreation to practically everyone. Seven miles to the south and east of downtown lay the pristine 1,354-acre Swope Park, a benefaction of the aged real estate multimillionaire, Colonel Thomas Hunton Swope. At its founding, it was nothing less than the nation's third largest municipal park, in a town that grasped eagerly at anything it could brag about. And on this warm first weekend of October, Swope Park would be thronged with families who would lay out blankets on the grassy picnic grounds, stroll in the shade of majestic hardwoods, or hire rowboats from the pennant-topped boathouse on the Lagoon. The temperature tomorrow, Saturday, October 2, would reach the 80s.

———•—•———

Jackson County, Missouri, in 1909 was a curious place, a sort of geographic time-culture warp. Leaving the boisterous, industrial Kansas City and entering the county-seat town of Independence, you landed suddenly in the rural nineteenth century. There was no transition, no midway between realities. It must have been like missing a stair in the dark.

Less than three miles of rock road and a single trolley line connected the eastern limits of the metropolis to the western edge of Independence. But the satellite community, with fewer than 10,000 citizens, maintained a tone and civic identity quite unlike those of its beefy, parvenu neighbor. Founded in 1827, before Kansas City was even a respectable hamlet, Independence remained in its soul a country town—and never mind that it housed the bureaucracy and trappings of county government. It got to be county seat, presumably, because it was there first.

Independence was also, in ways both seen and felt, a *Southern* country town. Any visitor would have quickly recognized both the externals and the social idiosyncrasies of its Dixie heritage—it was the same with many towns throughout this former slave state. Although the populace had shown split loyalties during the Civil War, many of its old families took pride in bloodlines and landed origins in Virginia and Kentucky. A separate if equally colorful heritage could be claimed by local votaries of Joseph Smith III's Reorganized Church of Jesus Christ of Latter Day Saints, an off-shoot of the Mormons, which had established its world headquarters near the center of town.

Two Civil War battles had slashed through Independence, one leading to its two-day occupation by Rebel troops, and it's easy to visualize the local partisans praying for Union or Confederate victory from the safety of their root cellars. Forty-five years later, the local United Daughters of the Confederacy were proposing to memorialize the Rebel invader of Missouri, General Sterling Price, with a statue on the Courthouse square.

The brick square might have been lifted of a piece from any county seat in Tennessee (except for the courthouse itself, a stolid, charmless pile that owed nothing to Greek Revival elegance). Among the shop fronts, a few steps from Ott's Furniture Store and Undertaking Rooms, stood the two-story jail that once housed the bandit Frank James, brother of the legendary Jesse. Here and there along residential streets a few antebellum homes remained, but a building boom after the Civil War had introduced Victorian architecture of one fashion or another. Among the more charming houses was a large, lacy, white-frame residence on Delaware Street, where a 24-year-old woman named Bess Wallace would soon be courted by her former high school classmate, a dapper young Harry Truman.

Domestic grandeur was not commonly seen along the town's leafy avenues. But there were exceptions, one of the most stately of which could be found standing alone a few blocks southwest of the square. If ever a home's mass and placement were in perfect metaphoric symmetry, it was the mansion—the only word for it, really—at 406 South Pleasant Street.

Like some fortress of an imagined barony, a tribute to wealth

406 South Pleasant Street—The Swope Home, ca. 1908.
Jackson County (MO) Historical Society Archives (jchs004367m).

and rank, it sat facing east on a nineteen-acre estate, high atop
the highest hill in Independence. It was separated from the street
by some 900 feet of winding walk and asphalt drive, of garden-
edged lawns planted in white maples, elms, and pin oaks. The
place held twenty-six rooms in three stories, including a library,
a music room, and a third-floor ballroom. It boasted a full-size,
manually hoisted elevator. And the home's massive exterior was
one that only an ardent fan of late Victorian design could love—a
dissonant symphony, you could say, of unmatched parts. Scholars
of the period might call it something like Romanesque, or else just
give up and fall back on the all-purpose "eclectic." It was built of
brownish-red brick and sandstone, a peculiarly macabre color—
reminiscent of dried blood—that somehow found favor with archi-
tects in the late nineteenth century. The front entry wore classical
columns and a Greek pediment, but the long porch running off it
presented four hulking arches, as black within as open mouths.
Above the second story arose tall, fussy Flemish gables in serious

Mrs. Logan O. (Margaret) Swope, ca. 1898.
Courtesy Jackson County (MO) Historical Society Archives (jchs016719m); gift of Mrs. D. J. Hyde Matheny.

conflict with a heavy corner tower, its domed roof resembling the lid of a Bavarian beer stein.

Impressive, yes. Ostentatious, perhaps. But not outlandishly large for the extended family that lived there. After all, the house had to accommodate not only its owner, Mrs. Logan O. Swope, widow of a prominent Independence banker, but a semipermanent ménage of eight other family members—five of her seven children ranging from early adolescent to adult, two gentlemen relations who had moved in some years earlier, and a cousin and former governess now serving as companion to the younger daughters. The black cook and her two house-servant daughters, one only 10 years old, lived out back in a one-and-a-half-story, two-room cabin. Two black men-servants were also "about the place," as Mrs. Swope put it, but seem to have lived off the property.

What's more, on this particular day, this first Friday of October, it happened there were others around the house on South Pleasant. A teenaged friend of the younger daughters had been invited for a

Colonel Thomas Swope, 1908.
Courtesy Jackson County (MO) Historical Society Archives (jchs004887m); from a 1908 engraving.

visit. A local seamstress came and went. A private nurse had come two weeks ago to help care for the frail, octogenarian Colonel (Uncle Thomas) Swope residing on the second floor. With all these relatives, dependents, and visitors under her roof, Mrs. Swope was doubtless grateful for the space at everyone's disposal.

Yet living in the big house was not without its little bumps and abrasions, even for a woman as redoubtable as the household's *grande dame*. For Mrs. Logan Swope (her given name was Margaret, usually shortened to Maggie) putting up with the plaints and peculiarities of Uncle Thomas, her dead husband's brother, must have been trying at times. In fact, the old bachelor occupying the southwest bedroom was about the worst houseguest—*permanent* houseguest—that one could imagine. At almost 82, he was cranky, melancholic, misanthropic, and practically friendless. He had no patience for sociable chitchat. Afflicted by dyspepsia, he sometimes vomited while swallowing rich food. Age had weakened his bladder, which would empty without warning.

Things had grown even worse in the last eleven months since

he'd abandoned his longtime drinking habit, those noontime shots of spirituous comfort that left him comatose on his office couch. Deprived now of that solace, he was given to lamenting life's woes, predicting his imminent death to anyone who'd listen, or bellowing curses through his bedroom door. After slipping on a rug in the mansion's library and injuring a shoulder, he seldom left his room except by necessity and the family saw less and less of him. Which was probably a relief to all.

Colonel Swope was truly close to only one member of the household, his genial cousin James Moss Hunton. Hunton was also a "colonel," a title granted to both men strictly as a gesture of respect, neither having served in any army. Old Swope was also friendly enough with his sister-in-law Maggie, who had taken him in after a lifetime lived mostly in hotels. But he didn't seem to care much for her children, nor they for him. The smaller ones he frightened. Even the grown nephew who'd been named after him and should have enjoyed that special kinship between namesakes had not had a conversation with the old man in four years.

Yet on this October Friday—and for several days previous—Uncle Thomas seemed in better-than-usual spirits, a bit improved both in mind and body. Perhaps it was the buggy rides he and Nurse Pearl Kellar had been taking together, the fresh air and sunshine he'd absorbed on these twelve-mile jaunts down country roads.

It is not even farfetched to imagine that this morning he had thrown open a bedroom window and let himself be drenched by the limpid perfection of all he beheld. So much *brighter* than the room at his back, really, although the chamber was spacious and handsome by the somber tastes of high-Victorian décor, its woodwork fashioned of rare bird's-eye maple. If Uncle Thomas needed Nurse Kellar, he had an electric button to summon her. She had planned for him another outing in the buggy this afternoon.

And thus, on a cheerier note than usual, began the shimmering final weekend in the worthy life of Colonel Thomas Hunton Swope, philanthropist, civic visionary, donor of the great Swope Park, and resident eccentric at the red-walled mansion on South Pleasant Street.

Chapter 2

Just about anyone would assume that Bennett Clark Hyde of Kansas City—surgeon, physician, a real up-and-comer in his field—would be an ideal match for the beautiful eldest daughter of Mrs. Logan (Maggie) Swope. He was handsome in a scholarly kind of way, with a wide, straight mouth, a strong chin and deep-set eyes often seen behind pince-nez spectacles. His hair, slicked down and parted near the center, was of reddish gold. He was six feet tall and of manly build. And my, how his smile could charm—patients, colleagues, friends. And young women. A female ex-patient, who had first met him when she was a child about to have her adenoids removed, called him "the handsomest young man I had ever seen." His voice was "so seductive that he made me feel I was doing him a favor when he asked me to let him give me the chloroform. I have thought since he had such an effect on a little girl, how he must have enchanted the young ladies."

And he was cultivated. A graduate of William Jewell College in Liberty, Missouri, he had excelled in his scientific studies and developed a taste for the classics. He knew his Bible, could deliver entire Shakespearean soliloquies, and could recite poems by Archilochus, Goldsmith, and Kipling. He was said to have a fine singing voice.

The fellow showed real professional promise, too. Right after earning his shingle from the University Medical College in Kansas City, he'd been trusted enough by city officials to win appointment as official police surgeon, handling all the sad and violent emergency cases that bloodied the town's meaner streets day and night. The job paid a decent salary—$125 a month. It afforded him not

Dr. Bennett Clark Hyde, Sept. 13, 1904. Courtesy Jackson County (MO) Historical Society Archives (jchs0088801); Strauss Peyton Photographic Studio Collection (negative no. 12821).

only a living but also enough left over to let him pay off his college debts, as any chap of character would insist on doing as promptly as possible. In 1898, with the help of unsecured loans from friends, Hyde went into private practice and was clearly a young man headed in the right direction.

By the time he began courting Frances Swope in 1903, he was starting to build a nice array of professional credentials: teaching posts in medical colleges, surgery affiliations in two of the city's hospitals, memberships in all the requisite medical associations. Six years later, he'd be elected president of the Jackson County Medical Society, the indisputable hallmark of respect among his peers.

As if all this weren't enough, his family pedigree could hardly have been better. The Swopes in their hilltop mansion may have possessed wealth and a distinguished Kentucky heritage, but Clark Hyde's ancestry (except for the wealth part; his family was closer to genteel poor) was no less notable by the standards of the day in this region of America. Son of a widely respected Baptist minister

**Frances Swope,
ca. 1904.**
Courtesy Jackson County
(MO) Historical Society
Archives (jchs016723m); gift
of Mrs. D. J. Hyde Matheny.

who'd served as a Confederate Army chaplain and was a trustee of two Missouri colleges, Hyde was born on a grandfather's farm called Cedar Lawn in Cooper County, Missouri. Both of his parents were descended from old-line gentry with origins in Virginia, Kentucky, and frontier Missouri. In fact, if the Swope and Hyde genealogies were viewed side by side, the parallels would be striking. The Swopes traced their lineage to the Hohenzollern kings of Prussia, the Hydes to the seventeenth-century Earls of Shaftsbury and Clarendon. The Swopes were linked to Virginia's landed aristocracy and Mrs. Swope herself was born into the eminent local Chrisman family of bankers, landowners, and judges. The Hydes claimed kinship to Revolutionary War hero General George Rogers Clark.

So it would appear, back in 1905 when 33-year-old Bennett Clark Hyde proposed marriage to the dark-eyed, 25-year-old Frances Swope, that their betrothal would have set off the usual rejoicing.

It was quite the opposite. Maggie Swope, Frances's mother, seems to have thrown what rural Missourians called a hissy fit. And all because of certain … indiscretions that hardly befitted a gentleman, let alone the son of a Baptist parson.

It was darkly—and accurately—rumored that Clark Hyde had shown himself to be a cad in his relationships with two Kansas City divorcées. Worse than a cad—a welsher. One Sarah Frank had accused the doctor of trifling with her affections, making a false promise of marriage, and borrowing $2,200 from her that he never repaid. Soon after, the former Mrs. Mike Heim, lately divorced from a local brewer, claimed Hyde had courted her, indicated a wish to marry, and borrowed $4,000 she had received as alimony from Mister Heim.

Somehow Maggie Swope had heard the whisperings about his past. Though she may not have known all the sordid details, she was not about to let the marriage proceed. Indeed, Hyde's chances of wedding Frances now appeared nil. Only after his lawyer provided a less dreadful version of his peccadilloes did the nuptial plans get back on track. The attorney acknowledged that his client had behaved like a bounder, but he denied that Hyde had bilked the women for money. Mrs. Swope was not mollified, but she agreed against her better judgment to let the engagement be announced.

What happened next was the calamity scene of an Edwardian melodrama. One of the cheated divorcées suddenly came forward demanding repayment of her money and crying lawsuit if it was denied. (Ultimately, the suits brought by both women were settled out of court.) The enraged Maggie Swope canceled the engagement forthwith and ordered Hyde never to darken her tile-floored front hall again.

In fact there had been a more disturbing incident involving the disgraced suitor, though it's doubtful it had come to Mrs. Swope's attention by 1905. The alleged offense was worse than womanizing or unpaid debts and it cast a demon shadow across the doctor's past that would haunt him for years to come. In 1897, when Hyde was in his second year as Kansas City police surgeon, he was accused of performing a most loathsome act of cruelty on a black woman named Annie Clements.

After ingesting or pretending to swallow morphine during a bout of depression, Clements had been taken to police headquarters where Hyde examined her. Moments later, by her account, a jail turnkey held her down while Hyde poured oil of mustard into her vagina and shouted, "Now, God damn you Annie, get up and get out of here and don't come back any more." Her agony was such, Clements said in her official complaint, that she could neither walk nor stand, and had crawled more than a block before a policeman came to her aid. The incident led to a hearing before the Board of Police Commissioners, which fired Hyde from his post. The doctor's story was that he had used the mustard-oil treatment simply to rouse the woman from her drugged stupor, and he insisted the cruelty charge had been trumped up by political enemies on the police board. There may have been some truth to the latter claim. Rival City Hall factions at the time did not exactly abide by lofty Jeffersonian principles in divvying up plum city jobs. A political shake-up of the police board had indeed occurred just before Hyde's dismissal.

Whatever the facts of the matter, it seems certain that the tale would have been too shocking even for the love-smitten Frances to stomach. As for Hyde's two erstwhile lady friends, about whom she must have been told, Frances was either disbelieving or willing to forgive. She made it quite clear to her mother that nothing would separate her from the man she loved.

Whereupon her mother took the usual steps favored by wealthy parents of obdurate daughters. First she played the family-elder card, appealing to old Uncle Thomas Swope to talk sense to the young woman. He apparently refused to get involved. Mrs. Swope's next move, according to some reports, was to banish her daughter to a female college called Monticello (which is questionable, given the fact that Frances had graduated from Monticello in 1899). At any rate the young woman's ardor was unabated, and she even rebuffed her mother's offer of a trip to Europe.

Another family member called in to exert his influence was Frances's dear Cousin Moss—Colonel James Moss Hunton. He had been living in the Swope mansion at the time her father died and was adored by all the children as a doting surrogate parent. Cousin Moss, too, got nowhere in changing Frances's heart, and her mother's final stratagem, to shuttle her off to Virginia, was equally unsuccessful.

Instead of accepting exile in Virginia, Frances made her way south to Fayetteville, Arkansas, to the home of a more liberal-minded male cousin of her mother's. The sympathetic relative at first tried to talk Mrs. Swope into letting the marriage take place after all, back home in Independence. Maggie Swope would have none of it, but soon enough the issue was moot. Clark Hyde had arranged to meet Frances in Fayetteville, and on June 21, 1905, the two were married by a Presbyterian minister in the elderly relative's parlor, before a passel of well-wishing cousins.

The outmaneuvered Maggie Swope did not accept defeat gracefully. There began a fourteen-month estrangement between mother and eldest daughter, during which neither visited the other's home. That a reconciliation finally took place in August of 1906 may be ascribed to a mother's tenderness—or perhaps to the newlyweds' skills for exploiting it. One day, after learning her son-in-law was stricken by a rheumatoid iris and confined to a dark room, Maggie Swope paid a sympathy call. It was the sort of thing a Christian lady just *did*. While she was there, Mrs. Swope also had a woman-to-woman talk with Frances, an intriguing scrap of which is preserved in court records. While discussing Hyde, according to the mother, Frances urged that she "assist her in making a man of him." No one can know exactly what making a man of him referred to. But Mrs. Swope was somehow touched by her visit with Frances and the ice floe between them began to break up.

Hyde's own elevation from pariah to accepted family member came shortly thereafter and was almost serendipitous. Mrs. Swope's second son, Tom Swope (named after his Uncle Thomas and sometimes known as Young Tom or Tom Junior), had been working at a mine in Tonopah, Nevada, when his right arm was mangled in a machinery mishap. When Mrs. Swope learned the arm had been amputated, she hurried to Nevada, bringing along her surgeon son-in-law for his medical expertise. Hyde treated the injured Tom with such gentleness and care that, as far as the Swopes were concerned, he was a redeemed man.

Redeemed but not *embraced*. Not *loved*—except of course by daughter Frances, who may have been oblivious to any family coolness shown toward her husband. At least the situation was peaceful enough that the newlyweds felt comfortable visiting the Swopes' Independence mansion every two or three weeks for Sunday dinner.

Still, something—what was it?—continued to distance the family from him. The Swopes' later comments about the young doctor didn't add up. Mrs. Swope recalled that he had never been affectionate or confidential with any of the family, yet she characterized the relationship after 1906 as "very friendly." The Swopes questioned whether Frances was happy in her marriage, yet Maggie Swope insisted that Hyde had enjoyed the family's "full confidence and trust."

This ambivalence people felt... surely it had as much to do with Clark Hyde's personal manner as with anything else. Court testimony, newspaper features, and other accounts suggest a personality in conflict with itself. Hyde is seen as both cordial and aloof, an amusing companion in a social setting, but cold and brusque with those he felt unworthy of his regard. With fellow doctors he showed collegiality and respect. In tense situations, he displayed less personable traits—an unseemly pushiness, a pride bordering on arrogance, and a defensive tendency toward snappishness and sarcasm. There were even those who claimed that the doctor had two different smiles. The first, the natural one, was endearingly genuine, everyone agreed on that. But the other was disconcertingly mechanical. *Click,* it flashed on, as if by some deliberate internal switch. And *click,* it would vanish. Or were those who remarked on it just imagining things?

The one dweller in the Swope residence who may truly have liked Clark Hyde was, oddly enough, crotchety Uncle Thomas Swope, who liked practically no one. At some point, perhaps even before the controversial marriage (which he hadn't approved of), the reclusive Colonel had somehow taken a shine to the doctor. On visits to the mansion, Hyde made a point of climbing the back stairway to the old gentleman's bedroom, where the two men would sit together discussing the classics and other learned subjects (Uncle Thomas, too, was an educated man with a passion for literature). It

16

didn't hurt, either, that the doctor had shown concern over Colonel Swope's health and offered bits of sound medical advice. In time he was even accepted as the Colonel's very own special physician. So instead of sharing the rest of the family's misgivings about the new son-in-law, Thomas Swope decided that Hyde was "a pretty bright fellow" and told a business associate he guessed the young man would make good.

No sooner had peace been restored in the family than Colonel Swope bought the couple their house on Kansas City's Forest Avenue, with its rough-cut stone, its small but sunny rooms, and its

THE HYDE HOME, 3516 FOREST AVENUE.
MRS. HYDE WAS A NIECE OF COL. T. H. SWOPE.
Kansas City Times, Sat., Jan. 15, 1910, p. 1.

east-facing porch where one could rock on a glider, shaded against the summer heat. The cost, including furnishings, was $10,000, which Uncle Thomas paid with a single check.

Two years later, the Colonel did his nephew-in-law another favor, perhaps a greater one. At the urging of Colonel Moss Hunton, who also appears to have decided Doctor Hyde was a good risk, Thomas Swope used his considerable influence with local authorities to get Hyde a position at City Hospital. For the doctor it was a significant professional advancement and a further lift to his reputation. One has to wonder, though, whether Uncle Thomas's contacts at City Hospital made any effort to check into Hyde's previous record as a public-service doctor. Or did they simply ignore the disagreeable business of the black woman he had treated with oil of mustard while serving as police surgeon?

If any of the Swopes had ever doubted Hyde's giftedness and worthiness as a medical man, there were no such qualms now. That much is certain. Had there been any lingering distrust, they would surely not have summoned Doctor Hyde on that balmy evening when something awful happened to Colonel Moss Hunton.

———•◦•———

For the last few days, 63-year-old Cousin Moss had been feeling unwell and uncharacteristically low-spirited. This was noticed by members of the household but was attributed either to an upset stomach or to wounded feelings over some recent mistreatment by his cousin, Colonel Swope. If the old grouch had subjected Hunton to one of his typical choleric outbursts, it was really unforgivable.

How could anyone find fault in Hunton? He was Swope's most loyal (and doubtless most long-suffering) friend, a confidant in all matters, an executor of his estate. For years Hunton had met the old man each evening at the Independence trolley stop—Swope always took the streetcar from his office in Kansas City—and had driven him in the buggy to the Swope residence three blocks south in order to spare his aged legs.

They all loved Hunton. Not just the Swopes, but the whole town. A stout, rubicund man only five feet seven inches tall, he exuded warmth and joviality—Santa without the beard, as one neighbor child described him. Later he grew a full, bushy one, though unlike St. Nick's it was dark colored. He was a natural with kids, distributing pocketfuls of gumdrops and small change. His debonair dress added a certain dash—always the black cutaway coat, the derby, and the red carnation winking from his lapel. And, as the wellborn often are, he was the very opposite of a snob.

The son of a New Orleans judge, related through his grand-mother to Thomas Jefferson, he grew up in Kentucky where, like his Swope cousins, he definitely qualified as a blue blood of the bluegrass state. But in the business and social circles of Independence, he fit right in. Hunton had been living with the Swope family for three years when Maggie Swope's banker husband died. He had made himself so useful and was so popular with the Swope children that there was no question he'd be urged to stay on. Now he was a director of the town's Chrisman-Sawyer Bank as well as manager of Mrs. Swope's financial affairs. Beloved. Indispensable. Linchpin of the Swope household. That was Cousin Moss.

Which would account for the family's utter shock and distress over the sudden crisis that disrupted the supper hour on Friday, October 1.

Sometime around 5:30, Cousin Moss had gone down to have supper alone. The dining room with its commodious table and massive built-in sideboard was much too large for solitary dining, but the servants had asked for the night off and Hunton, always considerate, was glad to finish up early and get out of their way.

As he sat eating, he noticed Nurse Pearl Kellar passing nearby and asked her to join him. That was typical. Moss always welcomed company—even that of the stiffly correct, sharp-featured, business-like Nurse Kellar, who had just brought Colonel Swope home from their afternoon buggy ride and gotten the old gent ready for bed.

Kellar was about halfway through her meal when Mrs. Swope and her third oldest daughter, also named Margaret, arrived home from the ladies' social ritual of "calling." They were joined in the dining room by one of the younger Swope daughters and a teen-aged friend. That's when the nurse heard Hunton say, "Things look

Swope Mansion Dining Room, ca. 1908.
Courtesy Jackson County (MO) Historical Society Archives (jchs016721am);
gift of Mrs. D. J. Hyde Matheny.

so queer; I feel so dizzy."

For an instant she thought it was just his biliousness acting up. But when Cousin Moss reached for his water glass, his right hand was shaking so violently that half the liquid sloshed out. "What do you reckon is the matter, Miss Kellar?" he said. She moved to his side and told him it was probably nothing. But he clung to her like a feverish 5-year-old and kept asking, "Don't you suppose I am awfully sick? I don't want to be sick."

Twenty-year-old Margaret Swope also rushed over to help, and someone produced a fan. The nurse advised against using it because Hunton was lathered in sweat and it might give him a chill. As usual, competent Kellar was taking charge. "Mister Hunton," she said, "I think you had better go to the library and lie down." He struggled to rise, but his right leg gave out, as if paralyzed, and he fell back. The nurse and a black manservant then hoisted the stricken man's chair and trundled him, seated, to the library, where they stretched him out on a couch.

Mrs. Swope, meanwhile, dashed up to the second-floor sitting room and telephoned Doctor George T. Twyman, the family's regular physician and trusted friend. She ordered another daughter to phone "Sister," Frances Hyde, in Kansas City, and urge her and Doctor Hyde to hurry to Independence. Then Mrs. Swope returned to the library and asked Hunton if he felt better. He said, "I don't know," and his left hand began wandering about his face as if some other force—invisible marionette strings—were dragging at it. "I would rather be dead than to be sick and be a burden to you all," he managed to say. His voice was thickening. His normally florid face was ashen. Then it grew red again—darker than red. Purplish.

Nurse Kellar remembered that Colonel Swope, in his room upstairs, hadn't been fed. She left the library just long enough to see that someone took up the Colonel's tray and let him know his Cousin Moss was seriously ill. When she got back to the library she found that Doctor Twyman had arrived. Hunton was twitching all over. Suddenly he gushed vomit onto his chest and the floor. Twyman suggested he be carried upstairs, and Mrs. Swope came up with the idea of using an ironing board as a stretcher. Thus the patient was borne by two menservants to Maggie Swope's own room at the southeast corner of the house, where she thought he'd be more comfortable than in his own bed. Comfort was now irrelevant, Hunton having lost consciousness.

Twyman, both the son and the father of doctors, was the kind of solid, old-fashioned practitioner who emanated competence and good sense—the Village Doc, stern-featured yet gentle, in a BBC mystery series. Before initiating treatment he preferred to consult with Doctor Hyde, who was on his way from Kansas City in a hired car. He didn't have to wait long. Within ten minutes after Twyman and Kellar had put poor Cousin Moss to bed, the Hydes were in the second-floor sickroom ready to go to work.

No one doubted it was apoplexy—the disabling shock of a cerebral hemorrhage. Doctors at the time routinely recommended bleeding to reduce the arterial pressure, like tapping off boiling water from an overfilled kettle. Pulling off his coat, Hyde borrowed a scalpel from Twyman's medical bag and proceeded to cut the incision on the inside of Hunton's right arm. At first the doctors had trouble getting a proper flow, but soon the blood was spurting nicely into the "pus basin" Nurse Kellar had brought to catch it.

Everyone was tense, on edge. For one thing, old man Swope had been yelling his usual curse-laden diatribes from his bedroom down the hall—no one was sure what had set him off. Then there were these loud, labored, guttural sounds from the patient himself, which were getting on Hyde's nerves. He ordered Kellar to hold Hunton's jaw a certain way to stop the noises, but she was having trouble getting the right grip because of her awkward position across the bed. Hyde, clearly annoyed, snapped at her impatiently. Kellar wasn't the type to lose composure but, as she later admitted, she was definitely unstrung until Frances Hyde stepped in to help her hold Moss's jaw.

About a pint of blood had been taken when Twyman said he thought that was probably sufficient. Hyde disagreed. He felt Hunton's pulse, told his colleague that still more should be tapped off, and resumed the bloodletting.

Twyman's uneasiness grew. Once or twice more he said to Hyde, "I think that's about enough." He and Nurse Kellar both checked Hunton's pulse and said they believed it was definitely softening. Hyde argued that the patient's ruddy coloring showed the pressure was still too high; the older doctor reminded him that Hunton's face was *always* ruddy. Twyman even told a little story about a patient he'd heard of whose doctor had mistakenly bled him to death. He hoped Hyde would take the hint.

If Hyde caught the hint, he wasn't acting on it. The bleeding continued. Finally, the exasperated Twyman picked up the slop jar into which Kellar had been emptying the blood, tipped it sideways, and told Hyde to take a look. "That is enough blood to take from any man," he said. "Let's quit." The appeal was seconded by a close friend of Hunton's who'd been invited into the sickroom, banker A. H. Ott.

Frances Hyde, who had been watching the whole thing closely, must have felt a bit of the same alarm. "Dearie, I believe I would quit," she told her husband. "Doctor Twyman seems to think you have bled him enough and I would quit."

"Very well, I will do so," Hyde said.

Minutes later, as the doctor was nearly done bandaging up the incision, Hunton went into a brief seizure, gasped, and was dead. It was around 8:30 p.m.

Kellar was out of the room when it happened. One of the doctors—most likely Twyman—had asked her to step out and measure the blood in the slop jar. Using a silver cup that held something under a pint, she had measured out six cupfuls. She later found that the total volume of blood in the jar amounted to four pints, or two full quarts.

Or did it? Hyde and his wife later swore that the slop jar had held much more than blood—it also contained the water that had been thrown there after it was used to wash Hunton's arm. The actual amount of blood drawn from Hunton's vein, Hyde claimed, was between two and three pints.

This wasn't the only discrepancy between Nurse Kellar's account of the night's events and Doctor Hyde's. Her story, told and sworn to at least four times in the next few months, varied hardly a word with each repeating and would prove more than a bit troublesome for the doctor.

The worst of it, from Hyde's standpoint, was the part covering the hours directly following Hunton's death. Kellar stated that twenty minutes after Cousin Moss had died, Hyde saw her in the hall, emerged from the upstairs sitting room, and said, "As soon as you have some leisure I want to have a private talk with you." She was busy preparing the body for the undertaker's arrival and really didn't have time for a conversation. After an hour and a half, however, the embalmer had shown up and begun his ministrations on the dead man, and Kellar was free to talk. The family had gone to bed and the sitting room was empty.

She and Hyde stepped in, and Hyde started off on a note of commiseration. "Isn't this awful?" he said. He offered a few words about Moss Hunton's many fine qualities, then smiled and got to the point: "I want you to do something for me tomorrow. Now, I am not a businessman, but I can be. And now that this man Hunton is gone, who was one of the administrators of Mister Swope's will,

23

I want you—you have influence with the old man—I want you to suggest me in his stead. Mister Swope has in mind putting in this man Hawthorne, who has been a justice of the peace, and who has a dirty record."

According to Kellar, Hyde also observed—significantly—that Colonel Swope in a few days would be making a new will.

Kellar's reply invited no argument. "Doctor Hyde, I came to care for Colonel Swope in a purely professional way, and the moment I begin to interfere with his private affairs I am overstepping my bounds."

Hyde let the matter drop until late the following evening, when audacity got the better of prudence. Meeting the nurse in the hall, he asked, "Miss Kellar, have you broached that subject to Mister Swope?" She said, "No, Doctor Hyde," and that was that.

Understandably, Hyde would deny that either exchange took place on those nights. It was his word against Kellar's, with no witness to say which of these powerful personalities possessed the truth.

On Monday afternoon, October 4, Moss Hunton received a lovely graveside service in Mount Washington Cemetery two miles west of town. Schools were closed for a day of mourning and hundreds of children attended the service. The casket was carpeted in red carnations.

There was one troubling distraction, however. The funeral-goers—indeed, citizens throughout Jackson County—had been shocked to learn that very morning of a second death in the hilltop mansion at 406 South Pleasant Street. The news had spread by headline, phone line, and talk on the street. It was bigger news even than the day's other big story—the launching of Kansas City's weeklong Priests of Pallas festival, the crowning celebration of the glorious year 1909.

Chapter 3

Colonel Swope knew he'd be dead soon. He wasn't sure when or how, but it wouldn't be long before the dark angel would come rapping at his chamber door. In fact he prophesied his demise so often in those last weeks, and to so many people, that you'd think he was yearning for his escape from the triple ordeal of old age, frailty, and sobriety.

Eleven months! That's how long he'd been off the bottle, except for one tiny relapse during an especially miserable day. His office mate and employee, Sylvester Spangler, who looked after his real estate holdings and served as a kind of private secretary, happened to have a bottle of apple brandy someone had left as a gift. Swope swallowed only one teaspoonful, lay back on his couch for a minute or so, and said, "It done me a world of good, Spangler." Apparently he never touched a drop again—which was quite an achievement for a man who'd fortified himself with generous tumblers of whiskey almost every day for at least twenty-five years.

By these final months of that life, however, Swope was feeling ganged up on by the demons of decrepitude. A year before, he'd had surgery for piles that left him much weakened. His gastric problems had become so acute that he complained of them constantly and kept tossing back digestive tablets called Pape's Diapepsin. He was hurting from an accidental injury inflicted by a doctor who was treating him for mucous discharges of the nose and throat. In an effort to build back his energy he was taking thrice-daily doses of an elixir of iron, quinine, and strychnine recommended by some sympathetic soul. There were no signs it was helping.

No wonder the old man was growing increasingly gloomy and fatalistic. Even before the fall in the Swope library that caused him further aches and immobility, Swope seemed ready to give up. On September 4, one of the last days he spent in his downtown office, a business acquaintance had congratulated him on looking so well and predicted he'd feel even better once the hot weather ended.

"I'm getting too far along for that now," Swope had replied. "My nervous system is so badly shattered and I suffer so intensely all the time that I expect to be dead and buried within ninety days. If I do not die within that time I shall be very much surprised—and a little disappointed. I am perfectly willing and ready to die. Life has held few pleasures for me, and few are left now. I must surely gain more by death than I'll lose. I'm tired of people and more tired of myself. I read a great deal just to keep my mind off myself."

One bit of reading material by his bedside was Metchnikoff's *Prolongation of Life*. Maybe he was scanning it for ideas to help him eke out a few more weeks. But his estimates of the time left to him—anywhere from one to three months—suggest that he had no illusions of stalling the inevitable. He told Spangler that an uncle of his who had given up strong drink had died exactly ninety days later. By that calculus, Swope should have been in his grave eight months ago.

It was clear to everyone that he was no longer the vigorous Thomas Hunton Swope who had seen Kansas City's future as a western metropolis and developed vast properties to make it happen. He didn't look well. His body, never robust, had noticeably lost flesh. His face with its patrician nose, slightly receding chin, and well-barbered mustache, was now a sickly gray that emphasized his baldness. He tottered when he walked. And there were more alarming physical signs. Swope suffered fainting spells on the street, in elevators, in the hall of the building. At times in the last year, peculiar noises would issue from his mouth—"oo-oo-oo," as Spangler imitated them.

Swope had not actually done much of anything in the seven years since he'd hired Spangler. The Colonel would come each day to his modest office on the fifth floor of the New England Building, would spend the morning reading (a black iron fireplace lent coziness in winter), would break for his midday libations in the bar of the nearby New York Life Building, and would take to his couch in the afternoon to sleep off the red-eye. At office-closing time, the 46-year-old Spangler—a model of patience and solicitude—would help the Colonel board a trolley car outside the New England Building, and soon after would drive his buggy a few blocks east to help his unsteady boss transfer to a second trolley for the ride home to Independence. Somehow one imagines Spangler as a meek, spindly Bob Cratchit figure, but in fact he was portly and plump-faced and wore the full mustache one associates with barbershop baritones.

It is tempting but unjust to write off Thomas Swope merely as an antisocial, self-pitying old grouch who happened to be one of the richest citizens of Jackson County. To do so would ignore the baffling complexities of a man who made his fortune with almost magical ease, who promoted scholarship and was himself highly learned, who dedicated much of his energy to improving life for the poor (especially poor children), who had an endearing affection for animals (especially mistreated ones), and who, above all else, was the most generous public benefactor Kansas City had ever known. Perhaps it would take a modern-day psychiatrist to make sense of, and to reconcile, the conflicting aspects of Thomas Swope's tormented being.

How, for instance, could one square the young Swope's itch for adventure with his delicate, bookish nature as a student at Central (now Centre) College in Danville, Kentucky? A fellow alumnus of the class of 1848, Senator George Graham Vest of Missouri, recalled that Swope was so fragile of spirit that he once fainted while making an oral presentation. Swope went on to study law for a year at Yale but found the legal calling was not for him. He could have returned to his old Kentucky home in Danville and become a merchant like his father. Instead, he obeyed a bolder inner voice and headed out West, invested in some mines, and made his way back to the raw, unruly, and quite dangerous Missouri-Kansas border. By 1857, he'd established himself in Kansas City, or what there was of it (population 2,500).

Though Swope had been credited with uncanny foresight, it didn't take a Nostradamus to see that the town had to grow south—could *only* grow south—from its perch on the river's south bank. Using his modest inheritance, he plunked down $7,500 for a large piece of Tom Smart's farm, started dividing his parcel into lots, and in no time at all, it seems, he owned nearly all the land that would become downtown Kansas City, Missouri.

It was as simple as that. Much of the property he sold too cheaply, but he held on to other prime locations where those proto-skyscrapers and retail emporiums would spring up like the palaces of Babylon. And the income rolled in—from newer urban properties, from farm investments southeast of town, from three mines in the Rockies. Even after giving away untold thousands in cash and huge tracts of land, he possessed a fortune of at least $3.6 million. In 1909 that was real money.

And it was not enough—*nothing* could be enough—to make Thomas Swope happy.

Maybe if he had married … but he told friends that by the time he could support a wife, no woman would have him. Did he take pleasure in his reputation as civic visionary and real estate wizard? According to a widely circulated story, he was once overheard muttering to himself, "You're an old fool, Tom Swope." A young passerby who heard the words could not let them go unchallenged and begged to disagree: Swope had certainly been smart enough to amass a fortune and assure the city's permanent gratitude for his magnificent public gifts.

"Me smart?" Swope is said to have countered. "I owned all of downtown, almost. I sold it here and there for a few hundred a lot. I have never done a day's work in my life; I have never earned a dollar in my life. There were two of these lots I couldn't sell. One was a deep hole in the ground, a pond; the other was an ugly clay hill. Nobody would give me anything for them, nobody thought they were worth anything, so I kept them—and they made me rich. That is no credit to me."

The tale sounds a bit pat, like the work of an over-inventive reporter. Still, the tone of it is accurate. Swope's self-effacement, his almost pathological shyness, his discomfort with public adulation, are underscored in every account of his life. One story has it that the Colonel even ducked out of the Swope Park jubilee—attended by 18,000 citizens—that marked the official opening of the great park on June 25, 1896. If the story is true, he may simply have preferred to walk away than to sit through two hours of embarrassing accolades from the speakers' rostrum.

What prompted Colonel Swope to become a chronic, almost compulsive civic benefactor can only be guessed. He was not an especially religious man. Some who knew him spoke of his innate, uncomplicated kindness, others of his desire to repay the town for the opportunities it had opened to him. In any case, he gave and gave.

He gave substantially to his alma mater, Central College, to which he donated half the cost of a new library. He gave the land for a badly needed new General Hospital. He gave a new building site and an impressive cash gift to a charitable institute that benefited the city's poor children and struggling mothers. He gave liberally to the Women's Christian Association, the YWCA, the YMCA, the Provident Association, and the Humane Society (he even hatched a plan to provide summer vacations for overworked draft horses). Among his innumerable smaller charities, he set aside a posthumous fund to provide annual picnics in Swope Park for thousands of slum kids.

And he almost gave Kansas City the most grandiose gift of all, a great art museum modeled on either Washington's Corcoran Gallery or Buffalo's Albright Museum (accounts differ as to which one he fancied). The dream museum was to have been erected near the front gate of Swope Park, but for reasons that remain somewhat vague, the project fell through. The most common explanation is that Swope backed off after he realized the staggering cost of the art palace's all-marble construction. Even the famous philanthropist had his limits.

Still, none could deny that Swope Park was legacy enough— this vast pleasure ground that was the city's pride and its favorite weekend retreat. It was a source of delight for everyone, it seemed, but Swope. As far as anyone knew, the man who'd begotten it never visited its pastoral acres again, not once, after that opening day in 1896.

Giving held no lasting joy, either. Late in life Colonel Swope felt unloved and unappreciated. Loneliness clung about him like a sodden blanket. He told an acquaintance, "I am rich but I am alone in the world. Nobody invites me to his home. Nobody wants to see me. Nobody comes to my office except to ask for something. I have given ground to institutions now known in the names of others. I don't care about that, but who remembers those gifts?"

The Colonel had made a will in 1905 bequeathing generous amounts of money and real estate to worthy charities and institutions. After his death, some citizens were surprised to learn there was no single super-gift along the lines of that dream museum, but they had to admit that old man Swope had long since paid his dues for sainthood.

In line for patrimonies great and small were various family members and a friend or two (loyal Sylvester Spangler would receive a mere $2,500). Swope's ten nieces and nephews, including the seven children of his sister-in-law Maggie Swope, would inherit blocks of high-rental real estate as direct bequests. These properties ranged in value from $136,000 to $270,000—not lavish but not insubstantial by the standards of the day.

It turned out that niece Frances Hyde's inheritance was right at the bottom—at least $100,000 less than her siblings got. The discrepancy was definitely noticed after the will was filed for probate and some took it as a sign that Uncle Thomas had liked her least or wanted to punish her for her marriage to Hyde, which he had initially opposed. Another explanation, perhaps as plausible, is that the property he had designated for her in 1905 had simply lost much of its value in the four years since.

Then there was the residuary estate—the $1,406,000 left over when all the individual bequests had been made. This portion was to be divided evenly among the nieces and nephews, giving each of them around $140,000 on top of what he or she received by specific bequest. Of particular interest, as it turned out, was the proviso that if any niece or nephew should subsequently die unmarried and childless, his or her piece of that residuary estate would revert to the surviving heirs to be shared equally.

The will was soundly drawn and apparently suited Colonel Swope just fine up until a year or two before his latest infirmity. That's when he started being nagged by second thoughts about the proper disbursement of his wealth. He got to asking himself whether the nieces and nephews really *needed* that extra $140,000 when they had already been left very decent individual bequests. Might they not become spoiled and seduced by luxury? He knew of young people with too much money who'd fallen under the spells of fortune hunters. And there was the simple fact that tens of thousands of other people needed the money—and deserved it— vastly more than they. It was a matter of principle.

To one visitor he said, "I am rich; I've got more money than I know what to do with, and I would like to do something for the poor people of Kansas City. The rich can take care of themselves; I have no patience with them anyhow; but the poor people—the laboring people of Kansas City—I feel that I owe more to them than to anybody else. I am going to draw a new will. I've got some nieces and other relatives to provide for, but I would like to leave most of my estate to the poor of Kansas City."

In this new will, Swope decided, he would set up a permanent fund for the sole benefit of the needy. The trouble was he didn't know how to make it work. He could deed the properties to the city to support programs for the poor, but that meant involving politicians, and politicians meant incompetence and waste. He'd rather create a trust to steer the income to the right charities. But where to find reliable trustees—good, reputable businessmen—who had the time to manage all the troublesome details?

Growing more fretful by the day, Swope started bringing his will home from the office, pinned to the inside of his vest pocket. He read and reread it in the privacy of his bedroom. He consulted friends about his quandary and almost certainly talked it over with one or more members of the family. It's doubtful that any adult in

31

the Swope mansion hadn't heard rumors, at least, of Uncle Thomas's urgent wish to do something about that damned will.

There's much reason to believe that Doctor Hyde had knowledge of the Colonel's plans too, although he would strongly deny it later. The doctor and the millionaire had had many long visits lately. After emerging from one of them on September 12, Hyde supposedly told Moss Hunton—in Maggie Swope's presence—that the old man intended to shift the residuary portion of his estate to charity. Then there was Hyde's remark to Nurse Kellar on the night Hunton died that Swope would very soon be drawing up a new will.

During the last three weeks of September, when the old man stayed away from his office entirely, Spangler would come out to Independence every two or three days to deliver the mail and discuss business. The main business they talked about was that infernal will. If Swope had any hope of fixing it, he'd have to act soon. He was a sick man.

Nurses' training by the early 1900s was rigorous enough to test any young woman's grit and noble aspirations. By the time novices had discovered the drudgery of night shifts and the stomach-turning realities of the sickroom, four out of five would have abandoned their bedpans and fled. Those who survived the two- to three-year program, however, tended to know their stuff, as Pearl Virginia Kellar indubitably did. A graduate of the Scarritt Bible and Training School for nurses, she was versed in basic anatomy, nutrition, medications, and clinical techniques—in everything a nurse had to know except the healing value of human warmth. She was skillful. She was conscientious. She was as starchy as her crisp white cap.

And she was precisely her cool, efficient self on the bright morning of Saturday, October 2, when she went to Colonel Swope's room to get him prepped for the new day. The octogenarian was already awake in his bed and may have been for some time. He had an anxious question: "How is Moss?"

Kellar replied, "Mister Swope, you know I told you Colonel Hunton was very ill, so you will not be surprised to know he died last night." Not one softening syllable, not one "I'm sorry to tell you … ." Maybe her tone was gentler than her blunt words, but it was no comfort to the old man who'd just lost his one real friend. Swope pulled up his bedclothes, hid his face, and groaned "Oh my God, poor Moss." He sobbed briefly. His frame shook. He wanted to know how Moss had passed away. Kellar told him, no doubt with her usual unsparing directness. Then she got him settled in a cozy Morris chair and went downstairs to get his breakfast tray.

Swope had one request for the rest of the day. It was, not surprisingly, to be left alone. He didn't wish to go out in the buggy, in deference to Hunton's memory. He asked to see no one except his nurse. Not a soul. Not even Hyde, who was usually welcome in the Colonel's room. Kellar hoped he'd reconsider. Hyde and his wife had stayed the night in the hilltop mansion and Kellar thought it would be only proper for Swope to let the doctor at least pay a sympathy call. After all, he was family.

The matter was settled a few minutes later when Hyde knocked at the door and asked himself in. Kellar stepped out so that Swope and his personal physician could speak in private. The two men spent the next thirty minutes or so in conversation, and then were joined briefly by Frances Hyde. What they talked about, whether it was the Colonel's health, his plans for his estate, or simply his grief over a friend's death, none but they would ever know for sure. Hyde's story was that they had spoken mainly of poor Hunton and the family's tragic loss and that he had offered what comfort he could as the old man wept.

At around 10 a.m. the Hydes boarded their hired car and headed back to Kansas City. For most of that Saturday, Nurse Kellar was Swope's only company. The two of them talked and she read to her patient, as she often did.

There was, however, one more visitor, whom the Colonel could hardly refuse to see. It was good, diligent Spangler, come to pay his respects in the hour of need. Swope was in bed, under the bedclothes and still in his sleepwear.

After Spangler had extended his sympathies, Swope changed the subject. He told his assistant that he felt well enough to return to the office Monday. Not only that, but he planned to spend Monday night there and keep on working through Tuesday. Most likely, he said, this would be his last visit to the workplace they had shared these seven years. But there was much to do.

"Spangler, I want you to have all your affairs put in such shape so you can be with me all the time," Swope ordered. "You see, I am a very weak man, and I can't get around, and I want you with me all the time because I have lots of things to go over, and you must go over them with me."

Spangler figured the Colonel's business had to be important, especially when Swope told him that great responsibilities were soon to be placed upon him. The old man said he had confidence that his aide was up to the task. But what task? It never occurred to Spangler that Swope may have been planning to name him an executor, now that Moss Hunton lay dead in an upstairs bedroom.

Despite the lack of details, the Colonel's basic message was unmistakable. If he were ever going to change his will, effectively depriving every niece and nephew of a $140,000 windfall, he'd be doing it on Monday and Tuesday of the coming week. It could be his last chance.

Chapter 4

Beyond the fact that death revisited the Swope mansion on the hot, cloudless Sunday of October 3, leaving two bodies laid out in separate rooms, certain details of the day would be disputed forever after. It was like the witnesses' testimony in *Rashomon*, the classic film of murder and the fickleness of truth. The stories of exactly what happened that Sunday don't just diverge—they turn on each other and collide.

There was Pearl Kellar's version, which was hard to dismiss given her air of cool-headed, no-nonsense rectitude. There was Bennett Clark Hyde's version, which could be viewed as so many self-shielding lies or, perhaps as reasonably, as a desperate insistence on facts that were being maliciously twisted by ill-wishers in the house. There were Mrs. Swope's and Frances Hyde's versions, as predictable as they were contradictory. But which had the truth?

Nurse Kellar was early to rise that morning, even before the dawn sun struck the east windows of the mansion. Scrubbed, combed, and crisply uniformed—can one imagine otherwise?—she went right to work in Colonel Swope's room. It was on the wrong end of the house to have caught much light yet, but she got the old man awake and proceeded to give him his morning bath. After that came the Colonel's breakfast, which Kellar dished up herself in the basement kitchen and carried on a tray to his bedside table.

Once her patient was settled and fed, Kellar headed to the dining room, found a chair nearest the folding doors, and made her pleasantries to those assembled. As she and Mrs. Swope later reconstructed the scene, the others at the table were the mother, daughter Margaret, and the second-oldest son, Tom, who lived on a farm but had spent the night at the family home. Mrs. Swope asked Kellar how the Colonel was feeling, and she replied that he seemed more chipper today.

About halfway through breakfast, Clark and Frances Hyde, who also had stayed the night, appeared through the room's doorway. Kellar's story was that Doctor Hyde had immediately rushed over to her and asked whether the old man had had his breakfast. When she said he had, Hyde said, "Come with me, then, I want him to have some of that digestive medicine that I have been promising to bring him." The reference was to a commonly prescribed preparation, Fairchild's Holadin, made of animal digestive glands that were powdered and put in capsules. Mrs. Swope clearly heard Hyde's request to the nurse, she later said.

Without finishing breakfast, Kellar followed the doctor up to Swope's room, where Hyde produced a pink prescription box, about an inch and a quarter square, took out a whitish capsule, and asked her to give it to the patient. Uncle Thomas was lying in his preferred position—his head at the foot of the bed, propped on pillows. Kellar tried to hand him the capsule and a glass of water, but he balked like a toddler refusing a spoonful of carrots. Kellar laid the capsule on the bedside table, turned toward Hyde and raised her eyebrows as a silent assurance that Swope would take it later—she knew the old man's quirks.

Kellar went back down to finish her meal, then returned to Swope's room with two Kansas City newspapers and two Independence journals filled with editorial eulogies to the late Moss Hunton. This time it took no cajoling: the Colonel swallowed the capsule at once, slipped on his nose glasses, and lay back on three pillows for a cozy perusal of the news. Kellar noticed the Colonel's large gold pocket watch lying on the table. It was 8:30 to the minute.

In light of what followed—what happened, in fact, just twenty minutes later—it will be no surprise that Clark and Frances Hyde would offer a quite different picture of events leading up to it.

Hyde's story would attack the nurse's account point by point. To begin with, he had *not* produced the Holadin package Sunday morning but had given it to Kellar the previous night—Saturday—when he had met her in the upstairs hall. During Sunday breakfast he had simply asked the nurse whether Swope had taken one of the capsules and Kellar had confirmed that he had. Hyde had *not* ordered Kellar to go up with him to the Colonel's room. He had *not* opened a pink box and taken out a capsule. He had *not* handed it to the nurse and instructed her to give it to the patient at that time. Indeed, he had not even set foot in the old man's bedroom until after he'd finished eating, at which time he had gone up to the sickroom alone.

Thomas H. Swope (Jr.), ca. 1905.
Courtesy Jackson County (MO) Historical Society Archives (jchs0038371); Strauss Peyton Photographic Studio Collection.

Corroborating her husband's story, Frances would swear that when she and Clark were at breakfast that morning, Mrs. Swope had not even been present in the room and obviously could not have heard anything spoken there. In fact her mother had still been asleep at the time, Frances said, and when she brought Mrs. Swope a meal tray later on, the older woman was just starting to get dressed. (Maggie Swope had slept in her daughter Margaret's bedroom because Cousin Moss's embalmed remains had not yet been removed from her own.)

Torn as their stories were by stark contradictions, the Hydes and Nurse Kellar would agree on what took place in the minutes between roughly 8:50 and 9:05 a.m.

Frances Hyde, who had come to Swope's room with her husband, left to give the servants some instructions downstairs, while Doctor Hyde strolled down to the front porch with his morning paper. After a few minutes he was back indoors to obey a call of nature in the lavatory off the back hall. Nurse Kellar remained alone with the patient.

Suddenly she was conscious of an odd sound—a kind of blowing sound, as she would later describe it. She asked Colonel Swope if he was ill, but he said nothing. She noticed that his face wore a "most peculiar" expression, the eyes fixed blankly on the west window.

Then the old man began quivering all over, his head thrown back, his eyes set and wide open, his teeth clenched. His skin was ghastly pale with a slight bluish cast, a condition known as cyanosis. The arms and legs shook. Guttural noises issued from his throat, as if he were struggling to speak. A ropy white substance exuded between his teeth, which Kellar wiped away.

Kellar knew a convulsion when she saw one and she knew she needed help. She opened the door, saw Frances Hyde approaching down the hall, and cried, "Come quick, Mister Swope is sick. Get Doctor Hyde." (Frances recalled Kellar's words as, "Mister Swope has had a stroke.")

Frances Hyde took one look at the patient, dashed back into the hall, and waylaid her little sisters Stella, 15, and Sarah, 14, as they descended the stairs from their third-floor rooms. "Run downstairs and get Clark, quick," she cried. "Uncle Thomas is worse."

While the teenagers and their big brother Tom were calling for Hyde through the bathroom door, Frances returned to her uncle's side and saw that his right arm and right leg were jerking. One of his arms was drawn up, the other extended. She bent near the Colonel's face and asked, "Uncle Thomas, do you know me?" She asked again, "Do you know me?" There was no answer.

Within two or three minutes Hyde arrived and found the old man much as his wife and Nurse Kellar had—still quivering, insensible, muttering incoherently.

The Colonel's throes were observed by at least one other family member, 31-year-old Chrisman Swope, the oldest of Mrs. Swope's children, who may have heard the commotion from his room across the hall. Mrs. Swope, still shaken and grieving over Cousin Moss's death, couldn't bear to peer into the sickroom, but she met Hyde in the hall outside and asked what had stricken her brother-in-law. Hyde told her what he'd just told Nurse Kellar: It was a clear case of apoplexy, the same brain attack that had killed Moss Hunton barely thirty-six hours earlier—"probably brought on by the shock of this dear old friend's death." Swope's demise was "just a matter of time."

Kellar had her doubts that apoplexy was the culprit. The Colonel's symptoms just weren't *like* Hunton's on Friday night. Swope's attack was a violent, wracking convulsion—if you'd ever seen one you'd never mistake it. Hunton's was far less intense—you'd hardly call it a convulsion at all. The nurse knew it wasn't her place to question a doctor's diagnosis, so she held her tongue. And if any family members shared her uneasiness that something wasn't quite right, none were saying so. Not then anyway.

The seizure lasted for another eight or ten minutes, after which Swope sank into a general collapse. He remained very pale but was semiconscious. In a sudden surge of nausea he began retching dryly, then was still enough for Kellar and Doctor Hyde to take his pulse. For the moment it was extremely weak. But a few minutes later it shot up, rather startlingly, to a rapid, bounding 140. The patient then started to urinate, and Kellar stepped out of the room briefly while Hyde collected the urine and covered the Colonel back up.

When she returned, Swope was more alert and for a minute or so he was even coherent enough to speak. His first words were the querulous plaints of the very old and feeble. He asked to lie flat— the stacked pillows annoyed him. Kellar and Frances removed them. He demanded that Kellar take away the bedpan he saw lying on his blankets. No bedpan was there, but Kellar did a pantomime of picking one up and carrying it off.

Swope's next words—if accurately quoted by Kellar—must have startled the nurse and the Hydes alike: "Oh my God, I wish I were dead. I wish I had not taken that medicine."

Months afterward, Hyde would deny that the second sentence— or any mention of the medicine—had ever crossed the old man's lips. Frances Hyde would swear she hadn't heard it either. Besides Kellar, there was no other witness; Chrisman Swope was out of the room when Uncle Thomas uttered what would turn out to be his last words. Again, as with so many details of that long, awful Sunday, it would all come down to whose story one chose to believe.

Immediately after Swope fell silent, Hyde ordered an injection of strychnine, to be followed by a second shot in fifteen minutes. This may have struck Kellar as odd, given the fact that Swope's pulse was racing so hard it was difficult to get an accurate count. Strychnine was normally given to *stimulate* the pulse, not reduce it. But whatever her misgivings, the nurse did as she was told, preparing the dosage from her own hypo case.

The truth is, her distrust of Hyde was already planted. She was troubled by the sudden onset of Swope's convulsion, coming just twenty minutes after he'd seemed so cheerful and relaxed. She was put off by the doctor's instant and dubious diagnosis of apoplexy. She couldn't rid her mind of Hyde's chat with her Friday night, when he had asked her to put in a word for his appointment as executor of Swope's estate. And then, as she would later testify, she made a discovery that all but clinched her suspicions.

The Hydes and brother Chrisman had left the room, and she was alone with the stricken Colonel. While they were out—no more than a few minutes—she felt an impulse to locate the pink box the capsules had come in. She wanted to read the label to verify the contents. Kellar looked for the box on the dresser top, where she thought she'd seen it last, then on the bedside table, then on the mantle. All she found was a brown bottle of another stomach remedy, Hinkle's Pink Pills. Next she checked the closet, where she saw, on a shelf, the tonic Swope had been taking, plus a jar of Stuart's Charcoal Dyspepsia Tablets. It crossed her mind that the pink box could be on top of the six-and-a-half-foot chiffonier, but that made little sense and she'd have to stand on a chair to investigate. The box was simply gone. Kellar suspected that someone had taken and disposed of it.

With Hyde's return it was time for the second strychnine injection. The nurse rechecked the old man's pulse and found it was still very high, although Swope had now lapsed into a coma. The Colonel's eyes were half shut, his mouth had fallen open, and he was making a peculiar snoring sound known in medical jargon as stertorous breathing. As ordered, Kellar gave the second shot and apparently gave a third not long after. Later she said her memory was vague about the third shot, while Doctor Hyde testified that she injected four or five strychnine doses throughout the day.

Whatever the case, the strychnine was having little effect on Swope's pulse, which by afternoon had reversed itself and dropped significantly. It was hard to say just how weak it got, since the patient's left and right wrists—if both witnesses' stories were true—were like two drums rapping out different beats simultaneously. Hyde tested the left wrist and concluded the sick man's pulse was failing irreversibly. Kellar held the right one and decided the pulse beat, while certainly weak, was "firm, good quality."

Neither of them, of course, could have believed that Uncle Thomas would pull through. Every physical sign said otherwise. As Kellar was cleaning up the patient's involuntary excretions, she saw that his legs below the knees had turned a dark, venous purple. It was as though Swope were dying from the feet up. The knees slowly contracted, first one, then the other. Kellar performed a routine test to determine whether any brain activity was going on behind the waxen brow. She struck a match, opened one eye, and passed the flame in front of the pupil. The eye stared back—not a flutter, not a blink.

At about three o'clock, Hyde suggested the nurse step outside and catch some fresh air. She spent a few minutes strolling on the lawn, then returned to the hushed cool of the sickroom so that Hyde could take a break. He had just gotten back, fifteen minutes later, when Kellar happened to glance at the Colonel's face. What caught her attention was a slight movement—a twitching—of the patient's eyelids. Her first thought was that Swope might be coming out of his coma. Her next thought was one she couldn't resist sharing. "I would hate to answer for the consequences if Mister Swope should rally," she said. Hyde asked her, "Why do you say that?" and Kellar replied, "Don't you know he connects that attack with the giving of that capsule?" Hyde reportedly said nothing.

Swope's rally was an illusion. The snoring sounds kept up, but the old man's breathing grew shallower with each hour chimed by the household clocks. From time to time a family member looked in on the dying philanthropist, and the household's routine upstairs took on the character of a classic deathwatch. All the players came and went, including Maggie Swope, who finally nerved herself to enter the room with her son Tom.

The lady of the house had more pressing duties downstairs, however, where admirers of the late Moss Hunton—there were scores, perhaps hundreds—were streaming in to pay their respects and view his body laid out in the parlor. The Swope family's attorney, John Gallatin Paxton, had come that morning to help Mrs. Swope greet visitors—he had, after all, been one of Hunton's dearest friends. At the same time he knew that a more pragmatic task awaited him later that day: As one of the co-executors of Colonel Swope's estate, he would be called to legal action from the moment the old man expired. Meanwhile, he stayed focused on his social protocols. Paxton was a gentleman, the son of a Confederate general. It wouldn't do to project morbid anticipation as the end approached.

At five minutes past seven o'clock, while Nurse Kellar was at dinner downstairs, Clark and Frances Hyde were alone at the Colonel's bedside. Frances described the scene as peaceful—so peaceful they hardly noticed the final passage. Thomas Swope's breathing grew softer and slower, the breaths now coming a half-minute apart. At one point Frances thought it was all over and said, "I believe he is not going to breathe any more." Her husband looked closer and said, "Yes, he is breathing again." They watched for a few more minutes, then it stopped. The time was 7:15.

Lawyer Paxton was in the upstairs sitting room, a few yards east and across the hall from Uncle Thomas's bedroom, when Hyde finally brought him word that the old man had breathed his last. The middle-aged executor—erect, sternly handsome, the very image of gravitas—may have welcomed his cue to take charge. "Well," he said, "now is the time to get that paper." Hyde asked him what paper and the lawyer said, "Mister Swope's will."

It seems the document had never left the inside pocket of Swope's vest, which the Colonel had worn on his last trolley ride home. With the will now in hand, Paxton led a cluster of family members—Mrs. Swope, sons Chrisman and Tom, Doctor Hyde and Frances—into the bedroom of daughter Lucy Lee Swope, who was off absorbing culture on a visit to Paris. There they enacted a ritual as hoary as the oldest dynastic melodrama of theater or fiction—the Reading of the Will.

Despite any anxious expectations, the scene may have been less than electrifying. Although the will did spell out a list of cash bequests, all the significant legacies were in real estate—blocks, single buildings, vacant properties. Not until the will was filed for probate six days later would the nieces and nephews even begin to know how much, in dollars, each one's inheritance was worth. It would take even longer for the appraisers to come up with their final figures. In the meantime, however, the children of Maggie Swope were assured of one happy outcome: The residuary estate—*their* residuary estate—was still firmly in Swope hands. Had Uncle Thomas lived a few days longer, just long enough to change his will, all that treasure might have rolled downhill to the poor folks below.

After the meeting broke up, Doctor Hyde had a nice surprise for the nurse who'd been working at his side all day. "By the way, Miss Kellar," he said, "when you present your bill, you present it to Mister Paxton for $35 per week." Correct as always, Kellar replied, "Doctor Hyde, we nurses never charge but $25 for ordinary cases, and simply because Mister Swope is a rich man is no reason why I should do this." She would not see the doctor again until December 11, on quite another matter.

———◦—◦——

Doctor Bennett Clark Hyde was well known to the proprietor and clerks of Hugo Brecklein's Drug Store in downtown Kansas City. For two years he had shopped there regularly to maintain his stocks of pills, tinctures, and tonics, as well as his favorite cigars (El Principe de Gales), whiskey, and other supplies. Not only was Brecklein's handy to Hyde's office—the store was in the nearby

Rialto Building at Ninth and Walnut—but it offered the modern convenience of accepting orders by telephone.

Doctor Hyde availed himself of this service on the morning of Monday, September 13, a full eighteen days previous to the dream-perfect October weekend when two men would go to their deaths in the Swope mansion.

Hyde's status as a valued customer may have been what spared him any awkward questions when he phoned in his order. Or perhaps if he'd spoken with the conscientious Mister Brecklein, who owned the store, he'd have been asked, at the very least, what he intended to do with his most bizarre purchase. But it fell to a mere clerk, John Massman, to answer the call and take Hyde's request: "Send over four 5-grain capsules of cyanide of potassium."

Massman was taken aback. He knew that cyanide was one of the swiftest, most lethal poisons in existence. He had never heard of selling it in capsules—the toxic crystals were always dispensed in bulk. Nor had he ever heard of any uses for cyanide by a medical doctor. In his experience, the purchaser was always a jeweler or a dentist, someone who used the substance as a solvent in working with gold. Nevertheless, despite his misgivings, he went ahead and put up the order, noting the transaction in the shop's daily sales log.

By chance it was Massman again who picked up the phone when Doctor Hyde called the shop the very next morning, September 14. This time, however, Hyde's order was as mundane as the other had been irregular. All Hyde wanted delivered to his office were two dozen capsules of a popular digestive compound sold by prescription under the trade name Fairchild's Holadin.

At the time, Massman scarcely gave it a thought. Why should he? It's doubtful that he even noticed a peculiar detail shared by these two radically different items purchased just one day apart. The harmless Holadin capsules were all but identical in size, shape, and color to the deadly cyanide capsules he'd sold to Hyde the day before. It might have taken a doctor to tell them apart.

Chapter 5

Call it an unworthy thought in the hour of grief, but it must have crossed the minds of Kansas City leaders and retail merchants that the death of Thomas Hunton Swope was poorly timed to say the least.

This very morning, October 4, was the dawn of the Priests of Pallas festival, the city's answer to New Orleans' Mardi Gras and the Veiled Prophet festivities of St. Louis. What the town didn't need just now was the passing of a great philanthropist, a citizen you couldn't just bury in the background while the carnival revelries rolled on. At the same time, scores of thousands of Kansas Citians and visitors were not about to let the death of a crotchety, reclusive multimillionaire spoil their six-day party.

The clash of official and public moods—of bereavement and mirth—would be awkward but easy enough to absorb. A real headache, however, would be the planning and execution of a suitable farewell for the sainted benefactor. There would have to be a lying in state, eulogies by area notables, a procession through the heart of downtown, the funeral rites themselves . . . and all of this while street galas and theatricals and shopping sprees engulfed the commercial district from morning till night.

Festivities would include the Hellenic-inspired Priests of Pallas pageant, two parades, two society balls (one masked), pyrotechnic displays, a lecture by the celebrated (and later discredited) explorer Dr. Frederick Cook, and a presentation of *H.M.S. Pinafore* featuring a full-size ship on stage at Convention Hall. And all week long the popular Electric Park, with its thrilling rides, games, and refreshment booths, would be the site of a Grand Fair and Exposition.

With pages of special ads, the great stores—Boley's, the Palace, Rothschild's, John Taylor, and Emery, Bird, Thayer—sought to seduce out-of-towners with all the big-city luxuries their dollars could buy.

Ladies need not visit Paris to find "Paris-model" hats, enormous concoctions of plumage, velvet flowers, medallions, and ribbons; "choicest Paris designs" in suits, demi-costumes and evening gowns; "dainty new foreign neckwear conceits"; and the chic new pumps that were fast replacing the matronly button shoe. Gentlemen visitors could go back to their hometowns in smart Hart Schaffner & Marx suits; "new fancies" in high-collared shirts; fine overcoats for the cold days ahead ("English, you know—just the thing for now"); and hats to every taste, from jaunty derbies with the D'Orsay curl to the low-crowned porkpies later adopted by Buster Keaton. For college-age dandies on lower budgets, $15 could buy "just the snappy ultra-styles you want"—suits with "dip-front coats, very peggy trousers, and swagger waistcoats." And fellows old and young who needed formal wear for the dressier Priests of Pallas events were assured that plenty of tuxes and tailcoats to suit any pocketbook were still available off the rack.

Colonel Swope's attire for the week—Prince Albert suit, white linens, and sober necktie—would befit both his rank as a revered personage and the solemnity of his passing. But before he made his postmortem debut before the mourning public, he required the immediate attentions of undertaker R. B. Mitchell of Ott's mortuary, who arrived at the Swope mansion around two hours after the old man's death.

Mitchell had brought along the instruments of his craft as well as three or four quarts of embalming fluid manufactured by the Frigid Fluid Company of Chicago. (Months later the fluid's manufacturer, Adelbert B. Krum, would be asked in court to divulge its formula: formaldehyde, glycerin, chili, saltpeter, synthetic oil of wintergreen, oil of cassia, oil of cloves, and oil of benzaldehyde.) He washed the body and placed it on a cooling board for the embalming procedure. He'd have to make a skilled job of it. Swope would lie unburied for days and the forecast was for continued unseasonable warmth.

When Mitchell returned the next morning, the Colonel's funeral finery was all laid out for him, as if by a diligent valet. With an assistant to help with the heavy lifting, the undertaker got the Colonel dressed, slipped into a basket, and carried downstairs to a casket waiting in the parlor. That the splendid coffin had been chosen, delivered, and set up on trestles with so little delay may be credited to canny foresight on the part of its purchaser. It seems that Frances Hyde, perhaps with her husband, had arranged for Swope's casket at the same time she'd selected Moss Hunton's on Saturday. It just made sense. The fact that Swope had still been up and about at the time, despite his health setbacks, didn't mean he could hang on much longer. Surely anyone could see that the end was near—weeks, months at most.

Swope Mansion Left Parlor through Hall, ca. 1908.
Courtesy Jackson County (MO) Historical Society (jchs016721cm);
gift of Mrs. D. J. Hyde Matheny

There in the parlor the Colonel's casket remained, right through Hunton's funeral on Monday afternoon and for two more days. Mitchell had fastened the lid of the copper lining over the old man's face, but on Tuesday it was reopened so an artisan named W. H. Jennens could take a plaster mold for a death mask. Someone discovered he had left some plaster on Swope's nostril and teeth, forcing the meticulous Mitchell to return and wipe it away. The next day Jennens made a mold of Swope's left hand as well. The idea was that sculptors could use the castings in creating statues of the Colonel, after which the molds would be destroyed.

While Kansas City officials were rushing through plans to make sure Thomas Swope was suitably displayed and memorialized—the very kind of pomp and physical exposure that would have horrified him in life—the local press was filling its pages with worshipful editorials, recaps of the Colonel's generosities, and fond anecdotes of his eccentric ways. *The Kansas City Star* extolled the civic optimism of the old man who had told a young acquaintance "you'll live to see more than a million people, perhaps two million, here." A *Kansas City Times* writer found the felicitous line, "His modesty was immoderate," and added, "The death of our benefactor has cast a cloud over our gaily dressed city and sobered the festivities of the week." A *Times* editorial argued that while the giver of Swope Park was a virtual recluse, "there is no reason why the city should not make his silent abode somewhat more conspicuous than he chose to make his daily life."

The silent abode favored by Kansas City officials and endorsed by the Swope family was of course Swope Park itself, and immediately the park board set about choosing a site. Swope had long since written his own epitaph: "In honor of Thomas Hunton Swope, who gave this park to the People of Kansas City Anno Domini 1896—Exegit monumentum perennius aere." (Swope paraphrased a classic Latin quotation, "I have erected a monument more durable than brass," changing the verb to the third person.) Meanwhile, Kansas City mayor Thomas Crittenden ordered that flags be flown at half-staff and government buildings draped in black.

Not that these shrouds threw a pall over Tuesday's Priests of

**THOMAS H. SWOPE'S OWN EPITAPH
(FACSIMILE OF THE EPITAPH AS WRITTEN BY COLONEL SWOPE).**
Kansas City Times, Wed., Oct. 6, 1909, p. 1.

Pallas Parade, the initial spectacle of the carnival week. For one thing the great whoop-de-do was held at night, when all that black bunting was more or less invisible. And far more to the point, the revelers at street-side—from Euclid to Main, Fifth Street to Nineteenth—were having such a royal, hooting good time. Here were the 128 Maids of Honor and the half-dozen Special Attendants, primped and poised like prize orchids on their twinkling floats. Here was Miss Maybelle Krebs, costumed as the Goddess of Liberty aboard the rolling North Pole display. And here, most radiant of all, was the helmeted, spear-bearing Pallas Athene herself, in the Homeric person (five feet eleven inches tall) of Miss Glendora Runyan, daughter of the secretary of the Elks Club. The streets were thronged. The hotels were thronged. There were so many out-of-towners competing for rooms— thousands arriving daily on 107 trains—that the overflow had to seek accommodations across the Kaw River in Kansas City, Kansas.

If any of the residents of 406 South Pleasant Street in Independence were tempted to join the big-city fun this week, it's certain that none were indelicate enough actually to do so. Out came the black crepes and woolens, the women's veils and nimbuslike funeral hats. White-haired, plump Maggie Swope, her fine eyes watchful behind dark-rimmed glasses, seemed born to wear the mourner's weeds, so stately was her presence in them. She would set the example. The family would behave like Swopes, with well-bred reserve, even if city officials insisted on turning the occasion into a necro-extravaganza of sorts. At sending off its dead, K.C. would take a backseat to no one.

Thus it was a blue-ribbon City Hall delegation—Mayor Crittenden, the deputy mayor, and five aldermen—who arrived Wednesday afternoon to meet Independence mayor Llewellyn Jones and his own entourage outside the mansion on the hill. The Independence councilmen carried the Colonel's casket out to the hearse on the asphalt drive, where four big touring cars and an honor guard of ten mounted policemen waited to make a parade of it. None of the Swopes came out to see them off, however, and none of the dignitaries was presumptuous enough to make a speech. In silence, the Colonel was borne to his next stop, the imposing Kansas City Public Library at Ninth and Locust Streets.

If one sought a proper venue for a lying-in-state, the rotunda of the downtown library could hardly have been more ideal. The classical space featured Ionic columns of marble hung with black fabric, and a massive stone fireplace that would fit nicely into Citizen Kane's Xanadu. It might have looked rather heavy—Wagnerian—had it not been for the flowers. The foot of the casket wore a sumptuous blanket of roses and lilies of the valley from the Swope family, while floral tributes from friends and organizations, including the Yale alumni group, crowded the sides. But the real showpiece was a ten-foot column of carnations and American beauty roses that loomed over the head of the coffin, its inscription reading "Kansas City Mourns."

When the library's black-draped doors swung open and the casket lid was raised at 9 a.m. Thursday, a line had already formed. School board president J. C. James and his family were the first ones in, but scores of the early arrivals turned out to be children, many so small that they had to be lifted up by the police guards in order to see into the casket. "Many Negroes were there," wrote the *Kansas City Star*'s reporter, who then quoted an elderly black man's remark that Swope "was the finest man I ever knew. I worked for him for twenty years and I loved him." Streets and sidewalks around the library were jammed, and all the more so when a Priests of Pallas event called the Flower Parade—legions of local beauties in floral costumes and cars bedecked with blossoms—broke up just in time to add its own throng to the Swope thousands. By closing time Thursday, librarian Carrie W. Whitney estimated, some 35,000 people had filed past the catafalque. Assuming the rotunda was open for eight hours that day, the librarian's estimate would translate to nearly seventy-three viewers per minute or more than one each second. Even though there were two lines of mourners, Mrs. Whitney's estimate would have them moving at quite a clip.

Friday was more of the same until just after noon when the library closed its doors and thousands of schoolchildren, released from classes and lured by free streetcar rides, swarmed into the district. Curbsides were jammed at 2 p.m. when the funeral marchers fell in behind mounted policemen and a military band for their procession to Grace Episcopal Church at Thirteenth and Broadway. No doubt about it, this was a cortège of civic luminaries—commercial and labor, political and patriotic, social and charitable—to rival any the city had ever assembled. There were militiamen and old soldiers, including Camp No. 80 of the United Confederate Veterans. There were pallbearers both active and honorary. There were carriages with cargoes of dignitaries, members of the Swope family and ordinary citizens (though none so ordinary that they couldn't afford a carriage). And of course there was the horse-drawn hearse itself, its sides varnished to a high, Stygian gloss.

The hearse's passenger, like all the Swopes, had been brought up Presbyterian, but any religious devotion he may have had was long gone by the last years of his life. Colonel Swope had studied Voltaire and expressed his doubts about the presence of a just and beneficent Almighty. As his days grew short, however, he told family members that he would like his last rites to be those of the Episcopal church, whose stately liturgy appealed to his literary tastes. At Grace Church he'd get the full ceremonial treatment at the hands of Bishop E. R. Atwill, splendidly robed and mitered; the bishop's chaplain, the Reverend E. B. Woodruff, bearing the pastoral staff; and the church's rector, the Reverend J. A. Schaad, in cassock, surplice, and stole.

The casket arrived to the muffled beat of a drum, after which the organ took over and the chief mourners slipped into their pews in the center section. It was just as well they had reserved seats; the rest of the sanctuary was packed with the benefactor's public admirers. Mrs. Swope sat beside the Colonel's nephew and co-executor, Stuart Fleming, in the same pew with her children and other close kin, among them Clark and Frances Hyde. As usual with the Episcopal Service for the Dead, it was all strictly by the Book of Common Prayer—no homily, no orations. The music embraced the scriptural (an anthem drawn from the Nineteenth Psalm), the sentimental ("One Sweetly Solemn Thought" rendered in solo), and the sepulchral (the funeral march of Chopin). Almost too neatly on cue, a thunderstorm broke out just as the hearse and carriages set out for the long ride to Forest Hill Cemetery on the city's south side. It would be years before Swope's permanent tomb in Swope Park was ready for occupancy. His temporary resting place would be the cemetery's receiving vault, buried in an earthen mound except for its Grecian facade, where bodies were housed while awaiting burial elsewhere.

It was pouring when everyone got there, so that besides the Swope relatives, the clergy, and the active pallbearers, not more than ten mourners left their carriages. With coat collars turned up, the burial party ducked through the rain into the vault's central chamber. The place was so dark people could barely make out their neighbors' faces, except when lightning flared from the doorway across the stone floor and against the wet cloaks of the onlookers. A little organ managed to wheeze "Nearer My God to Thee" over low rumbles of thunder. Then it was Bishop Atwill's turn to read the somber sentences spoken at Episcopal gravesides.

The trouble was, the bishop's prayer book was practically use-less in the dark, and no one had thought to bring a candle. The oversight might have caused serious embarrassment had the rector of Grace Church, the Reverend Mister Schaad, not been carrying a supply of matches. These he struck one after another above the pages while the prelate intoned the lofty words: "Unto Almighty God we commend the soul of our brother Thomas departed, and we commit his body to the ground; earth to earth, ashes to ashes, dust to dust...."

It was a fine send-off for the soul of Thomas Hunton Swope. But the great philanthropist's mortal remains, handsomely coffined and shelved in an outer casing of stone, would not lie undisturbed for long.

Exactly what passed between Frances Hyde and Maggie Swope in the hours and days following the Colonel's death is in some dispute. What's almost certain is that the daughter and mother did get into subjects—and say things—that couldn't help striking sparks, given the tensions beginning to crackle through the Swope mansion. If nothing else, their encounters suggest that Mrs. Swope's animosity toward Doctor Hyde was well advanced by the time Moss Hunton and Uncle Thomas were in their coffins.

The first flare-up—probably the milder—seems to have occurred on Monday, October 11, shortly before the Hydes returned home after their ten-day duty visit in the Swope house. Frances had already told Clark she'd like to see him named an executor of the Swope estate. Now she approached her mother: "Have you any objection to Clark being made an executor?" Maggie Swope's snappish reply, as quoted by Frances, was, "I do object." She added that if anyone were chosen, one of her own brothers would be more suitable. The idea of Hyde's appointment was never broached again.

Harsher feelings evidently sprang up over a proposal to do something generous for Cousin Lizzie Moore. The elderly Mrs. Moore was a sister of Moss Hunton's and a resident of Kentucky.

She was apparently not well off and could have benefited nicely had a modest bit of the Swope estate been signed over to her. Her brother Moss had not lived to receive his own bequest in the Colonel's will, around $60,000 in real estate. Now his piece of the Swope fortune would pass to the Swope nieces and nephews.

According to Mrs. Swope, she and Frances had discussed Cousin Lizzie's situation at Hunton's funeral. Magnanimously, Frances had offered to give Mrs. Moore her share of what she and her siblings would inherit through Hunton's death. Her mother was delighted: "Daughter, I think it would be beautiful, and nobody would appreciate it more than Cousin Lizzie."

Frances's story differs from Mrs. Swope's both in fact and tone. She said it was her mother, not she, who had suggested the favor for Cousin Lizzie. Frances wanted to think about it before going along with the idea, and she discussed the matter privately with her cousin Stuart Fleming, one of the executors. Fleming's advice was quite clear: Don't do it.

Frances agreed, and she made up her mind—not for the first time—to defy her mother's formidable will. In early November, when she told Maggie Swope of her decision, the latter's response was not gracious. "This is Clark Hyde's work," her mother allegedly said. "He doesn't love you and he never did love you. He simply wants your money, and I will see that he never gets any of the Swope money."

Mrs. Swope later denied she had said any such thing. Whether she did or not, the remark seems very much in character with the determined, strong-tempered woman who had fought so hard to keep Bennett Clark Hyde out of the family.

Chapter 6

Who could blame any ambitious medical man, especially a forward-thinking younger fellow like Clark Hyde, for wanting to set up a laboratory for the study of disease bacteria? Not many doctors made the effort, to be sure, but the advantages to anyone who did were obvious. To have a lab right in his own office would free the doctor from reliance on outside bacteriologists for diagnostic and other necessary work with germs. Even better, it would offer him the opportunity to expand his knowledge through microscopic study, over time, of these minuscule killers. It was the wise principle of knowing one's enemy.

Thus Hyde had made arrangements, when he leased his new office in the Keith and Perry Building in August of 1908, for sufficient working space to accommodate a modest laboratory. His three-room suite on the fifth floor had ample room, and after fifteen months of occupancy he finally found time to put his plan into action.

At a dinner on November 1, 1909, he mentioned his idea to a physician and bacteriologist, Doctor Edward L. Stewart, whose laboratory in the Shukert Building was a short walk from Hyde's office. Hyde had known Stewart, a dark, dramatically handsome man of 34, for several years as a colleague and fellow officer of the Jackson County Medical Society. The bacteriologist encouraged Hyde to pursue his plan and volunteered to provide him a sort of starter collection of germ species.

Nine days later Hyde appeared at Stewart's office with a half-dozen glass tubes of sterile culture jelly. Into these, Stewart transplanted six specimens he had scraped from his own bacteria colonies with a platinum wire loop. He then instructed Hyde to pick them up the next day, November 11, after he had nurtured them overnight in an incubator to make sure they were alive and vigorous.

Sure enough, when Hyde returned he found that the specimens had grown nicely—fresh, virile broods of microbes, ready to serve whatever purposes the doctor had in mind. To the layperson they might have seemed an odd mix—one harmless bacterium, two humble species known generically as "pus germs," and three more sinister varieties: *Bacillus anthracis, Corynebacterium diphtheriae,* and *Salmonella typhi.* Typhi meaning typhoid.

Of all the bacteria in Hyde's collection, the typhoid germs probably had the greatest practical utility. Typhoid fever was still common in an era when many families still used outdoor privies and when Missouri River water—settled in basins but untreated—ran from household taps. While medicine offered no cure, doctors could prepare a fairly successful vaccine from the dead bacteria. Perhaps as importantly, the germs were used in a procedure known as the Widal blood agglutination test, the first reasonably accurate means of diagnosing the disease.

The numbers of known cases in Greater Kansas City at the time would be alarming by modern standards. Three months after Hyde had set up his lab, health officers in the Missouri metropolis counted six hundred patients under treatment, while Kansas City, Kansas, at one point picked up twenty-five new cases in three weeks. At Park College, the small Presbyterian school located just across the river, afflicted students filled the infirmary and many dormitory beds.

Although health officials advised taking precautions, anything approaching public panic was plainly absent. Typhoid outbreaks drew only a few stories in the local press, most of them brief and restrained. One exception was a *Kansas City Post* article headlined "Typhoid Scourge Becomes Menace Because of Water," but even that wound up buried on page 8 near the sports and cartoons.

Two factors may have accounted for the general calm. Only a small percentage of typhoid victims died—figures cited by doctors at the time were around 5 percent. And the ailment was … well … old hat. A year without typhoid would have been as hard to imagine as a year without chicken pox. It had killed countless thousands throughout history—some scholars believe it was the plague that wiped out one in three Athenians in the fifth century BC—and it was no respecter of rank. Notables felled by typhoid since the beginning of the nineteenth century included President Zachary Taylor, Franz Schubert, Archduke Karl Ludwig of Austria, industrialist Mark Hanna, and Queen Victoria's consort, Prince Albert. But most patients, of whatever class, endured nothing worse than three to five nasty weeks of high fever, headaches, constipation followed by diarrhea, muscle and belly pains, and a general malaise. Sometimes the afflicted broke out in rose-colored spots. In extreme cases they might become delusional, wildly agitated, even convulsive, but those symptoms were rare.

Most enlightened people knew that typhoid was transmitted through ingesting food or water contaminated by the feces of infected persons, but ideas for meeting the menace could border on the bizarre. Sextons in Kansas City were informed, for example, that public funerals for typhoid victims were banned from homes, churches, and chapels, as though the corpses might rise up mid-service and spew their germs over the mourners. Doctors recommended that householders use boiled or distilled water only and urged special care in the handling of milk, especially when flies were active. All that failing, there were the standard treatments: hot packs and sweat baths, oral analgesics and "intestinal antiseptics," even shots of strychnine, nitroglycerine, digitalin, and morphine in cases of convulsion. If you got well, you got well. Most did.

Outbreaks around the area were spotty, of course. While there may not be records to prove it, there seems little doubt that better-off homeowners, those with indoor plumbing and educated standards of cleanliness, were freer from infection than the residents of poorer, crowded, inner-city districts. Some outlying communities must have been safer, too, unless the City of Independence was a unique exception. Doctor George T. Twyman, among the town's most established physicians, said he had not known of a single case in Independence throughout most of 1909. Until their change of luck near the year's end, the Swope family had escaped the disease far longer than that. Maggie Swope said that no one in her aristocratic line had had typhoid since 1865, the year the Civil War ended.

What no one had given much thought to, apparently, was the illness that struck 10-year-old Carrie Copridge in February 1909. Carrie and her older sister, Leonora, were the children of Ida Copridge, the Swopes' black cook, with whom they lived in the two-room servants' cabin behind the great brick residence. The three of them also shared an outhouse roughly fifty feet to the north of their wood-frame dwelling. On the late winter day when Carrie came down sick with an intestinal complaint, her mother decided the child had worms and proceeded to "doctor" her for the parasites. She also took the precaution of summoning a local black physician named Griffin, who disagreed that worms were the problem. Doctor Griffin concluded that the child had a light case of typhoid fever, although no Widal tests were taken to verify his diagnosis.

During the three weeks Carrie was ill, her mother and 19-year-old sister had cared for her while continuing their duties in the Swope mansion, Ida in the kitchen and pantry, Leonora throughout the house as maid and meal server. The sickbed duties cannot have been pleasant. "Slops" had to be carried out and emptied into the servants' privy, a primitive and noxious affair. Built on a low stone foundation, the tiny shed was enclosed on only three sides, the open west side invisible from the mansion's rear windows. There was no pit to contain waste. Excrement discharged through the three seat holes fell directly onto the ground.

By contrast, the Swope family enjoyed the huge comfort and health benefits of indoor plumbing. By November of 1909, the mansion had modern toilet facilities on the first and second floors (in December a third "closet" was installed in the basement, near the kitchen and laundry room). There were also two sources of water. For drinking, the family relied on a twelve-foot-deep cistern— professionally cleaned each year—fed by rainwater that passed through a charcoal filter. For washing and other household uses, there was the clear but untreated "faucet water" purchased from the city.

No matter the advances in hygiene practiced in the Swope house, there were chinks in its shields against disease. Besides the servants' latrine, an old cesspool near the outhouse remained unfilled, capped only by a loose wooden lid. Milk from the family's three cows, though probably handled with care by the usual dairy standards, could have been a seasonal attraction to flies. These conditions may or may not have been known to Bennett Clark Hyde, but he certainly had asked his mother-in-law, as far back as the fall of 1908, whether she had considered boiling the family's drinking water. She hadn't and didn't plan to. At the time, Doctor Hyde did not press the issue.

Meanwhile, the Hydes' frequent practice of taking Sunday dinner at the mansion—partaking freely of Ida Copridge's cooking and the water pumped from the cistern—had continued right through September of 1909 without anyone's saying another word about sanitary precautions.

Then, sometime between October 1 and 3, Clark and Frances Hyde arrived at the house bearing a five-gallon jug of Fountain of Youth double-distilled drinking water. It was the weekend of Hunton's and the old Colonel's deaths, and the Hydes had come to help out with the numerous tasks that always accompanied family tragedies. At least once during their ten-day visit, the doctor recommended strongly that the Swopes drink only boiled or distilled water. If they didn't, he warned, they'd be inviting typhoid fever.

The warning didn't take. While the Hydes now drank exclusively from their bottled supply, the rest of the family—who may have disliked the flat taste of the distilled stuff—stayed with their usual water poured from a wooden cooler in the butler's pantry. (The Hydes kept their bottles in the kitchen refrigerator.) Apparently Mrs. Swope was of no mind to switch over. Water from her cistern, after all, had proved its wholesomeness over all these years. As a matter of fact, she recalled, Doctor Hyde himself had once praised its quality.

The slightly eccentric drinking arrangements were barely noticed at Thanksgiving dinner on Thursday, November 25. Indeed, about the only unusual thing about this year's feast was the hour it was served. Normally a midday affair, it had to be put off till evening so that guests could attend the annual football game between the University of Missouri Tigers and the University of Kansas Jayhawks. The teams, symbolic bearers of an interstate enmity going back to the Civil War, played at Association Park in Kansas City, Missouri. It was the perfect game day—sunny and 64 degrees at kickoff. Among the 14,400 in attendance were Clark and Frances Hyde and 50-year-old Cousin Stuart Fleming, who had come up from Tennessee to help execute Colonel Swope's will. All of them, of Southern heritage, must have cheered when the Tigers won it twelve to six.

The dinner bell at the Swope mansion rang at seven o'clock. From the second-floor sitting room, the family's informal gathering place, everyone headed downstairs for the ritual repast. It is not known whether, at dinner, anyone remarked on the sad absence of poor Cousin Moss or the (no doubt) less regretted absence of Colonel Swope. The holiday socializing ended at 9 p.m., and the Hydes retrieved their coats—Clark's from the hall closet, his wife's from sister Margaret's room—for the ride back to the city.

———•◦•———

Witnesses' recollections of Thanksgiving Day would be of some interest in the criminal case that would embroil the Hydes and the Swopes in months to come. Testimony about another family dinner, however, would prove more intriguing and far more contentious. The conflict came down to this: Had—or had not—Clark and Frances Hyde come out to Independence four days earlier, on Sunday, November 21, to enjoy one of their routine Sabbath dinners at the family place?

The Swopes and their ménage would insist the Hydes had dined there on that brisk, sunny fall day. And the Hydes, as tenaciously, would insist they had not—that they'd been somewhere else altogether, and could prove it.

Mrs. Swope was adamant. Besides herself, Clark Hyde, and her daughter Frances, a half-dozen others had been seated at the family table. Elder son Chrisman was there along with three other sisters. Then there were two cousins—Stuart Fleming and spinster Nora Belle Dickson, the girls' companion and former governess. The house girl, Leonora Copridge, had served the meal, which arrived on a dumbwaiter from her mother's basement kitchen.

As young Margaret Swope reconstructed the day, the Hydes had shown up in late morning, had dined at around one o'clock, and had stayed well into the afternoon if not the early evening. Cook Ida Copridge said she had seen Doctor Hyde in the kitchen that Sunday and heard him pouring something—presumably distilled water—

Margaret Swope, ca. 1907.
Courtesy Jackson County (MO) Historical Society Archives (jchs003619m);
gift of Miss Grace and Miss Eleanor Minor.

from a bottle he kept in the refrigerator. Both of the Swope teenagers, Stella and Sarah, said they remembered Clark Hyde at dinner, discussing his plans to attend the Missouri-Kansas football game the following Thursday, Thanksgiving Day. Nora Belle Dickson was equally certain the Hydes had dined at the Sabbath table on November 21.

Could they all have misremembered? Or been coached or coerced into spinning some elaborate lie? What other conclusion could be drawn if one believed the story that was sworn to afterward in a court of law by Clark and Frances Hyde?

The Hydes' account was so prosaic really—almost too commonplace to be something dreamed up. They had had lunch at their Kansas City home on the day in question and had left around 4 p.m. for a dinner engagement with friends. Their hosts, a Mr. and Mrs. Cleary, lived close by at 3533 Tracy Avenue, and there the Hydes remained until 10:30 or 11 that night. In short, not once on Sunday, November 21, had they been within eight miles of the Swope mansion in Independence. And if one chose not to take the Hydes at their word, the Clearys themselves would later swear that everything their friends had recounted under oath was absolutely true.

All of which might have been dismissed as a pointless, rather silly family squabble, had it not been for three seemingly routine illnesses reported in the Swope household in the final days of November.

On Monday the twenty-ninth, Margaret Swope and her oldest sister, Frances Hyde, spoke by phone about a shopping excursion they had planned for later in the day. Margaret said she was feeling unwell and just wasn't up to the ride to Kansas City and a tiring afternoon in crowded downtown stores. The two agreed to postpone their outing a few days and meanwhile, Frances insisted, Margaret must phone the family's physician, Doctor Twyman, to make sure her ailment was nothing serious.

While Margaret nursed her aches and fever and passed the time doing fancy needlework in the mansion, one of the servants suffered similar distress in the wooden cabin out back. Leonora Copridge, the 19-year-old house girl, had felt poorly for a day or so, but was ordered to do the cooking that Monday while her mother Ida was tied up with other chores. In the afternoon she complained to her mother that her head was hurting so badly she had barely been able to do her work. Two days later she'd be bedridden.

Less noticed at the time was Chrisman Swope's vague indisposition on the morning of Sunday the twenty-eighth. Whatever ailed him did not seem serious and it's likely that he attended services as usual at the First Presbyterian Church just up the street, where he served as a deacon. By Tuesday or Wednesday, he'd be off his feet as well.

When Doctor Twyman finally confirmed what had sickened them—at first he hadn't suspected it—he must have wondered how the germs of typhoid fever had invaded such a clean, well-ordered residence as the Swopes'. And he must have wondered when.

No one could point with absolute certainty to the exact day or even week of typhoid's incursion, but one might narrow the possibilities simply by counting back. Doctors in 1909 knew that the usual incubation period for typhoid—between exposure and the appearance of the first symptoms—was rarely less than one week or more than three weeks. If one counted back seven or eight days from the onset of the three illnesses, the probable exposure date would have been no later than November 22. It was certainly possible—wasn't it?—that *Salmonella typhi* had somehow gotten into the food or drinking water served on November 21, the very Sunday of the Hydes' disputed presence at dinner.

In time, some would wonder: If Doctor Hyde had been at the Swope house that day—with full freedom of the pantry and the kitchen and the family watercooler—then why would he and his wife so vehemently *deny* it? Unless he had been up to something to feel guilty about?

In late November, of course, no one was thinking the unthinkable. Even those who had misgivings about the suave son-in-law would not, for several weeks, begin to suspect that Bennett Clark Hyde had introduced typhoid bacilli into their home in a cold, meticulously scientific scheme to destroy them.

Chapter 7

Had matriarch Maggie Swope so much as dreamed what would happen during her absence over the next week, she would never for an instant have considered joining several friends on a long-planned trip to Chicago. But everything seemed in order, everyone reasonably well when she boarded the train in Kansas City at 5 p.m. on Sunday, November 28.

Her elder son, Chrisman, though a bit under the weather, was well enough to ride with her to the Grand Avenue station. It wasn't unusual for him to suffer bad days. He had always been frail, subject to ailments that bypassed her other children. At 31, he *looked* vulnerable with his soft, benign features. Chrisman had never left the home where he was born, except to attend Westminster College in Fulton, Missouri (his brothers in Phi Delta Theta had thought him "different"). Nor had he ever really worked, except as bookkeeper for the family farm. If anyone thought him a weakling, however—one of those languid, wellborn layabouts familiar in Victorian novels—it probably went unsaid. He appears by all accounts to have been much loved, most ardently by his mother. He was the first of her children to survive past infancy. She doted on him and would have canceled her trip at the slightest hint that he was genuinely ill.

Mrs. Swope had heard that the house girl, Leonora, was down with some malady or other, but a sickness in the servants' quarters was hardly of urgent concern. As for her other children, all seemed as fit as ever when they saw her off that afternoon. It would be another day before daughter Margaret's symptoms would make their ominous appearance.

In light of what followed while Mrs. Swope shopped and socialized in Chicago, it is a bit surprising that no one bothered to inform her by telegram. Loved ones were coming down sick—sick enough to need medical attention—but for most of the week doctors still hadn't verified the cause. Perhaps the family wished to spare her needless anxiety. In any event, it wasn't until Sunday morning, December 5, after she had detrained in Kansas City and ridden the streetcar to Independence, that she learned the facts from Cousin Stuart Fleming. He laid them out as he drove her from the trolley stop to the roofed carriage entrance on the south side of the house. Even inside the big door, Maggie Swope was unprepared for what awaited her upstairs. Her home had become a virtual hospital.

Five nurses, none of whom she'd ever seen, scurried along the corridor with their armfuls of towels and trays and bedpans. Doc Twyman and her son-in-law Clark Hyde were both making rounds and administering pills. So far there were five diagnosed cases of typhoid, including the servant girl Leonora and an 18-year-old seamstress, Georgia Compton, who had been employed at the house in late November. Chrisman, Margaret, and the children's companion, Cousin Nora Belle Dickson, were ill enough to be confined to their beds on the second floor; Leonora Copridge was being treated in the servants' quarters, and the seamstress had gone home to her parents.

Waylaying a nurse, Mrs. Swope inquired about the patients' conditions and was told that only one of them, her daughter Margaret, was seriously sick. The nurse explained that Margaret was the "fleshier" of the victims and that "it always goes harder with fleshier people." As the anxious mother passed from sickroom to sickroom, she found that Chrisman was the liveliest. "Mother, don't be uneasy, we'll all be well soon," he assured her. "I think I will be up tomorrow. I am not sick much. They are just keeping me in bed." Chrisman did indeed look well and had only a low, persistent fever. Because the other victims were obviously worse off, Mrs. Swope spent more of the afternoon seeing to their needs.

All in all, the doctors and nurses seemed to have matters well

**William Chrisman
Swope, ca. 1899**
Courtesy Reeves Library,
Westminster College,
Fulton, MO.

in hand. From the start, Hyde had deferred to Doctor Twyman as
the physician in charge, even though Twyman had been the slower
to grasp the true nature of the outbreak. Early on, Hyde had suspected typhoid, but the older doctor at first maintained that Margaret's ailment was nothing worse than a cold "with myalgia or La
Grippe infection." Then, as patients' symptoms grew more troubling, Widal tests on blood drawn from Chrisman and Leonora
Copridge turned up positive. There was no denying that typhoid
fever was afoot in the Swope mansion.

Hyde had recruited the nurses, all of whom had excellent
credentials, and had then managed to antagonize them within an
hour of their arrival. They had hardly settled into their third-floor
dormitory-style room and changed into their uniforms when he
summoned them to a meeting. Hyde's aloof manner can't have
helped, but what really chafed the nurses was the work schedule he
had drawn up. Instead of assigning each to a single patient for the
duration of her stay—the standard practice in cases like this—he

informed them they would each share duties with all the sick over sixteen-hour shifts. The women objected: It would sacrifice continuity of care, make record keeping a mess, and leave them only eight hours for sleep and recreation. Hyde was unmoved.

Whatever resentments the nurses bore, they kept the feelings among themselves. Certainly Mrs. Swope noticed nothing of the kind in their demeanor. In the first hours after her homecoming, she found the general mood of the caregivers and patients surprisingly upbeat. Even Margaret, the most ill, was in good spirits. Chrisman could hardly stop repeating how strong he felt.

Then, at around three o'clock, things started to unravel.

Frances Hyde, who'd been staying at the mansion several days to help out, called Nurse Anna Houlehan to Chrisman's room, where Doctor Hyde was with the patient. Frances told her that Chrisman's temperature had taken a sharp climb and the nurse was to give him a bath. When Houlehan explained that she was assigned to Margaret at the time, Doctor Hyde, with a brusqueness the nurses were growing used to, overrode the duty roster and ordered her to Chrisman's care.

Houlehan would later testify to a remark Hyde made just before leaving the room: He told her he had given Chrisman "his capsule," which, she assumed, referred to the harmless "intestinal antiseptic" given to all the patients. In time the alleged statement would take on a sinister significance and be strongly denied by Hyde and his wife.

With the doctor out of the room, Houlehan spent twenty minutes or so bathing Chrisman with a sponge. At one point another of the nurses, Elizabeth Gordon, came in to offer help and was asked to run downstairs and prepare a glass of orange juice for the patient. Houlehan was just finishing up, changing Chrisman's bed linens, when Stuart Fleming arrived to check on his sick cousin. It was a few minutes later, right after Nurse Gordon reappeared with the orange juice, that the convulsion struck with the sudden force of a released spring.

Chrisman's body stiffened into boardlike rigidity, the arms and legs flung straight out. His eyes were set, his head thrown back. Every muscle was quivering, as though jolted by an electric current. "Peculiar sounds"—Houlehan could only describe them later by imitation—erupted from his throat. His pulse simply vanished, as far as she could tell.

Houlehan stepped into the hall, where she saw Mrs. Swope and cried, "Call Doctor Hyde quickly, quickly." The frightened Maggie Swope screamed her son-in-law's name, and Hyde came running back to the sickroom. Houlehan stepped aside to let the doctor feel Chrisman's pulse. Instantly, he ordered her to inject a fortieth grain of strychnine. "Doctor," Houlehan said, "it looks like meningitis." Hyde answered, "That's what it is."

The seizure lasted around twenty minutes, after which Chrisman, his body still rigid, sank into apparent unconsciousness. The violence of the attack had shaken Cousin Stuart, who had also been disturbed by Hyde's diagnosis. When Hyde stepped out for a moment's rest, Fleming tracked him to another room. "Doctor," he asked, "isn't this very unusual in typhoid?" Hyde seemed sure of himself: "Oh, not at all unusual. Typhoid frequently brings on meningitis."

The sight of his cousin's convulsion had added to Fleming's worries about his own health. All day he'd been hammered by a vicious headache, which had gotten still worse after he'd tried to walk it off on a four-mile hike in the freezing cold. In the minutes after Chrisman's attack, however, he was less concerned about his headache than about Maggie Swope, who was waiting outside in a state of near-hysteria.

She hadn't gone into the room—simply hadn't been able to face it—while her adored son was seized by those awful electric spasms. When she finally did enter, escorted by the solicitous Fleming, Mrs. Swope seems to have misunderstood, or simply refused to grasp, the gravity of Hyde's verdict of meningitis. As if the disease were no more threatening than a bad cold, she remarked that "whenever my poor boy [is] sick, it always [goes] to his head." She laid a hand on his face and noticed that his skin was less hot than she'd thought it would be. Chrisman had slipped into the coma that would enshroud him all night.

One tiny incident the nurses would claim they witnessed that Sunday—and that Hyde would irately dispute—illustrates the nurses' growing readiness to look for the worst in the overbearing doctor who had hired them. Anna Houlehan, who had worked with Hyde a time or two before, and her colleague Miss Gordon were giving Chrisman's inert body a rubdown under the doctor's orders. Once or twice Hyde interrupted to take the patient's pulse and administer shots. The first two hypos, of digitalin and nitroglycerine, he himself gave, and it was the second of these, according to the nurses, that drew their startled attention. As the women would tell it, Hyde prepared the second shot by dissolving a nitroglycerine tablet in some dirty water left over from Chrisman's bath. The nurses said he could have used sterilized water from a chafing dish sitting on the dresser. His only explanation, Nurse Gordon said, was that he had chosen the bath water because the basin was handier and he wanted "quick results."

Chrisman's condition was worrisome enough that someone placed an urgent call to Doctor G. T. Twyman, who not only came right away but brought along his physician son, Elmer. They found the patient in a tetanic state—his rigidness similar to a tetanus victim's—with his eyes still open, turned to the right and upward. His skin was flushed and slightly bluish—cyanotic. The pupils were dilated and showed no response to a lighted match held close to them. Chrisman's pulse was running at such fierce speed that the elder Twyman had to give up trying to get an accurate count. Hyde, who was in the room as the two other doctors probed and examined the patient, repeated his opinion that the malady was meningitis as a dangerous spin-off of typhoid fever.

The Twymans were far from convinced. Many weeks afterward, in his quaintly formal diction, G. T. Twyman would recall, "I did not gainsay that diagnosis, although I thought that the picture of meningitis was not complete to my mind and so expressed myself to my son afterward." Elmer Twyman put his conclusion more bluntly: "Well, he did not have meningitis."

The senior Twyman also took issue with Hyde's choice of medications and told him so. He was troubled by the injections of strychnine, which he felt were contraindicated in a case of tetanic stiffness. Hyde agreed to substitute shots of morphine, but he apparently resumed the strychnine injections sometime later.

On Sunday night, Nurse Elizabeth Gordon took charge of Chrisman's care so that Anna Houlehan, who'd been on duty far beyond her normal shift, could finally get some sleep. Gordon was joined around midnight by Nurse Rose Churchill. What they saw during the long hours would reappear in sworn statements, one of which would raise the real or imagined specter of criminal intent. Chrisman's rigid state, Nurse Gordon would declare, "was just such a seizure as I am considering in connection with strychnia poisoning. ... His face twitched in an awful and awesome manner. I have read, as all well informed nurses have read, about the symptoms of strychnia poisoning; and among other things, I have read about the sardonic grin that appears on the face, and it seems to me that these words more perfectly describe than anything I know the expression on his face at these times."

If Chrisman's condition had been grim throughout Sunday night and the following morning, it turned positively alarming on Monday afternoon. At around two o'clock, a minute after Doctor Elmer Twyman had taken a leukocyte count, the patient suddenly emerged from his coma and corpselike stiffness and reared up with the macabre animation of a spook-show skeleton. Something seemed to terrify him as he struggled to get out of bed. Crawling over the mattress, bumping the headboard, he managed to clamber to the floor. It took two people, young Twyman and Nurse Houlehan, to wrestle him back onto the mattress, where they tied his legs together. His temperature was a frightening 107.8.

Again, Maggie Swope couldn't force herself to enter the room, but her second son, the heavyset, one-armed Tom Swope, had stationed himself near the sickbed, a horrified onlooker. Mrs. Swope could hear Tom crying, "Oh, brother, brother, don't do that way. Do you know me?" Amazingly, the sick man replied, "Oh yes, I know you."

The frenzy had left him exhausted and semiconscious—even talkative, in the surreal non sequiturs of delirium. Sometimes the words made sense. When Chrisman's attack had obviously passed and his body had relaxed a little, Maggie Swope let herself be escorted to his bedside by young Elmer Twyman. As she sat by her son, stroking his face, he said, "Mother, don't worry, we will all pull through all right." His eyes were closed, as if he had slipped into a gentle doze. Mrs. Swope remained with him, speaking to him quietly.

Chrisman grew downright chatty a bit later in the afternoon. With nurses Gordon and Houlehan in the sickroom, he offered a cheerful apology for his bout of craziness. "How in the world did you hold me when I had that fit?" he said. "That was a regular fit I had, and I know it must have taken about eight men to hold me." Miss Gordon said, "Mister Chrisman, you must not do that any more." He told her he had tried not to, "but I could not hold it back."

Mrs. Swope felt so reassured by her son's rally that she had to tell Clark Hyde the moment he returned from a visit to his Kansas City office. She was downstairs in the front hall to meet him, and as Hyde removed his overcoat, she cried, "Doctor Hyde, Chrisman is better—he is conscious and is going to get well." He answered, "Isn't that fine?" and pushed on up the stairs.

Hyde and the senior Twyman were at the bedside when Chrisman suddenly had another disturbing episode. Somehow he had gotten the idea that Hyde planned to operate on him for appendicitis. Both doctors tried to assure him it wasn't true, but his paranoia was in full swing: "You are trying to deceive me, you are going to operate, I have appendicitis, and you are all deceiving me." He demanded to see John Paxton, the family lawyer, so he could make a will—he was sure he would not recover. Maggie Swope was beside herself: "My dear son, you must not get nervous, so much depends on your being quiet. You will get well if you just keep quiet. Try not to get nervous for Mother's sake." Her oldest child promised, "All right, Mother, I will."

Doctor Hyde seemed undiscouraged by Chrisman's state. After meeting with Nurse Houlehan to review the day's developments, he left the room and stayed away for some minutes. On his return, Houlehan would later state, the doctor told her, "If the patient is getting along all right it is time to start his medicine." He then handed her a capsule and requested that she give it to Chrisman with a glass of orange juice.

Hyde would swear there had been no such capsule and no such order to Houlehan. He would fight the allegation as adamantly as he'd fight her claim that he had given—or said he'd given—another mysterious capsule the previous day, shortly before Chrisman's convulsion.

Whatever Chrisman's doctors and nurses did to stabilize him, nothing worked for long. For a while the patient did appear more relaxed. But according to Houlehan, half an hour after she'd given the capsule Chrisman became "restless" again—her euphemism for an agitation bordering on violence. He thrashed about so wildly that, again, she had to hold him down. When she got a chance to ask Hyde if anything more could be done, he replied, "No, let him alone." Ten minutes later the doctor reappeared in the sickroom and volunteered to stay with Chrisman while Houlehan and a second duty nurse, Mae Pierce, took their dinner breaks.

Both were gone for half an hour, perhaps longer, during which Hyde was alone with the patient. In the absence of other witnesses, legal officials would have only the doctor's word for what happened while the nurses were downstairs. Still, Hyde's account seemed reasonable enough. Chrisman was gripped by another powerful spasm that stiffened his fever-wracked body more cruelly than ever and set off a burst of maniacal babbling. Whether the seizure amounted to a second full-scale convulsion was never entirely clear. Hyde himself declined to use the term in subsequent court testimony, but he was quoted by the two nurses as having called the attack a convulsion minutes after it occurred.

In any event, the paroxysm was over by the time Houlehan and Pierce returned to the patient's bedside. They found Chrisman lying crosswise on the bed, apparently having flung himself into that position during his seizure. He was unconscious, his eyes set as they had been after the first convulsion on Sunday. Hyde told the nurses what had happened and directed Houlehan to give Chrisman a hypodermic of morphine. She did as she was told, though it struck her that morphine, a depressant, was an odd drug to be injecting given the patient's extreme weakness.

Hyde's next order was to give Chrisman a hot-water enema. Houlehan thought it was a "brutally cruel" measure to take under the circumstances. Chrisman's legs were so rigid, she later said, that she had "an awful time trying to give it to him," and his bowels failed to discharge most of the fluid. He just lay there, unconscious, still positioned on the bedpan, for another ninety minutes. Nurse Gordon, who had been summoned from Margaret's room, found him breathing shallowly and nearly pulseless.

At some point Mrs. Swope returned to her son's room, sat down beside him, and put her hand over his eyes. They were open but rolled back in his head. She stayed for a while, praying, and then left for the sitting room where her son Tom and Frances Hyde were waiting.

The nurses later recreated the death scene. Houlehan was sitting at Chrisman's head, her hand on his pulse, while Hyde sat on the opposite side of the bed. The doctor spoke the words everyone was expecting, "He's gone," but Houlehan wasn't so sure. "Why, Doctor Hyde, he is breathing yet," she said. And then Chrisman slipped away. It was 9:50 p.m. on Monday, December 6.

Was it a fact—or simply the misperception of nurses who thoroughly disliked the doctor—that Hyde seized the dead Chrisman's ankles and dragged him roughly to a lengthwise position on the bed? They would insist he had, he would insist he hadn't. At any rate he reportedly told Houlehan, "Just leave him for the undertaker," before stepping out to inform the family. At the open door of the sitting room, he said to his wife and mother-in-law, "It's all over." Mrs. Swope said, "What?" and he repeated, "It's all over."

It might have helped Maggie Swope through her hours of anguish had the gentlemanly Stuart Fleming been there to offer comfort. Unfortunately he had boarded a train the previous night for his home in Tennessee, stricken by such pain and fever that there was some concern he might have to get off in St. Louis to seek emergency treatment. His case of typhoid would keep him bedridden and under a nurse's care for more than a month.

It is relevant, in light of subsequent events, that Chrisman had died without progeny and made no will. His share of the Colonel Thomas Swope estate would thus revert to his brother and five sisters, among them Mrs. Bennett Clark Hyde.

Kansas City pharmacist Hugo Brecklein undoubtedly appreciated Doctor Hyde's loyal business, but this latest purchase bothered him. One of the clerks, J. Glazier Williams, had taken the phone order that morning for six 5-grain capsules of cyanide of potassium. Williams knew how swiftly and surely the stuff could kill, and he was hesitant to put up the order before telling his boss.

Brecklein instructed him to call Hyde back to verify that this was really what he wanted to purchase. And why in *capsules*? As Williams spoke with the doctor, he also asked what use he had for cyanide and Hyde answered that he needed it to get rid of some pesky dogs. Later, when Hyde arrived to pick up his lethal purchase, he repeated the dog story to Brecklein, who was waiting for him in the front of the shop. Brecklein had not known of Hyde's previous cyanide purchase on September 13, but even so he felt uneasy. He would sell the capsules to Hyde only if the doctor promised to handle them himself. What if they wound up in the hands of someone else, who took one thinking it was ordinary medicine?

That was on Saturday, December 4, two days before Chrisman Swope departed his devout and gentle life.

Chapter 8

Of all Jackson County's burial places, Mount Washington Cemetery, near the west edge of Independence, may be the most idyllically situated and artfully landscaped. The two hundred acres of plump hills and lawns, sylvan glades and curvy lanes, are so inviting that death itself might seem a reasonable requirement for occupancy. Winter, however, is not Mount Washington's best season. A ground-hardening cold had settled in by the time Chrisman's funeral party arrived on Wednesday, December 8, following services at the First Presbyterian Church (the Reverend C. C. McGinley officiating). A four-inch snow had also fallen two days earlier, icing the road to Chrisman's plot near the crest of a hill. It was just as well that the casket would lie for the time being in the cemetery's receiving vault carved into an earthen slope from the flat ground below.

Maggie Swope's farewell to her son in that cold place must have been unimaginably painful. So too her ride home in the carriage with her eldest daughter, Frances, and her son-in-law, Clark Hyde. Yet the matriarch seems to have held herself together throughout the ordeal of recent days—discounting a few moments of hysteria—and displayed the fortitude expected of her role and rank. She and Frances had issued orders to abandon the household cistern in favor of bottled water and to discard the old wooden coolers in the pantry. She had engaged a temporary cook to replace Ida Copridge, although the family cook had shown no signs of disease. And a day before Chrisman's death, she had dispatched a cablegram to her second eldest daughter, Lucy Lee, instructing her to book the next steamer home from France.

Even during the carriage ride from the cemetery, Maggie Swope had to look past her grief and concern herself with the practical. Someone, for instance, would have to meet Lucy Lee at the dock in New York and look after her during the two-day train ride to Kansas City. Mrs. Swope mentioned the matter to the Hydes as they rode east toward South Pleasant Street, and the response she got from Clark Hyde did not sit well: He told her he would gladly take on the mission himself. She made it clear—politely enough—that she'd prefer someone else. She wanted a woman to go, a sensitive relative or friend who could console and sympathize with Lucy Lee after breaking the news of Chrisman's death. The mother was really hoping daughter Frances would make the trip—able, dependable Frances, who always seemed to step in and take on the big jobs in times of family crisis. But, for the moment, the subject was dropped.

Concern for Lucy Lee's emotional welfare may not have been Maggie Swope's only reason for opposing Hyde's suggestion. Her longtime coolness toward him, plus an uneasiness that would soon swell into full-blown suspicion, were clearly working against the doctor. And then there was Hyde's unseemly behavior of the previous night. Worse than unseemly—scandalous, in the Swopes' eyes.

It was one of those unaccountable slips that revealed a curious flaw in Hyde's personality—the social equivalent of a tin ear. Newly named president-elect of the Jackson County Medical Society, Hyde was to acknowledge the honor at the society's regular meeting on Tuesday night, December 7. Unfortunately, that was the eve of Chrisman's funeral and only one day after the eldest son's death. Given the social conventions of the time, Hyde's decision to attend the meeting, even as his brother-in-law lay in his coffin in the parlor, struck the Swopes as outrageously callous.

As if that weren't insensitive enough, Hyde had treated some colleagues to supper after the meeting to help him celebrate. The late meal had hardly been an extravagant affair, just sandwiches and beer at the newly opened Densmore Hotel in downtown Kansas City. But somehow the family became fixated on the idea that he'd hosted a veritable banquet at the swankier Baltimore Hotel. Hyde later tried to convince his detractors that the "banquet" had been no such thing and that professional courtesy had left him no choice but to attend the society's meeting. Still it was a serious gaffe, suggesting that Hyde's hunger for the applause of his peers had simply overridden his regard for good form. Or perhaps he lacked the social antennae to sense other people's feelings in times of high emotion. Or maybe he just hadn't cared.

It is possible that, by the second week of December, nothing Hyde could have said or done would have won over any of the Swopes except for his wife, Frances, whose loyalty remained absolute. Qualms about the doctor, still short of open mistrust, were spreading throughout the family like whispered rumors. As far as the in-laws were concerned—not to mention the already-suspicious nurses—it was starting to seem that Hyde could do no right. From Tuesday night's social fiasco to certain events later in the week, incident after incident kept impugning whatever the doctor did (or didn't) do.

How could he have been so unresponsive, late on Wednesday night, December 8, when Margaret's condition appeared to take a turn for the worse? The duty nurses, Anna Houlehan and Elizabeth Gordon, noticed that their patient was suffering a severe chill and immediately feared that it might signal a hemorrhage. Their first response was to wrap the shivering Margaret in hot blankets and dose her with sips of whiskey. But the chill persisted and Gordon asked Houlehan to alert Doctor Hyde, who was asleep in the bedroom he was sharing with his wife.

As Houlehan recounted the scene, she approached Hyde's bed in the dark, woke him up, and asked if he could suggest any further medication to relieve Margaret's distress. What she got for her midnight trouble call was little more than a curt "No." The next morning, she said, Hyde tried to excuse his unhelpful response by explaining that he'd been only half awake at the time and hadn't really grasped all that she was saying. Hyde's version of the incident was that he assured Houlehan that she and Gordon were giving exactly the right treatment but insisted they awaken him immediately if Margaret's condition got worse.

A bit less portentous—at the time—was the episode of the sickening sweets. On December 4 and again a few days later, Hyde brought gifts of candy to the still-healthy teenagers, Sarah and Stella. He had purchased them at Dempsey's Candy Store downtown, he said, while waiting for the streetcar to Independence. Both girls sampled the sweets and shared them with an overnight guest from Kansas City, 16-year-old Mildred Fox. None of the children showed any immediate ill effects, but Nurses Elizabeth Gordon and Rose Churchill, who had helped themselves to the treats, were seized by violent nausea that incapacitated them the entire next day. Mrs. Swope decided the candy was to blame.

So far, no one had suggested—out loud at least—that Hyde was behind the typhoid contagion, which spread to its seventh, eighth, and ninth victims in the days following Chrisman's death. The adolescents, Sarah and Stella, developed clear symptoms of typhoid fever on December 10 and 11. So did their guest of the previous weekend, Mildred Fox, who was taken sick after returning to her family home in Kansas City. However, it was just a matter of time until Doctor Hyde's candy (by then long eaten) would become the object of horrified conjecture. What sort of man would give young girls—children!—gift boxes of sweets laced with potentially lethal bacteria?

From the Monday of Chrisman's death until Saturday of that terrible week, Maggie Swope continued to fret over the same dilemma—whom could she find to meet Lucy Lee's ship and see her safely home to Independence? The steamer from Cherbourg, the *Oceanic,* would arrive on Wednesday, December 15. Wealthy relatives in New York, M. D. Hunton (Cousin Mac) and his wife, volunteered to meet Lucy at the dock but could not spare the time for the trip to Missouri. Mrs. Swope considered sending her dairy-farmer son Tom but feared the journey would cause him serious inconvenience. She kept hoping Frances could go, even after Clark Hyde insisted the trip would be too exhausting for his wife, who was feeling weary after her exertions of recent days. In fact, Frances was in a "delicate condition"—her second month of pregnancy—which Hyde may or may not have told Mrs. Swope at the time. He later said he had; she claimed he hadn't.

Late in the week, someone came up with the idea that Mary Hickman, a young woman friend who lived near the Swopes, would be more than suitable for the mission. Hickman, who had never been to New York, might have gathered her nerve and made the trip if the Hydes had had the least intention of letting her do so. Instead, Frances turned over the tickets and the $250 in expense money—provided by her mother—to the last person Mrs. Swope wanted to send. Clark Hyde would escort Lucy Lee home, just as he'd planned to do all along. The outmaneuvered Maggie Swope was not pleased.

As the hours and days wore on, further events added weight to the family's apprehensions that Hyde was somehow a subversive presence, a person they could not trust. The most damning development, in its long-term impact, grew out of two midweek phone calls from Hyde to a Kansas City pathologist, Doctor Frank Johnson Hall.

Hall had already known of the typhoid outbreak in the Swope house, having run a Widal blood test the previous week on one of the patients, at Hyde's request. Then, on Tuesday, December 7, he received a call from Hyde informing him that Chrisman Swope was dead. Hall was astonished. He had never known a typhoid patient to die so early in the course of the disease and his first thought was that Hyde must have made a diagnostic error. At once he asked permission to conduct a postmortem on the chance of discovering some other, overlooked cause of death. Hyde replied that an autopsy was out of the question—the family would never permit it. But on the following day Hyde telephoned Doctor Hall again to enlist his expertise on another matter: Could the pathologist visit the mansion himself and examine the premises for some possible source of the typhoid infection? Hall agreed to meet Hyde at the house as soon as his schedule permitted, and on Friday or Saturday (the exact day is uncertain) he showed up at 406 South Pleasant Street.

After making the rounds of the sickrooms, Hall headed outside for a walk around the property. As he reported later, he found the estate "wonderfully free from the usual factors that introduce typhoid into a household." The cisterns were situated so they weren't subject to surface drainage. The stables were down a slope to the southwest of the house. Placement of the milk house ruled out any seepage of household waste. Everything about the premises that Hall could see—or was told about during his visit—led him to conclude that conditions there were "perfectly sanitary."

Inside the mansion, Hall took a sample of the cistern water remaining in the old wooden cooler. He would examine it that evening for bacteria of fecal origin. He would find none.

Meanwhile, during his conference with Mrs. Swope and Doctor Hyde, Hall inquired about the residents' food habits, which varied: Some drank milk, others never touched it; some ate green vegetables, others didn't. The germs, he reasoned, must have come *en masse* from something nearly everyone had eaten or drunk. He wondered aloud whether the victims had consumed tainted food, perhaps oysters or raw vegetables, during one particular family meal. Mrs. Swope told him she didn't think so. The date Hall fixed for the infection was November 20 or 21—which would raise eyebrows later on as witnesses disagreed over the Hydes' presence or absence at the Sunday dinner on November 21.

All in all, the pathologist's investigation at the Swope mansion left him feeling troubled and frustrated. As he put it to Hyde, the disease seemed to have "walked in," deposited its cargo of germs, and "walked out" without leaving a trace. In the absence of hard facts to explain it, Hall resorted to a more unsettling analogy. It was, he said, "as if the infection had been administered to the family with all the precision of a scientific experiment."

Or maybe it wasn't an analogy after all. Maybe it conveyed what he was truly starting to suspect. The fact was, Doctor Hall (in his own words) didn't "feel right" about the case. If Hyde or the Swopes wanted him to get more deeply involved in it, he made up his mind to refuse. Some instinct told him to stay out of it.

Hall's report of his findings—rather, lack of findings—must have given pause to Maggie Swope when she thought about them. *As if administered with all the precision of a scientific experiment.* As distracted by grief as she was that day, the words stuck with her. She would remember them in months to come, when Hyde's accusers would use them to chilling (and highly newsworthy) effect.

However methodically Hall had searched the grounds and out-buildings, he had in fact overlooked one possibly relevant detail: He had failed to notice that the privy had recently been moved. While no one later agreed on exactly when the work was done, it had evidently been just days before the typhoid invasion. The crude latrine had stood well back of the mansion but also far enough to the north to be visible from the Swopes' front lawn. This offense to the eye had led Mrs. Swope to hire a carpenter to move the outhouse thirty feet to the south. A manservant named Peyton was given the task of scooping up the waste at the original site, dumping it into the abandoned cesspool, covering the filth with dirt and stones, and replacing the cesspool's wooden lid. It was conceivable that Peyton had brought in typhoid germs on his hands or clothing, and everyone knew he sometimes helped Ida with the cooking. By the time this theory was advanced, of course, the family would have settled on a much more sensational explanation.

It is too much to believe that Doctor Hall's report—especially his line about "a scientific experiment"—failed to reach other family members that same day. The talk may have started even as Hall was pulling away from the curb on South Pleasant Street. What is all but certain is that everything the investigator had to say added further tension to the already charged atmosphere inside the great house.

Such was the state of uneasiness when a person familiar to all the Swopes, Nurse Pearl Virginia Kellar, showed up on Saturday, December 11, for her second stint as an in-house caregiver. The nurse who'd been at the deathbeds of Moss Hunton and old Colonel Swope had been asked days earlier by Frances Hyde to return to the house to assist in the typhoid crisis. At the time she'd been involved with another case but promised to come back as soon as she was free. On the late Saturday morning when Kellar arrived at the mansion, sickness seemed to be everywhere. Margaret was in her second week of the fever, Nora Belle Dickson was bedridden in the same room, 14-year-old Sarah was ill for the second day, and

16-year-old Stella was flushed and running a temperature of nearly 102. Chrisman, of course, was in the receiving vault at Mount Washington Cemetery.

The eldest son's death had caught Nurse Kellar by surprise. Only five days previous—the early evening of Monday, December 6—she had telephoned the mansion and reached Stella, who was still in good health. The nurse had heard that Chrisman was down with typhoid and asked about his condition. "He is getting along very nicely, thank you," Stella replied. The teenager was either putting a good face on her brother's dire state or was unaware that he was at the point of death. The following day Nurse Kellar read in the *Kansas City Star* that Chrisman had succumbed.

It was quite by chance that Kellar learned on Tuesday the seventh how death had come to the Swope heir. She had just left the lunchroom at Emery, Bird, Thayer, the elegant, arcaded department store on Kansas City's Petticoat Lane, when she spotted Stella Swope in the crowd of shoppers. They greeted each other and Kellar said, "Why, Stella, didn't Chrisman die awfully sudden?" The girl confirmed that he had and Kellar followed up with the next question that might occur to a nurse: "Did he have a hemorrhage?" Stella's answer—"No, he died in a convulsion"—caused something to click in Kellar's mind.

Not surprisingly, one of her first acts after reporting for duty at the mansion was to ask her nurse colleague, Anna Houlehan, if she had noticed anything mysterious about Chrisman's last hours. Houlehan recalled the conversation later: "I told her a few things I didn't like at the time, but never thought of questioning a medical man." Kellar then related what she had observed at Colonel Swope's bedside—among other things, that the old man had swallowed a whitish capsule only twenty minutes before he was seized by the convulsion that led to his coma and death.

One can only speculate as to why Pearl Kellar agreed to return to the Swope house at all. When she had left it two months ago after attending the old Colonel's funeral, her anxiety for the family may have been as great as her relief at being out of the place. So much of what she'd seen there had left a stark conviction that Doctor Clark

Hyde was up to something diabolical. And now she'd be assisting Hyde again! Was $25 a week really worth it?

At the same time, she must have come to like various family members during those early autumn weeks in their home. She had been of admirable service to them and they undoubtedly had responded with gratitude and respect. The fact that ghastly things were happening to them again—another death, more illnesses, hints of something wicked afoot in the house—must have roused her instincts to protect and warn the family, as well as care for the sick. In accepting her second tour with Doctor Hyde, Kellar could keep an eye on him.

———•·•———

It would later be documented that on Thursday, December 9, the day after Chrisman was laid to rest in the Mount Washington vault, Clark Hyde made another purchase at Brecklein's Drugstore. This time he increased the order of cyanide capsules to a round dozen.

It would also be stated in testimony—and denied by the doctor—that on the following evening, Friday the tenth, he had tried to foist another of his mysterious capsules on an ailing member of the family.

According to the story, Hyde approached young Stella Swope in the sitting room, handed her the capsule, and said, "Will you please give this to Miss Gordon to give to Sarah if she is restless in the night." Sarah, the youngest, had just been bedridden with typhoid, while Stella was still symptom-free. She did as Hyde asked and the capsule was duly delivered to Nurse Gordon in the sick child's room.

That was as far as it got. Sarah slept well, so the next morning Gordon threw out the capsule to keep it from getting mixed in with the other medications. Much later she told a jury there had been another motive for her precaution: She had heard about those capsules given to two other Swopes—on Hyde's orders—shortly before they convulsed and died.

Chapter 9

Maggie Swope's headaches were so common that she accepted them as just another of life's tiresome burdens. In fact, during this last week of grief and anxiety she had been too distracted to notice her pains at all. Still, shortly after breakfast on Sunday, December 12, she agreed to try a new headache powder recommended by Doctor Hyde, which he had brought to the house some days earlier.

She and the Hydes were in the second-floor sitting room when the doctor excused himself to fetch an empty capsule to help the medicine go down. He found none in his medical bag, however, so his mother-in-law would have to take the potion in powdered form. Hyde measured out a dose and sprinkled it on her tongue. Mrs. Swope then washed it back with a large swallow from a glass of water he had brought from downstairs.

Instantly, she made a grimace of disgust. The water tasted horrible, she cried. It was bitter, sour, nasty. She demanded to know where Hyde had found it. He said it was from the cooler in the downstairs hall—it was only the Fountain of Youth distilled water that she never had liked. Mrs. Swope was unconvinced. "There is something radically wrong with that water, no matter what you say," she declared. And then, turning to Frances: "Daughter, have that water emptied out of the cooler and don't allow anyone to drink it because it is the vilest stuff I ever put in my mouth."

Her next command was, "Give me an emetic."

Hyde stepped into the hall, followed by Mrs. Swope and his wife, but he appeared to be taking his time filling the order.

Frances urged, "Hurry, Clark, go and get mother an emetic—she is so nervous she will go crazy." Maggie Swope decided to take matters into her own hand—quite literally—and headed for the bathroom, where she ran a finger down her throat.

Having ejected both medicine and breakfast, she saw Hyde approaching with a small box in hand. He identified its contents as alum, pronounced it an excellent emetic, and poured her a heaping teaspoonful of the white powder. Mrs. Swope had never heard of this use for alum, but she swallowed the stuff anyway with another glass of water. It didn't taste as bad this time, but the alum wasn't doing its work. Again she induced vomiting with a finger to the throat.

"Why Mother, don't get so nervous," Frances exclaimed. "Clark would never try to poison you."

Later, in a sworn statement, Maggie Swope insisted she had not at the time feared poisoning at all. Why, she had said as much to daughter Frances right after the incident took place. She had no doubt that Hyde had brought her the wrong water only through some innocent mistake. Or perhaps the foul flavor had come from something previously left in the glass.

Her statement seems more than a little disingenuous—unless, by some unlikely change of heart, she had shed her growing distrust of the son-in-law about whom she'd had serious qualms for years.

Whatever Hyde's intention or fault in the matter, if any, the episode of the vile-tasting water was insignificant compared to what happened that evening after dark in the sickroom of 20-year-old Margaret Swope.

The sheer creepiness of the second incident would grip jurors and newspaper readers in months to come, and part of its weird fascination—like that of the bedchamber scene in a silent *Nosferatu*—must have sprung from the nature of the victim. Supine on her sickbed, Margaret was just so helplessly, pitifully … sacrificial. Her very features and form—the doleful, equine face, the melancholy eyes, the soft, sloping shoulders—implied a meek submissiveness. She also seems to have been, by far, the least spirited and confident of the three older Swope girls. (Months later, as a timid-voiced trial witness, she would have to be asked repeatedly to speak up.) She was the first of the siblings to get sick. Her relapses appear to have caused special concern among the nurses. She was terrified of hypodermic injections, so much so that gentle Doctor Twyman had ordered them discontinued in her case.

And then came the Sunday night of December 12, sometime around 8:30. Several facts of Margaret's ordeal were beyond dispute; other details would be debated in court.

Without question the patient was conscious and alone in the room, while her primary nurse, Elizabeth Gordon, was having supper downstairs with fellow nurses. Without question the chamber was close to dark, the only light provided by an electric floor lamp near the dresser, its shade wrapped in dark paper for added dimness. Without question Hyde entered quietly, without turning on any additional light, closed the door behind him, and said something to Margaret about a hypodermic shot. As she recoiled in dread, he pulled up her left sleeve and, apparently without preparing the skin, drove the needle into her upper arm near the elbow. In the same instant she tried to jerk the arm away, and a sharp pain drew tears to her eyes.

Hardly had Hyde withdrawn the needle and started from the bed when Nurse Rose Churchill, who had just come up from supper, opened the door, stepped inside, and met the doctor emerging from the shadows. As she later described the scene, he seemed off-guard and clearly in a hurry to leave. Hyde told her, "I just gave Miss Margaret a hypo of camphorated oil. I found her pulse weak." Then he slipped past her into the hall.

Churchill's immediate concern was for Margaret, who was weeping from pain. As she bent over the patient and tried to comfort her, the nurse noticed there was no scent of camphorated oil. She was quite familiar with the medicinal smell of the stuff, which was sometimes injected as a heart stimulant. She also was surprised by Hyde's mention of a weak pulse. Churchill herself had tested Margaret's pulse earlier in the day and found it normal. She asked Margaret if the doctor had checked it before giving the shot. The sobbing patient said he hadn't so much as touched her wrist.

Nurse Gordon, who had spent the most time with Margaret

that day, reached the northeast bedroom only minutes behind Churchill. She too found the patient crying and obviously frightened. As Margaret told what had happened in those minutes alone with the doctor, Gordon made her mind up to approach Hyde and get his version of the story. She found him in the hall just outside the sitting room. Above all, she wanted to know whether he had checked Margaret's pulse before administering the needle. "Yes, I found her pulse was intermittent," he answered, "and I gave her a hypodermic of camphorated oil."

Gordon was immediately skeptical. As she would later testify, Margaret's pulse that afternoon had not been the least bit intermittent. Nor was it intermittent when she rechecked it shortly after the hypodermic injection, and again later in the night.

Like her fellow nurse, Gordon had noticed not the faintest whiff of camphor—not from the arm itself and not from Margaret's bedclothes, where a few drops likely would have spilled. As a matter of fact she had never once seen a bottle of the medication around the house, although she had recently looked for some. It turned out that brother Chrisman had asked for camphorated oil one day during his final illness, but the nurses had failed to locate any in the bathroom cupboard.

Inspecting Margaret's arm, Gordon found it badly inflamed around the point of injection, with a red, swollen, "feverish" spot the size of a dollar. And it was getting worse. As the nurse applied a dressing of bichloride of mercury, Margaret could barely stand to have the sore area touched. The only way she could get any sleep was to cradle the arm on a pillow at her left side.

The next morning—Monday—Margaret was still in severe pain. A large section of the arm was shockingly swollen and colored an angry red. When Mrs. Swope looked in on her, the mother's reaction was predictable. She called to Hyde, who was in the sitting room with Doctor Twyman, and demanded, "Come look at Margaret's arm and see what suffering you have caused her to have." Clark Hyde's later statement that she spoke the words "with a smile" would strain the credulity of practically anyone who knew the passionate, fiercely protective mother.

But then Hyde and other witnesses to Margaret's misery would go *mano a mano* over several key points. Among other things, the doctor would assert that shortly before supper, while standing at the top of the stairs, he and Nurse Gordon had discussed Margaret's pulse and she had told him clearly that it was intermittent. To buttress his account, Hyde would claim that his wife, Frances, was at his side at the time, had heard Gordon's report, and could verify the substance of it.

Furthermore—regardless of Margaret's statement to the contrary—he insisted he had personally examined her pulse while the nurses were at supper. Upon finding it was intermittent, he had taken the obvious next step—to prepare an injection to stimulate the heart. Camphorated oil was a widely accepted remedy for an irregular pulse and a one-ounce vial of it was in the bathroom just down the hall. He had put it there himself, he said, after purchasing it recently from a Kansas City drugstore.

Hyde would downplay the injection's effect on Margaret's left arm, later testifying it had left only "a red spot." But a week after the shot the arm was still badly swollen—at one point from shoulder to finger tips and nearly twice its normal size—and it continued to throb painfully. To the nurses who changed Margaret's dressings, the condition of her arm suggested that something other than camphorated oil may have entered the flesh. Something more like the "pus germs" found in common sores.

The nurses were growing more anxious and indignant by the day, and their indignation was heightened by the knowledge that Hyde had told one story—to Doctor Twyman and Mrs. Swope— while their own eyes told quite another. Rose Churchill had been less willing than the others to think the worst of the doctor who'd hired them. But now she joined those who clearly believed Hyde was up to no good. Without specifying just what evils she felt were astir in the mansion, Churchill was convinced there was "something wrong going on around here."

Nurse Anna Houlehan, who had arrived at the same conclusion from "the many things I had recalled that seemed so peculiar," grew all the more alert for signs of suspicious activity on

Hyde's part. Her watchfulness was sharpened by a plea from Margaret never to leave her alone with the doctor.

But of all the nursing team, it was strong-minded, blunt-spoken Pearl Kellar who reacted most angrily. After hearing her colleagues' stories the morning after the mysterious injection, and after examining Margaret's bloated, bandaged arm supported on a pillow, Kellar spoke to the nurses as a group: "Girls, just one thing more has got to happen and I will not be here. Doctor Twyman has got to share this thing. I will not be here and see these people murdered."

Kellar's declaration was a call to arms. Her sister nurses made it clear they would stand by her in the event of one more outrage.

———————

On Monday, December 13—the very day Hyde left for New York—the popular young Kansas City physician and bacteriologist Doctor Edward Stewart found himself startled by certain details of a medical case just brought to his attention.

A colleague and close friend, Doctor J. Q. Chambers, had told Stewart he was treating a 16-year-old girl named Mildred Fox, whose symptoms clearly indicated typhoid fever. There was every reason to believe, he said, that the Kansas City teenager was infected during an overnight stay at the Independence home of the prominent Swope family. The time between her visit to the great house and the onset of symptoms was precisely seven days, a typical incubation period for typhoid infections. The teenager had been rushed back home immediately after three of the mansion's occupants were diagnosed with typhoid fever.

And things had gotten worse. In the days following Mildred's departure, the disease had rampaged through the Swope household, striking family members, guests, and a servant. One victim, an elder son, had gone to his grave. Yet, as far as Doctor Chambers knew, *not one* other case of typhoid fever had been recorded in the City of Independence during the entire year. The epidemic—if that was the word for it—was confined to a single family's home.

Stewart pondered the matter all afternoon and couldn't stop thinking about it, even after he'd closed his office for the day and reached his home at 2524 Jackson Avenue. Snow had fallen again—it would be a fine evening to take his small son sledding. After dinner the two of them headed for a neighborhood slope, where the boy romped until nearly bedtime. When they returned, Stewart found that his wife, mother, and infant son were already upstairs. He sent the older child up as well and was now alone, free to settle into a cozy chair and read the evening paper. But the moment he sat, a thought struck his mind with disturbing force. Actually it was two thoughts in sudden convergence: the weirdly isolated typhoid outbreak in the Swope house, and the cultures of typhoid bacillus that he himself had furnished Doctor Hyde back in November. Surely Clark Hyde, his respected colleague and president-elect of the Jackson County Medical Society, could have had nothing to do with. . . .

Stewart tried to dismiss the idea and get on with his reading, but the newspaper columns were a blur. He climbed the stairs, undressed his little boy, and tucked him in. Then he headed for his own bedroom. It must have been a relief to find his wife still awake—he needed badly to tell someone what was on his mind. After laying out his troubling hypothesis, he cautioned her to say nothing about it to anyone, and Mrs. Stewart likewise cautioned him. But it was after midnight before the handsome doctor could fall asleep.

When he awoke on Tuesday, his brain was already at work formulating a plan. It would be a simple matter to visit his colleague's office and take a look at the typhoid culture he had prepared for Hyde's use, as a friendly favor, a little over a month ago.

Stewart was busy with other tasks until three o'clock, but then he walked the two blocks north to Hyde's office. The secretary-receptionist, Bessie Coughlin, informed him that Hyde was on a trip to New York. Stewart explained that he had recently given a typhoid culture to her employer, but subsequently his own stock culture had died. Would Miss Coughlin kindly permit him to scrape off a bit of Hyde's typhoid colony for replanting in his own laboratory? The obliging secretary opened a cabinet door to reveal the entire germ collection in glass tubes. Stewart took them to the window and lifted the samples to the light, one by one.

None appeared to have been disturbed until he came to the typhoid culture, which was planted on a slant in an agar tube. The lower half of the gelatinous medium had not been touched, but the upper half had been—in Stewart's phrase—"swept clean." This had probably been done in two long strokes of a platinum loop "such as would be made if one was desirous of removing a vast number of bacteria."

Stewart later described the amount of missing bacteria a bit more colorfully. Enough typhoid germs had been skimmed off, he said, "to inoculate the whole of Kansas City."

The bacteriologist slipped the tube into a pocket, having decided to have it photographed at a studio at Eleventh and Main Streets. However, the proprietor, a Mr. Coffey, told him that no camera could capture the object in clear detail. Careful to keep the tube's contents as close as possible to the condition in which he'd found them, Stewart then returned to his office and asked his associate, Doctor H. O. Leonard, to examine the sample and take notes on everything he saw. Leonard's observations were the same as his own.

From that point on, Doctor Stewart's involvement in the Hyde case began to evolve from the simple inquiries of a troubled onlooker to the direct actions of a rescuer and medical detective. His immediate duties were clear enough: first, to hold on to Hyde's tube of bacteria as possible legal evidence; and second, to replace it in Hyde's germ collection with a harmless substitute. After scratching tiny marks on the glass for identification purposes, he locked the original tube in his desk. Next he planted a new tube with an identical typhoid culture, to which he added potassium permanganate and formaldehyde to destroy the germs. This dead typhoid colony—a virtual twin of the live culture—would wind up in Hyde's office cabinet.

Unfortunately, on Wednesday, Stewart found that a few live bacilli were still swimming in the new culture medium. Worried that Hyde might return at any hour, he decided he had no choice but to revisit Hyde's office without delay and place the tube of devitalized culture in the glass holder where the virulent specimen had been kept.

It was during this maneuver that he noticed something he had missed on the first visit. Another of the culture tubes, labeled "Diphtheria," had also been molested. Some of the germ growth had been scraped from the top, apparently with a single stroke of the loop. Stewart thought little of it at the time, however, and left the tube where it was.

Chapter 10

It was almost as if a gust of clean, bracing wind had swept through the Swope mansion at midmorning on Monday, December 13, when Clark Hyde headed out the door to begin his journey to New York City. Indeed, throughout the five days of his absence, it seemed that every patient in the house began to feel more fit and cheerful than they had since the epidemic began. Margaret's sudden return to strength and her much-improved mood were noted in particular. Despite the persistent pain and swelling of her arm, she was chatty and lighthearted with everyone who dropped by to see her or dispense care.

The occasion of Hyde's trip, to meet Lucy Lee's ship and escort his young sister-in-law back home, would prove a pleasant interlude for the doctor, as well. His train pulled in to New York's West 23rd Street Station at 7:15 p.m. on Tuesday the fourteenth. He had just finished dinner on board and in all likelihood was in the best of spirits. For one thing, he had left the all-but-hostile atmosphere of the Swope mansion some 1,250 miles behind him. For another, he would have an evening and half of the next day to enjoy the city before the White Star liner *Oceanic* was scheduled to dock.

Hyde checked into the Hotel Woodstock on West 43rd Street—the same hotel where his wife's Hunton relatives, Cousin Mac and his wife, had their apartment. Hyde's room on the eleventh floor was just across the hall from the Huntons' flat, although the cousins were at dinner in the hotel restaurant when he arrived. After trying unsuccessfully to phone two old friends from his room—one was the husband of a former sweetheart—Hyde dispatched a bellhop to deliver his card to the Huntons' table. A few minutes later he joined them in the restaurant, where they offered to treat him to dinner. Hyde declined, but stayed on for a leisurely conversation as they finished their coffee.

Clearly, the three of them hit it off. Rather than cut short the evening, the Huntons invited the doctor to their apartment, where he remained until nearly eleven o'clock. At one point Hyde asked Mrs. Hunton for the pleasure of her company on a Christmas-shopping excursion he had planned for the next morning—they would not be meeting Lucy Lee's ship until early afternoon. Mrs. Hunton happily accepted.

After breakfast on Wednesday, December 15, Hyde and his new friend were making the rounds of New York's fashionable department stores. It was the jolliest of outings. In fact, it is inconceivable that the Manhattan relatives would have welcomed their visitor so graciously if they had known of the sullen cloud that hovered over him back home in Missouri.

Their shopping tour over, Hyde and Mrs. Hunton made their way to the White Star docks on the Hudson River, where the liner *Oceanic* had just slipped into berth. It was 12:45. They were in perfect time to greet Lucy Lee Swope, who'd been summoned home nine days ago with an urgent cablegram from her mother. She'd been told only that typhoid fever had invaded the household and sickened two of her siblings, Margaret and Chrisman. It was unpleasant news but hardly catastrophic.

Then, as she was about to debark, she was amazed to see her brother-in-law, Clark Hyde, waiting near the foot of the gangplank. Lucy Lee had sailed home from Europe on a previous trip, and no one had greeted her at the wharf that time. But Hyde had come *all the way from Missouri* to meet her. His surprise appearance had to mean something terrible had happened. With the flawed logic of panic, she assumed that her entire family must have died.

That the only one dead from the typhoid was poor Chrisman may have given her some perverse relief, but she was nevertheless stunned. And it didn't help that Hyde broke the news to her with something less than brotherly tenderness. He did so as they

**Lucy Lee Swope,
ca. 1912.**
Courtesy Jackson County
(MO) Historical Society
Archives (jchs003618m);
gift of Miss Grace and
Miss Eleanor Minor.

stood on the sidewalk a block and a half from the dock. His tone
was unemotional—she would later describe it as "cold-blooded."
He was wearing his ... smile. The one that looked as simulated—to
some people, anyway—as the painted grin on a mask. In contrast,
Mrs. Hunton threw her arms around Lucy's neck, poured out her
warmest condolences, and suggested they all take a cab to the Wal-
dorf for lunch.

One of the comelier of the Swope daughters, a less equine version of her sister Margaret, Lucy Lee could not have looked her
best that afternoon. The shock of Chrisman's death had left her
shaken and weary. If Mrs. Hunton had not offered a room in her
apartment where Lucy could rest and be alone, it's doubtful she
could have faced the next leg of her journey starting in just hours.

It was 6:15 p.m. when she and Hyde arrived by taxi and ferry at the Pennsylvania Railroad Station in Jersey City. Lucy Lee was feeling more composed as she boarded the Pullman car and settled into her private stateroom. Soon Hyde joined her and spent some time recounting the events that were plaguing her family back home. She had been informed, while in France, of Cousin Moss's and Uncle Thomas's deaths.

The truth was, she had never much liked her brother-in-law. But there he sat, trying to be attentive and sociable, and she could hardly be less than civil. As a boy selling candy passed down the aisle, Hyde stopped him to buy two boxes of sweets—peppermints for Lucy Lee, cream chocolates for himself. Then, some forty minutes into the journey, she said she was thirsty and stood up to get a drink of water from the cooler down the aisle.

Hyde said, "Wait a minute."

He not only volunteered to fetch the water himself, but produced a silver folding cup to bring it in, a clever travel gift sent along by her sister Frances Hyde. While he was out of the stateroom, it crossed Lucy Lee's mind that Hyde was taking his time for such a simple errand. He returned soon enough, however, and she drank down the whole cupful, which tasted quite normal. Lucy's next sip of anything was at table in the dining car, where Clark Hyde ordered wine—he had a weakness for the finer things—and poured a ladylike portion into her glass. After dinner, Lucy asked Hyde to call the porter to make up her berth. Then they separated for the night.

The train reached St. Louis early Thursday evening, leaving them three hours to kill before they boarded the Chicago & Alton for Kansas City. Lucy read a telegram from home, Hyde made phone calls, they dined at a restaurant. Shortly after their train pulled out, Lucy Lee was feeling faintly headachy. Hyde offered to give her a powder "to open her bowel," but she decided instead to take some pills made up by a Kansas City, Kansas, "herb doctor" known by the improbable name Chasing Hatred Chase Jordan. Jordan would eventually become a kind of comic bit player in the Hyde-Swope drama, setting off a minor rivalry among newspapers over the correct rendering of his name.

As Lucy Lee's train approached Kansas City on the morning of Friday, December 17, the anticipations of family members and others in the mansion were decidedly mixed. Of course Lucy's homecoming would be welcomed by all—it would draw together the full circle of Swopes to share mutual comfort and fellowship in their hour of need. On the other hand, the prospect of Hyde's return threw a shadow of foreboding, especially among the cadre of nurses. Anna Houlehan, who had remarked on how well the patients had all done during Hyde's absence, said to her colleague Elizabeth Gordon, "Miss Gordon, I have a presentiment that something is going to change our conditions." The other nurse replied, "Doctor Hyde is coming home. You wait and see if something don't happen."

A hard sun glinted off the snow on the east-facing hill when Lucy Lee Swope and Clark Hyde arrived at the Independence mansion at midmorning. After the cries of greeting and the scurry of servants bearing suitcases, Mrs. Swope expressed her concern that Lucy Lee would now be vulnerable to typhoid infection. There was no such worry for Hyde, who had been heavily exposed for many days and remained healthy. Hyde offered right away to give Lucy Lee and her mother vaccinations against the disease.

Mrs. Swope was definitely leery about the idea and decided she'd better consult with Pearl Kellar, the family's most veteran nurse. Kellar looked her hard in the eyes and said, "Don't you permit it." Then Kellar turned to a fellow nurse, Lou E. Van Nuys, and asked, "You would not, would you?" and Van Nuys answered, "No indeed."

That settled it. Maggie Swope told Hyde that vaccinations wouldn't be needed and a few minutes later he headed off to his office in Kansas City. Mrs. Swope then decided that Lucy's best hope for avoiding the disease would be for her to spend a few days with the family of her bosom friend, Eleanor Minor, whose house on Spring Street was in walking distance from the Swope estate. That evening, the homecoming daughter removed herself to a safer lodging, where she would wind up spending the next three nights.

Nurse Anna Houlehan's dark apprehensions over Hyde's return had left her unprepared for the surprising cheerfulness that saturated the dawning hours of Saturday, December 18. She had been on duty in Margaret's room since midnight, and to her satisfaction had found the patient's temperature a perfect 98.25 degrees and her pulse normal. Margaret was chatting and laughing and told Houlehan that she hadn't felt so fine since before her illness. Her buoyant mood could have sprung in part from her 7 a.m. medication—orange juice and two drams of whiskey.

Then, as the nurse was writing up her log, Hyde arrived. He was in glowing spirits. Almost flirtatiously, he announced that the first thing he'd seen on entering the room was the sunshine on Houlehan's face. The morning radiance was pouring in through a space between the shutters.

Hyde glanced at Houlehan's chart, set it down, and stepped over to the mantle, close to where the nurse was standing. From it he picked up a box of capsules and asked Houlehan if Margaret was still taking them. She was, the nurse confirmed. Houlehan didn't know their contents, only the prescription number, but she'd been giving them to Margaret several times daily under Doctor Twyman's orders. They had produced no ill effects. Hyde asked her when the next capsule was due and Houlehan told him she'd be giving it in about an hour. At this moment Frances Hyde appeared at the door and informed the nurse she was to go downstairs for breakfast.

At 8 a.m., Houlehan was back on duty at Margaret's bedside. Hyde had left for his office in Kansas City, and the nurse and patient were now alone together. Following the usual morning routine, Houlehan bathed Margaret and gave her an alcohol rub. Then she noticed it was time for Margaret's capsule and picked one from the box that Hyde had examined earlier. Margaret swallowed it as the nurse stood by, and lay back on her pillows. Close to twenty minutes passed. At some point Houlehan wandered to the window, its shutters now open, and gazed out over the snowy lawn to Pleasant Street below. A buggy was parked in front of the house, she noticed, and Doctor Twyman was making his way up the landscaped hill. Both patient and nurse heard his arrival at the big front door. When Margaret was told it was Twyman in the entry hall, she remarked casually that he always visited her room first on his morning rounds.

Just as Houlehan turned to step closer to her patient's bed, the young woman lying before her—without warning—began to shudder, her body an electric arc of quivering motion. Margaret's neck had gone rigid, her head was jammed back into the pillows, her eyes were open in a dead stare toward the ceiling. Sounds tumbled from her mouth, nonwords spilling out in a senseless muttering. Houlehan immediately grabbed Margaret's wrist to find a pulse. She found none.

As far as Houlehan could tell, the convulsion was identical—sounds and all—to the one she'd observed firsthand at Chrisman's bedside and the other she'd been told about, the old Colonel's seizure. From professional experience, she knew all the ghastly symptoms. But Margaret's attack got to her. It took an effort of will to suppress her anxiety as she dashed into the hall. Mrs. Swope was in the sitting room with the door open and it wouldn't do to frighten her. At the same time, hearing Doctor Twyman climbing the stairs, Houlehan couldn't help calling for him to come with her—come quickly—into Margaret's room.

Mrs. Swope heard the commotion. "What in the world is the matter, is anything wrong?" she cried. As Twyman and the nurse rushed into the northeast bedroom, she followed right behind them ... and then took one look at her daughter's clenched body on the bed. She forced herself not to scream. If she screamed the whole family would be alarmed. All she could think to do was retreat down to the basement two floors below, where no one would hear her wailing.

Twyman realized instantly that Margaret was in a "severe clonic convulsion." Without delay, he ordered Houlehan to prepare an injection of a fourth grain of morphine and a hundredth of nitroglycerine. Houlehan discovered there was neither nitroglycerine nor a hypodermic needle in the room—she'd have to borrow the items from her sister nurses, who were scattered in various parts of the upper floors. Twyman, meanwhile, attempted to check Margaret's pulse, but the twitching and rigidity of her arm made it impossible to get a count. Margaret's skin had a slightly bluish cast—cyanotic blue.

Word of her attack immediately shot through the house. Houlehan raced to the third-floor nurses' dormitory "all in a trimble" (Nurse Gordon's term), where she found the nitroglycerine. The needle she obtained from Rose Churchill, who was on duty with the bedridden children's companion, Nora Belle Dickson. Nurses Lou Van Nuys and Pearl Kellar were summoned from other rooms.

As Kellar stepped into Margaret's room, she saw Doctor Twyman seated by the patient's bed, looking less anxious than simply dumbfounded. He peered up at her and said, "I cannot see any cause for this convulsion." Kellar replied—as if it were fresh news—"Doctor Twyman, have you ever noticed this is the third one in this house to have convulsions lately?"

Twyman estimated that the seizure lasted fifteen minutes, after which Margaret lapsed into a coma, her eyes still wide open. The morphine-nitroglycerine injection finally did its work at 10:15 a.m. Margaret began sweating heavily and vomited an opalescent, milky substance, which Houlehan caught in a large silver cup. (Nurse Gordon later transferred the vomit into a corked bottle, which she placed under the bathroom washstand.) At once, Margaret was deeply asleep. The crisis was over.

The incident, however, had left Twyman feeling shaken and frustrated. The sicknesses and scary surprises were getting out of hand—he needed help. As soon as Margaret had drifted off, he went to Mrs. Swope's room and told her he would like to engage another physician, a Doctor Ayers, whom she herself had once recommended. To Twyman's dismay, Ayers turned out to be tied up with another case. Mrs. Swope then informed him she had put in calls to Doctor Hyde and a colleague of his, Doctor John W. Perkins, asking that they hurry to Independence. She had arranged with a Kansas City garage to have a car waiting for them. Why Maggie Swope summoned her son-in-law at this of all times is a puzzler, given her deepening conviction that he was behind much of the family's misery.

Though Margaret was clearly out of danger, Doctor Twyman had no time to relax and take his mind off the family's troubles. First came Nurse Anna Houlehan's distressing news that she'd be quitting the Swope house—permanently—that very day. Twyman didn't ask her why and Houlehan didn't tell him. It was as if they had made a silent pact to steer around a mutually distasteful subject. Then Frances Hyde showed up in time to catch the last of their words. Twyman repeated what the nurse had said to him, and Mrs. Hyde also asked no questions. "Very well Miss Houlehan, if you feel that way," she said. "We certainly appreciate what you have done for us."

The next incident to rattle Twyman's composure began with a request to come upstairs to the nurses' dormitory. There he found three of the nurses waiting for him and sensed right away what they were up to. Before they could open their mouths, he said, "Girls, I know what you are going to say."

Kellar, the obvious peer leader and spokesperson, came right back at him: "Doctor, you don't know all, and we can't stand it any longer."

That morning they had huddled in pairs and threesomes, venting their anger and consternation among themselves. They knew of—and supported—Houlehan's decision to leave the house and its escalating horrors. Sternly, as though reciting the articles of a criminal indictment, Kellar spelled out for Twyman each one of the nurses' causes against Hyde. She spoke of the capsules, the three similar convulsions, the doctor's midnight injection of *something* into Margaret's arm. And, of course, the typhoid outbreak, which, they had no doubt, was Hyde's wicked doing.

Twyman asked for time to think—he had to get his bearings, he said—and for the time being the matter was dropped. There were visitors in the mansion. Clark Hyde had returned to Independence in the hired car, accompanied by Perkins, a Harvard-educated doctor with some expertise in typhoid transmission. The two of them would be visiting with patients, nurses, and others in the house, looking for the source of the contagion. Perkins also planned to poke around the premises checking objects and places where disease bacilli might yet be hiding.

The doctors' investigations went into early afternoon, with nothing to show for it except—most interestingly—nothing. Both Perkins and Hyde offered the usual theory that the typhoid was food-borne. Perkins mentioned unwashed lettuce. The physicians talked it over at lunch, during which Perkins told Mrs. Swope the typhoid germs seemed to have been "brought in and walked out again"—the same phrase she had heard from a previous investigator, the suspicious pathologist Doctor Frank Hall.

Hyde and Perkins also took time to look in on Margaret, who had gradually come awake and was still under Houlehan's care. Perkins asked to see the patient's swollen arm, which Houlehan exposed by undoing the bandage. "What have you got on it?" Perkins inquired, and she answered, "Antiflugestine." Hyde flashed one of his smirks at Perkins and said, "Just to have something on it." Whether or not he'd meant it that way, Houlehan took it as a gibe at her for having overreacted to a mere sore arm. Worse, she saw it as a slur against Doctor Twyman, who had ordered her to apply the antiseptic ointment. In Houlehan's mind, Twyman was a more capable, conscientious physician than Hyde could ever be.

Hyde's sarcasm—if that's what it was—may have reinforced Houlehan's already firm decision to leave. At around four o'clock, after Hyde and Perkins had left the mansion, Houlehan spoke with Mrs. Swope for the last time. The latter had been told of her unhappiness with events in the house, but the official reason for Houlehan's departure was that she'd been called home to Kansas City because of an illness. After handing the nurse her paycheck, Mrs. Swope was gracious, as usual: "Miss Houlehan, I am sorry you are going. I hope there is no unkind feeling in regard to anything." Houlehan's reply, as Maggie Swope recalled it, was that she held no ill feelings at all but simply had to go home. Houlehan remembered her farewell line as a bit harsher: "I told her there were too many mysterious things happening—I couldn't stay."

Whatever Houlehan told Mrs. Swope on her way out the door, her words were undoubtedly less blunt than those of her fellow nurses when they confronted Doctor Twyman a second time since noon. He had been home for an hour and returned to the mansion around 5:30. After hearing that the nurses wished to speak with him again, he no doubt felt a certain dread as he climbed the stairs to their room. All five remaining nurses were there in a defiant cluster. Again it was Pearl Kellar who led off.

What they demanded to know, she said, was precisely what Twyman intended to do about Hyde. Great wrongs were being done. Now it was up to him.

Twyman said he hadn't had time to think the matter through. He wondered if they were needlessly alarmed, and he said so, which probably ruffled them further.

Kellar reminded him of what had led up to Colonel Swope's death—the mysterious capsule, the convulsion minutes later. She told him what Hyde had asked of her on the night Moss Hunton died—to help secure his appointment as executor of the old Colonel's estate.

It was all too much for Twyman. He said he could not see "how any man could be so low on the scale of humanity as to think of such an enormous crime." One of the nurses suggested that perhaps Twyman's life had been more innocent than Hyde's.

Then Nurse Kellar put everything on the line: "Now, Doctor Twyman, you may talk all you please, you are not going to convince us at all, because we think we know that Doctor Hyde is responsible for the death of Colonel Swope and Chrisman Swope, and the inoculation of this family with typhoid."

What it came down to was that the nurses would not—could not—stand by in the Swope mansion to see the whole family murdered. They would give Doctor Twyman until morning to devise a plan for ridding the house of Bennett Clark Hyde.

"If he goes, we will stay," Kellar added. "If he stays, we go."

Chapter 11

xcept for the absence of a moon it was a Christmas-card evening, crystalline and vivid with stars, when Doctor George Twyman made the long walk downhill from the mansion to the street. For the moment he was free of the nurses, the sickroom crises, the dreads and rancors that filled the house like sour odors. But it's doubtful he took much pleasure in the picturesque snowscape that lay about him in the early dark of Saturday, December 18. It had been a rotten day. Given all that he'd witnessed since morning, he had little hope that things would be much improved the next time he dropped in on the Swopes.

Twyman's buggy and a servant "boy" driver were waiting at the curb to deliver him home for supper. The prospect of some rest and a hot meal must have been welcome—precisely what he needed to settle his mood. But even that modest respite would have to wait. As the buggy rolled along Pleasant Street, it overtook a middle-aged couple walking briskly on the sidewalk. Twyman recognized the Swope family's attorney, John Paxton, and Mrs. Paxton, heading in the direction of their home at 614 Delaware. Seeing an opportunity to confide in a trusted adviser, Twyman ordered his driver to pull up beside the couple. He then proposed that Paxton walk with him for a few minutes while Mrs. Paxton received a ride home in the buggy.

The few minutes turned into nearly half an hour as the two men, bundled in heavy overcoats, conversed in the privacy of the frozen residential streets. By 6:30, Twyman had related everything about the turbulent day, right up to the nurses' ultimatum and his

**DR. G. T. TWYMAN
OF INDEPENDENCE.**
Kansas City Times, Tue.,
Feb. 8, 1910, p. 1.

own quandary over what to do next. Paxton recalled later that he
was "thunderstruck... shocked and overcome" by the whole tale
of alleged treachery. He felt attached to the entire Swope family,
including Frances and her husband. His hope from the outset,
he said, was that Hyde was innocent of wrongdoing and that the
suspicions were no more than the poisonous spillover from some
awful misunderstanding.

Whether Hyde was falsely accused or not, the two men agreed
it was no time to take chances. Paxton's counsel was that Doctor
Twyman return to the mansion that evening and lay his information and concerns before Mrs. Swope. The mistress of the house
had to be told, especially what the nurses were threatening to
do if Hyde remained in residence. If they actually acted on their
threat and deserted their posts in the morning, several seriously ill
patients would be left unattended.

The men ended their walking conversation at Twyman's house at 401 North Pleasant, some eight blocks from the Swope mansion. Before they parted, the doctor promised Paxton that he would speak with Mrs. Swope after he'd had supper.

Twyman's evening meal was not the relaxing interlude he'd have liked. Within half an hour—if that—he had finished eating, was wrapped in his overcoat, and was heading back south by buggy to the Swopes' hilltop estate.

Maggie Swope was in the back of the house when she heard the doorbell's ring. As she admitted Doctor Twyman into the front hall, neither of them wasted words on social niceties. Twyman said he needed to speak with her privately, and they stepped into the adjoining music room. It was semidark, but as Mrs. Swope reached to switch on the light, Twyman asked her not to do so. The conversation would be highly confidential. He didn't wish to attract notice.

Twyman started off: "You know there's been some trouble with the nurses." Mrs. Swope denied knowing anything about it, although she'd been told of Anna Houlehan's unhappiness and had personally seen the nurse out the door. "Well," Twyman went on, "don't you know that Hyde is in trouble, that the nurses say they will not stay here?"

"Oh God, can it be true?" the black-clad matriarch said. She reminded Twyman of a recent conversation in which she had asked him, "Is Doctor Hyde all right?" and he had answered, "Yes, I think he is." Tonight's visit told another story. As Maggie Swope later recounted it, "A great many things flashed over me. Everything seemed to open up like a great revelation to me, and a different light was put on things I had not thought of."

Clearly she *had* thought of Hyde's possible villain's role in the chain of family disasters. Why else had she asked previously whether Hyde was "all right"? Still, she later maintained it was not until her meeting with Twyman in the darkened music room that all parts of the macabre puzzle began falling into place. She was now convinced that the nurses had every reason to feel as they did and to take their stand against the diabolical—as she firmly believed—son-in-law. Little wonder that these conscientious caregivers refused

Swope Mansion Right Parlor, ca. 1908.
Courtesy Jackson County (MO) Historical Society Archives (jchs016721em);
gift of Mrs. D. J. Hyde Matheny.

to stay in the house with Hyde and, in her words, "be used as tools towards getting people out of the world."

Twyman left the decision to her: "What should I do?"

Without a beat, she replied, "Tell him to go."

At this point they were interrupted by a woman's voice. Frances was calling "Mother!" from somewhere on the second floor. A minute passed and the eldest daughter appeared at the music room door. She had heard there was a visitor in the house and had come downstairs to investigate. She entered the room, turned on the light, and asked her mother what she and Twyman were talking about—was something wrong?

They mumbled a few guarded words and Twyman got up to leave. As he walked into the hall to get his coat, the doctor asked Frances what time her husband was expected back at the Independence mansion. She told him she wasn't sure. "When he comes,"

Twyman said casually, "tell him I want to talk to him about a case." He would be at his office all evening, he added. Then he was out the door.

In any other emergency, Mrs. Swope would have gone straight to the sensible Frances for advice and strength. Of all the children, this daughter was the closest the mother had to a trusted confidante. But in this crisis, obviously, any disclosure to Frances was out of the question. Maggie Swope had to speak with *someone* about her visit with Doctor Twyman, about the nurses' accusations and their threatened rebellion. Fortunately there was a mature family member she could confide in. Her stolid but reliable son Thomas, whose dairy farm was four miles east of town, happened to be staying the night at the mansion. She found him in the sitting room and proceeded to tell him everything.

The furtive discussion ended abruptly when Frances, passing along the hall, stepped in to join them. She had already sensed that something was in the air, an atmospheric change that made her uneasy. The tensions in the room must have been almost tactile as the three of them sat there, elaborately skirting what was really on their minds. No doubt they reacted with a start when the doorbell rang shortly after eight o'clock. The person at the door was Clark Hyde, unimpeachable healer and loving husband or agent of unspeakable evil, depending on whose ears heard him arrive from his medical office in Kansas City.

As Frances headed downstairs to let her husband in, her brother Tom was heading out. Their sister Lucy Lee, who had spent part of the day at the mansion, needed an escort back to the home of her temporary hosts, the Minors. Tom and Lucy were on their way toward the Minor house on Spring Street by the time Hyde was warming his hands in the Swopes' front hall.

Hyde had not even removed his coat when Frances relayed the message to call Doctor Twyman. The husband and wife talked for a few minutes, then Hyde placed the call from the downstairs telephone. Frances, at his side, heard him say, "All right, doctor, I will be right up"—just those words, with nothing in the tone to suggest apprehension. Hyde hung up the earpiece and told Frances he'd been asked to drop by Twyman's office ... something about a case the older physician wished to consult him on. The couple spoke together a while longer, after which Hyde left for his appointment with the family doctor.

Three streetlights—electric, kerosene, and gas—shone along Pleasant Street between the entrance to the Swope estate and Kansas Street, two blocks to the north. While their glow was limited, the freshly fallen snow added its own pale luminescence to the night. Conceivably, a person walking along that stretch of pavement could have seen another pedestrian approaching him from as much as a block away.

Of all the questions raised later in court testimony, the issue of who saw whom doing what along those two blocks would be one of the critical points of dispute between the enemies and the defenders of Bennett Clark Hyde. If the story sworn to by the Swope family was believed, Hyde's claim of innocence could very well crumble before a jury. Conversely, if Hyde's account should be accepted as true, a key weapon in his accusers' hands would misfire.

Hyde's version of events between the time he left the Swope home and arrived for his meeting with Doctor Twyman could be summarized in two words: Nothing happened. He simply turned north at the bottom of the Swope hill, walked up Pleasant Street to Electric Street (since renamed Lexington), and followed Electric eastward to Main Street, where Twyman's office was located in a two-story brick building. Hyde claimed to have seen no one along the route. At no point, he would testify, did he pause or do anything that might be construed as suspicious.

The Swopes' version—originating with Tom Swope and strongly backed by his family—was a prosecutor's dream. Tom had just delivered Lucy Lee, the story went, and was walking back south on Pleasant Street when he spotted a dark figure heading toward him half a block away on the opposite side of the street. In light of what happened next, Tom concluded that the approaching man hadn't seen him—which was possible if a bit unlikely. Perhaps the other walker *had* noticed Tom but merely failed to recognize him. In any event, the man allegedly stopped, took something from an overcoat pocket, dropped it at the edge of the sidewalk, and stamped it vigorously into the snow. A moment later the figure passed under a streetlight and Tom got a clear view of the face. It was Clark Hyde.

As Hyde continued north up the street, Tom would recall, he himself kept walking south until he was opposite the spot where Hyde had halted. Then he crossed over to investigate. Reaching down into the disturbed snow, Tom felt about with his one hand and came up with a tiny object—an empty, broken, gelatin capsule. It might have seemed innocuous enough, but Hyde's manner of getting rid of it struck a nerve. Tom decided he'd better tell someone what he'd found, and his next move was to do just that.

An acquaintance of Tom's, a druggist named Jim Clinton, lived in a square brick house at the southeast corner of Pleasant and Kansas Streets. Although Clinton was working late that evening, his wife was in the sitting room with her sewing and heard the doorbell ring. Jim had warned her about opening the door to strangers after dark, but she recognized Tom Swope as a neighbor, and all he wanted was to use the telephone. She let him in just as the clock chimed 8:30.

Tom explained that he needed to reach Doctor Twyman and Mrs. Clinton volunteered to place the call herself—she was Twyman's patient, too. When she handed Tom the receiver, he had trouble holding it. She noticed he was clutching something else in his hand, something small, which forced him to grip the earpiece awkwardly with his thumb and forefinger. Tom didn't speak for long. Then he made a brief call to his mother, hung up, and headed home.

He would hardly have dawdled on the way. With his suspicions activated by what he'd witnessed and his fingers still clenched around the mashed capsule, he undoubtedly strode as quickly as his body's bulk would allow—south to the Swope hill, up the 900-foot walk to the mansion, and up the grand stairway to the sitting room where his mother waited. He must have been out of breath, but he got out the tale of Hyde's mysterious behavior and displayed the remains of the capsule. Maggie Swope, who now believed that any act of her son-in-law must spring from some evil design, placed the tiny item on a card as potential evidence.

Within minutes of Tom's return, according to legal statements, Mrs. Swope and one of the nurses, Lou Van Nuys, helped him wash his hand in the downstairs bathroom. Both of them, as well as Tom himself, would claim to have smelled something on the hand—a "peculiar, sweetish, bitterish odor," the nurse said, which she couldn't quite place at the time. Mrs. Swope compared the smell to "bitter almonds…it was very perceptible." Tom would testify that he had found the scent familiar yet elusive. It would soon come out, of course, that the odor they referred to—whether they'd actually smelled it became a matter of contention—was that of cyanide. Tom had encountered it back in his mining days in Nevada, where cyanide was used for treating silver ore. Nurse Van Nuys had once worked in a jewelry shop where the deadly substance was kept as a cleaning agent.

Clearly Tom and his mother had much to talk about in the sitting room, where they felt safe speaking in confidence. They were alone. The upstairs was quiet. Hyde was still absent at Doctor Twyman's office and the nurses were attending their patients. At some point Mrs. Swope paused to pen a message to John Paxton summoning the lawyer to the mansion at his earliest convenience. Even in 1909 it must have seemed quaint to send a note by servant courier to Paxton's residence. Especially since a perfectly functional telephone hung near a north window of the sitting room, a few feet from where Maggie Swope was sitting.

She and Tom were still talking when Frances Hyde—again showing her penchant for invading private discussions—walked in and settled into a chair. The whispered conversation across the room struck her as "funny," she later remembered, but she did not inquire what was wrong for the simple reason that "I didn't know anything was wrong."

If Frances didn't know by then that something was terribly wrong—was that possible?—her husband, seated in the Main Street office of George Twyman, was hearing there was *plenty* wrong. What the Swope family doctor had to say to Clark Hyde that night would devastate any up-and-coming physician who

111

valued his career, let alone his life and liberty. Yet the older man's opening words and Hyde's initial response bore a strangely decorous restraint, as if the two men were discussing nothing more dire than an embarrassing social gaffe at the club.

As soon as Hyde was seated, Twyman began, almost apologetically: "Doctor Hyde, the matter I have to talk to you about tonight is a very delicate one and I am very loath to do so, but I don't know any way around it.

"I have studied the matter over, and from the standpoint of duty there is nothing to do but tell you that the nurses are up in arms and are going to leave Mrs. Swope's unless you go. They have an idea that you are the cause of all the trouble there. They refuse to stay any longer if you stay in the house."

Hyde appeared more curious than ruffled. "Well, that is pretty bad, isn't it?" he said. "Tell me some more. Talk some more about it."

Twyman obliged. The nurses believed that old Colonel Swope's convulsion and death were induced by a capsule—Hyde's capsule—"which he first refused to take and finally took under pressure…and they think you killed him."

If Hyde's face showed any hint of alarm, Twyman's later account of their meeting didn't mention it.

Twyman continued: "In the second place, Chrisman Swope on Sunday morning had a temperature of 101, pulse about 80, feeling fine, and between three and four he had a convulsion and they think you doped him. And he died as you know on Monday, and they think you killed him.

"Now then, doctor, the nurses believe that you have inoculated this family with the typhoid germ and brought the typhoid culture there and fed it to them, and they think you are doing this because your wife will be a beneficiary, and that you are trying to kill the family for their money."

Hyde's response this time was more animated. "Well, that looks pretty bad, that is a terrible accusation. I could sue those nurses for a criminal accusation like that."

Twyman advised otherwise. "Doctor, what would you gain if you did sue the nurses? If the nurses leave or you make this thing public, people are aware that you married Frances under a strong protest, and you have personal enemies. This matter would be a sweet morsel in their mouths. And I want to say to you further, Doctor, that if this thing is made public there are thousands of people in Kansas City and Jackson County who will believe you guilty."

Hyde conceded this was probably true.

Twyman enforced his point with an anecdote. A German servant girl in Kansas City had accused her employer of sexual mistreatment and sued him for damages. Fortunately, Twyman found medical evidence "that the girl had gone wrong before" and she was charged with blackmail. "Now then," he added, "you see how easy it is for anyone to make an accusation and how hard it sometimes is to refute it."

Hyde had heard enough. "Doctor," he said, "what do you think I should do?"

"Doctor Hyde, there is but one thing for you to do and that is to leave," Twyman said. "If you don't want this thing to become public, you will have to leave. If the nurses leave, they are going to tell why they left."

Hyde acquiesced with a final display of good form. He would quit the Swope house as Twyman suggested, he said—then he thanked his fellow doctor for doing "the manly thing" in sharing the bitter news. With that, he headed back into the cold.

As events over the next two hours would reveal, Clark Hyde's fall from grace (if he'd ever known anything resembling grace) was picking up speed. Minutes after the meeting with Hyde, Doctor Twyman was on the phone with John Paxton to report every nuance of the conversation. Both men were intrigued by two aspects of Hyde's reaction to the grim interview. First, he had shown no more than a brief flare of indignation when told of the nurses' charges against him, and secondly, he had offered not a single word in his own defense. There had been no stunned incredulity. No furious denials. No demand for an investigation to clear his name.

But then, Hyde's coolness under hostile conditions had served him in the past. It served him fifteen minutes later on his return to the Swope house. No one heard him arrive except Frances, who let him in the front door, and Tom, who retreated upstairs. Quietly, the Hydes sequestered themselves in the library, which had been converted into their temporary bedroom (they had vacated Lucy Lee's room on the second floor when she returned from France). The husband and wife spoke together for an hour while they packed their bags, not once leaving the room or uttering a word to anyone else. Yet their muted exchange behind the library door—undoubtedly of grievance and mutual support against Hyde's accusers—was easy enough to imagine.

Paxton, meanwhile, was on his way to the mansion, arriving there on foot at around ten o'clock. Mrs. Swope and Tom must have greeted him with both relief and urgency. The three of them hastened upstairs to the sitting room, which again became the site of a family strategy session. Paxton, of course, passed along Twyman's account of the meeting with Hyde, which helped reinforce Maggie Swope's resolve to banish her son-in-law from the house that night. The conference lasted around forty-five minutes, after which the mother, son, and lawyer adjourned to the downstairs hall, presumably to wait for Doctor Hyde to appear from the library.

At close to eleven o'clock, he—or rather they—did just that. Clark was laden with luggage and Frances, like her husband, wore a heavy coat. Hyde's only comment was addressed to Paxton. "The solution of this difficulty is for me to go," he said, "and I am going."

The exact words spoken between Frances and her mother were never recorded, but the gist of their parting dialogue was remembered by both. Mrs. Swope, apparently surprised to see Frances dressed in coat and hat, asked her daughter where she was going. Frances said she was returning to her own home in Kansas City. Her husband had been unjustly accused, she said; she could no longer remain in a house where Clark was not welcome. She reminded her mother that she had practically run the Swope household and cared for the children since the typhoid broke out. Maggie Swope declared her gratitude. She implored Frances to come back. But the daughter she had always been closest to—the daughter she had tried to rescue from Hyde's avaricious grasp—was leaving this sanctuary on the arm of the heinous interloper her mother despised.

Never one to omit the courtly gesture, John Paxton stepped across the hall and shook Doctor Hyde's hand. As he later explained, he had still hoped Hyde was guiltless and wanted to grant him the benefit of the doubt. With that, Clark and Frances were on their way. At the trolley stop three blocks north of the mansion, they caught the late-night streetcar for Kansas City, arriving at their home on Forest Avenue at 1 a.m.

However inclined he was to presume Hyde's innocence, Paxton was still the Swope family lawyer and the Swope family was in a prosecutorial mood. The obvious starting place toward seeing justice done, Paxton knew, was to investigate "this horrible story…just as much on the theory of innocence as of guilt." As a modest first step, he asked Tom Swope to take him to the spot on South Pleasant Street where Hyde had been seen throwing something into the snow. They headed there at around 11:30, Paxton having remembered to bring along a clean, empty envelope. They found the site and started sifting through the snow. Paxton came up with shell fragments of other capsules and Tom discovered a few tiny shards of glass. All were collected in the envelope. At no point, either then or back at the mansion, did Paxton notice any odor of bitter almonds.

On the day of her return from New York—Friday, December 17— Lucy Lee Swope had eaten a late breakfast or lunch at home before taking refuge with the Minor family that evening. She remained a guest of the Minors for the next three nights, although she made daytime visits to her own home. During more than one of those visits, she joined her mother for luncheon and probably remained for dinner. Her friend Eleanor Minor later said that Lucy Lee had taken all her meals at the mansion. But whether she had breakfasts with her host family—which they surely would have offered—is not clear.

What drew attention to Lucy Lee's meal schedule during that period was the onset of illness on Wednesday, December 22. It had begun with a general feeling of malaise, followed by the chills, hot flashes, and a pounding headache that proclaimed Lucy the tenth victim of the Swope family's typhoid epidemic. A Widal test soon confirmed the diagnosis.

Perhaps she'd been infected at home. Perhaps she'd ingested tainted food or caught the germ in the sickroom of an ill sister. If not at home, where *did* she pick up the bacillus? There had been no typhoid, to anyone's knowledge, aboard her ocean liner from France or among the people she'd encountered briefly in New York. John Paxton, however, had his own theory—backed up by medical authority—that would add considerable weight to the case against Clark Hyde.

By the reckoning of most physicians at the time, the gestation period for the typhoid bacterium was almost always between one and three weeks. While it was not unknown for symptoms to appear just a few days after exposure to the germ, such rapid maturation was quite rare. A quick finger count would indicate that Lucy's infection—if she had picked up the germ at home—had reached the sickness stage with unusual speed, in five days or less.

The only other likelihood, it seemed, was that she had been exposed to typhoid sometime between her ship's arrival in New York and her homecoming at the Swope mansion. It was only natural that Paxton and others would start asking about every detail of every hour of her return journey with Doctor Hyde. The meals. The medicines. The candy purchased from a vendor on the Pullman car. The drink of water that her brother-in-law had kindly fetched for her as their train clicked over the rails forty minutes out of Jersey City.

The question had to be raised: What if the tiniest speck of typhoid culture had been added to the water Hyde brought to Lucy Lee in the silver folding cup sent along by his wife?

Given what the family already knew of Hyde's motives and conduct—or thought it knew—or definitely suspected—there was no doubt among Hyde's in-laws that Clark was capable of such demonic mischief. If that was how and when it happened, the awful act had occurred precisely seven days before Lucy Lee took sick.

Seven days.

Chapter 12

To advance the case against her hated son-in-law, Maggie Swope had no choice but to face a grim necessity. The corpses of her beloved son Chrisman and old Colonel Swope would have to be slipped from their respective cemetery vaults and put through the indignity of autopsies. Her attorney, John Paxton, had made it clear that the procedures, as disagreeable as they were, might be the only means of proving Hyde's role—if any—in the two deaths.

In fact, Paxton had already begun making arrangements two days after the Hydes' hasty departure from the Swope mansion. While asking the advice of friends in Chicago, he kept hearing references to one man as the leading forensic pathologist in the city. Professor Ludvig Hektoen of Chicago's Rush Medical Center had conducted hundreds of postmortem surgeries and testified in scores of criminal trials. Holder of an MD from the acclaimed school where he now taught, he had also pursued medical studies in Berlin, Liverpool, Prague, and Sweden. He had co-authored an authoritative book in his field. He headed a Rockefeller-funded institute for the study of infectious diseases. He had close professional ties with the best chemists and toxicologists, whom he could call in for help on special cases. In short, if the Swopes wanted a top-notch medical expert on their prosecution team, Doctor Ludvig Hektoen was their man.

On Tuesday, December 21, Paxton and Tom Swope rode a train to Chicago and the following day they presented themselves at the office of the renowned pathologist. The middle-aged man who greeted them was the very image of the gentleman scientist, his eyes so aglow with intelligence they might have been backlit, his sober tailoring and his grooming impeccable. Lawyers who put him on the stand undoubtedly treasured his striking demeanor before a jury.

As Hektoen listened gravely, Paxton laid out key details of the family's ordeals by death and disease. He added the usual disclaimer—so far he had formed no theory as to Hyde's guilt or innocence. All he wished, he insisted, was to have certain physical aspects of these tragedies examined scientifically. He had brought with him a corked, six-ounce bottle of yellowish fluid that young Margaret Swope had vomited following her convulsion. Then there were the two envelopes containing mashed and broken gelatin capsules, which Hyde had thrown into the snow on the night of December 18. Paxton's first request was that they be tested for poison. Hektoen explained that he was no chemist but agreed to assign the job to a colleague, Doctor Walter S. Haines, a widely respected toxicologist.

Paxton's second request was, as it were, closer to the bone. Could the eminent pathologist also find time—sooner, rather than later—to visit Missouri to conduct autopsies on the late Thomas Hunton Swope and his nephew Chrisman? It went without saying that Mrs. Logan O. Swope would cover all costs and compensations.

It was settled, then. Chrisman would be first to go under the pathologist's knife, the procedure to take place on December 30 at Ott's funeral parlor on the Independence town square. Dissection of the Colonel's cadaver would occur at a somewhat later date, still unscheduled.

In the meantime, the surviving Swopes, their kinfolks, and retainers would be honoring the birth of their Savior from the heights of their turreted fortress above South Pleasant Street. The holiday would later be remembered throughout the Kansas City area as the White Christmas of 1909. Perhaps all the fresh snow did have a softening effect on the mansion's brooding walls and arches, the bare trees and the lifeless flower beds. But if the people inside the house made an effort to celebrate the Yuletide, it's doubtful they had their hearts in it. The fact that poor dead Chrisman had his appointment with Doctor Hektoen on the following Thursday cannot have helped anyone's mood.

At midafternoon on the day of the autopsy, undertaker R. B. Mitchell, who had embalmed all three of the Swope family's recent dead, pulled his carriage up to the superintendent's house at Mount Washington Cemetery. There he requested Chrisman's removal from the cemetery's receiving vault for transport to Ott's undertaking establishment. The superintendent and an assistant helped with the heavy task of pulling the casket from its "catacomb" (the fanciful term for holding compartment) and lifting the body into a sturdy basket for the ride to the square. In the process, Mitchell got his first look at Chrisman since the funeral. Much to the embalmer's credit—with help, to be sure, from the frigid weather—there was no visible deterioration.

Doctor Hektoen was waiting in the back room of the funeral home, along with a small delegation of others involved. John Paxton was there—he was sensitive to gruesome sights and would sit out most of the postmortem procedure in an adjoining office. The Swope family's physician, Doctor G. T. Twyman, had made a point of attending and was asked by Hektoen to take notes. The senior partner of the undertaking firm, Henry J. Ott, had come as a witness but would spend more of his time keeping Paxton company in the office. Mitchell and an assistant embalmer would serve as general helpers and scrubbers.

They got to work shortly before dark. Hektoen did the cutting and made a cursory examination of all the organs as they were exposed (detailed laboratory analyses of the tissue would take place later). Lungs, heart, liver, and kidneys appeared to be normal. The intestines showed evidence of typhoid, but not of such severity, Hektoen believed, as to have caused death by itself. The stomach was removed and both ends tied like a sausage casing for subsequent study of the organ and its contents. What really focused the doctors' interest, however, was the brain. If meningitis had stricken Chrisman Swope, as Hyde had stated unequivocally just moments after Chrisman's first convulsion, the brain would have been congested with turbid, infiltrated matter. The pathologist found no such condition. The dead man's brain, he would state later in court, "was found normal in every respect."

As Hektoen placed organs and organ parts in sealed jars to take with him to Chicago, the workmanlike Mitchell put what was left back in place, sewed up the incisions, and got Chrisman re-dressed in his coffin clothes for the long sleep in Mount Washington Cemetery.

Except for a few family members, no one received word of the autopsy in the days immediately following the event. It wouldn't do to alert other parties—especially Clark Hyde—of this first decisive act in building the case against him.

Doctor Bennett Clark Hyde's jolly spirits on the evening of Wednesday, December 29, were noted at once by a colleague who'd been summoned to Hyde's Kansas City home. What struck the visitor, bacteriologist Edward Stewart, was the incongruity between Hyde's mood—he was downright bubbly—and what Hyde had just disclosed about his health. It seems he had been experiencing some ominous symptoms in the last few days and was now certain he had come down with typhoid fever. Yet here he was, discussing his disease with the lightheartedness of a man in full vigor emerging from a perfect checkup.

Also present that night at the Hyde residence were Doctor John Perkins, Hyde's friend and personal physician, and a nurse named Mrs. Von Bachmer. Along with Doctor Stewart, they made up a delegation of three health professionals. It was almost as if Hyde and his wife, Frances, who had called Stewart that afternoon to ask him by the house, wanted to guarantee a full audience when Hyde's illness was announced.

By the time Stewart got to the house at 8 p.m., Doctor Perkins had just finished examining Hyde and concluded that the patient did indeed have typhoid, though only a light case of it. Stewart, who had had a suspicious eye on Hyde since learning of the Swope

DR. E. L. STEWART. WHO TESTIFIED THAT HE GAVE TYPHOID CULTURE TO DOCTOR HYDE.
Kansas City Times, Thurs., April 28, 1910, p. 1.

family's epidemic, intended to take a much closer look at his symptoms. If Hyde truly had the disease—or was able to convince others he did—his position could change dramatically from suspected bacterial poisoner to just another innocent victim. No wonder Hyde seemed pleased to be certifiably ill.

Stewart checked out the patient himself. Hyde's skin was reddish. His tongue, though coated, did not look to Stewart like a "typhoid tongue." The bacteriologist asked Doctor Perkins about Hyde's temperature; it was a relatively mild 101. Stewart took blood in a pipette for a white cell count, more blood in a tube for a Widal agglutination test, and a final smear to examine for malaria. He and the nurse then left the bedroom to let the Hydes confer privately with their personal doctor. After twenty minutes, Perkins reappeared and invited Stewart to join him on the ride back downtown. Late as it was, both men had errands to run—Perkins to pick up something at a drugstore and Stewart to leave off the newly drawn blood samples at his office.

During their ride to Eleventh Street and Grand Avenue, the two doctors discussed the Swope typhoid mystery, in which both of them, one way or another, were now involved. Perkins repeated his conclusion that Hyde definitely had the disease that plagued his in-laws and again predicted it would take only a light form. This time Stewart thought of asking him—but didn't—how he could be so sure he was right with so little diagnostic evidence. Perkins also said he was all but certain of the fever's origin on the Swope estate. He now believed the germs had spread from the servants' privy to the family's milk supply (earlier he had suggested that unwashed lettuce might have been the bacterial Trojan horse).

Stewart would need much more convincing. Over the following days, right through the frozen first week of the new year, the bacteriologist shuttled between the Hyde residence and his own laboratory, drawing blood from Hyde's hand and head and belly, running tests, checking temperatures. During one house call, Hyde displayed unusual peevishness. He grumbled that Stewart had taken enough blood—it was time to spare the syringe. He implied that his own physician, Perkins, was far too skilled to need second-guessing. He recited his symptoms as if no one had heard them before: the constant headaches, the fever, the nosebleeds, the gas in his bowels. Perhaps embarrassed by her husband's testiness, Frances handed Stewart a cigar on his way out.

Stewart, the consummate professional, was not about to sign off on a final diagnosis until he had followed every lead and clue and possibility—*everything*—with his usual exacting care.

His first use of the Widal test, in which typhoid bacilli were introduced into a blood sample, failed to produce the telltale clumping of the germ culture that indicated infection. Another test the next day did produce a Widal reaction but didn't necessarily prove anything. Everyone knew the test was less than surefire. Its result could have been triggered by a bout of typhoid fever that Hyde had suffered years before. Stewart next attempted to grow typhoid bacteria in flasks of Hyde's blood mixed with beef broth. The experiment turned up nothing. Yet Hyde's symptoms, as light as they were, could only suggest … what?

At Stewart's request, a colleague, Doctor Scott P. Child, had also tested Hyde's blood and found it Widal positive. Again, the test results and the patient's mild condition just didn't add up. As the two doctors conferred, they found themselves heading toward the same conclusion. The likeliest cause of Hyde's illness, they decided, was the very recent introduction of dead or devitalized bacteria into his body, causing an extremely light version—a sort of pale masquerade—of the dangerous disease. But how had the devitalized germs entered Hyde's system? The only answer Stewart and Child could come up with would give no comfort to Hyde and his defenders. It was all too likely that Doctor Hyde, with cunning premeditation, had squirted them into his own bloodstream with his very own needle.

———•—•——

Like all medical researchers, Stewart had some of the detective's instincts. He was nagged by one great question, perhaps the central enigma of the tragic afflictions of the Swope family. By what means had typhoid fever invaded the great house in Independence? If it was Hyde's doing, the doctor had done a far worse evil than simply imperiling a large family, its guests, and its servants. He had caused the prolonged, excruciating death of a young man and brought a daughter so near the precipice that only the chance arrival of her physician had saved her. The idea was almost too grim to entertain, but it lent urgency to Stewart's quest for answers. Then too, he may have felt driven by a sense of guilt. It was he, after all, who had furnished Hyde with a thriving colony of typhoid bacilli back in November.

Until this point, Stewart apparently had shared his suspicions only with his wife and two close colleagues, one of them his office partner. He certainly had not discussed them with Doctor Perkins. The latter's questionable haste in diagnosing Hyde's illness as typhoid fever made the bacteriologist uneasy. Though he had long admired Perkins's professional skills, Stewart was starting to wonder whether the physician was acting as a purely objective scientist or as a biased friend and ally of Clark Hyde's. Could Perkins's medical judgment—could Perkins himself—be wholly trusted?

Had Perkins known of Stewart's suspicions, it's doubtful he

would have consulted with him freely, almost daily, on the progress of Hyde's illness. Nor was it likely that Perkins would have asked Stewart to join him on an investigation of the Swope house, grounds, and outbuildings to search again for the cause of the typhoid outbreak.

Perkins had telephoned Stewart on the evening of New Year's Day to recruit him for the field study the following afternoon. But early the next day, a Sunday, Perkins called to say something had come up and he couldn't go to Independence after all. He hoped that Stewart could go without him and handle the investigation on his own.

Stewart was willing. If only he could pin down some sign, some trace of concrete evidence of the typhoid's source, he would be free of these gnawing uncertainties. Like every scientist worth the name, he knew that to test any hypothesis, including his own of Hyde's possible guilt, he had to take every measure to *disprove* it. Having packed his bag with instruments for the collection of water and other samples, he set out well prepared to do his work objectively and thoroughly.

What Stewart wasn't prepared for was the reception he met with upon reaching the mansion at 4 p.m. The woman servant who answered the door, all but radiating hostility, kept him standing on the porch until he'd stated his business. He assured her that Mrs. Swope was expecting him—Doctor Perkins had telephoned the day before. That got him as far as the front hall, where he saw the *grande dame* herself descending the stairs with a starchy escort of nurses. "She did not seem overjoyed at my visit," Stewart later said. It was an understatement. Right away, Mrs. Swope demanded to know why he'd come to her house and who was paying him. He replied that he had "certain ideas as to where the infection originated" and wished to make a bacteriological survey of the premises to test whether his theory was true. At the moment he could tell her no more—except to assert, emphatically, that no one was paying him a thing.

If Maggie Swope was mollified, she wasn't showing it. The matriarch—in fact the whole household—was in a state of bitter resentment and guardedness, and Stewart couldn't blame them. In their eyes, he was not only a stranger but quite likely a medical hireling engaged to get Hyde off the hook by coming up with some other, natural cause of the typhoid scourge. The Swopes may also have gotten word of Stewart's recent visits to Hyde's bedside accompanied by Doctor Perkins, whom they now suspected of working in league with the sinister son-in-law.

Stewart told his unwilling hostess what he'd come for: samples of milk from the crocks on hand, of water from the cistern, and of dirt from the site of the old privy. He also wished to examine the teats of the family cow, which was kept in a small dairy barn behind the house. She granted her reluctant consent and agreed to let him sterilize his collecting pipette in the basement kitchen.

The moment he stepped into the room, behind Mrs. Swope, he saw he was in for a bad time. Two or three nurses and a cluster of servants crowded the kitchen like sullen protesters at a strike meeting. Someone—presumably the cook, Ida Copridge—agreed grudgingly to kindle a fire in the stove and boil a pan of water. At the same time she acted as a sort of "master-of-ceremonies"— Stewart's term—issuing a stream of "improper remarks." She hinted that Stewart should pay her for her help. (He didn't.) She intimated that he might have brought in typhoid-tainted bottles to deliberately infect the family's milk supply. She demanded that he boil every vessel, even those he had already sterilized back at his lab. All at once the cramped space got even tighter as portly, glowering Tom Swope pushed in, ready to make sure the bacteriologist was up to no tricks. "I saw," Doctor Stewart later said, "that I had one more inspector."

He was, in fact, monitored at every step—when he drew off pipettes of milk from the crocks, when he poured beef tea over the cow's teats and collected it in a flask, when he tried to lower a bottle into the cistern for a water sample. The latter effort was sharply vetoed by Mrs. Swope, who apparently feared the bottle could be contaminated and made him use the pump instead. Before heading for the site of the old privy, Stewart asked one of the help to take two sealed bottles of water to the kitchen, where he had left his satchel. The servant's insolent rejoinder drew not a word of reprimand from the lady of the house. Maggie Swope did condescend to escort him to the spot where the privy had stood, but it was growing dark and Stewart could see only that the dirt was sprinkled with quicklime. He'd have to put off his probe for a reliable soil specimen until another day.

Stewart packed his grip to go. Nothing would relieve him more than to get out of this place "where I could see I was suspicioned strongly." Yet he felt he should linger long enough to reassure Mrs. Swope and her son that he was not the villain they imagined him to be. The three of them met in the sitting room, where Stewart did most of the talking. He had not come to do them harm, he promised, and in the end they'd understand the real purpose behind his investigation. But until he'd finished the job, he added, he would not be free to explain his mission.

He continued his study the next day in his Kansas City laboratory. Under microscopic scrutiny, the samples of milk, cistern water, and the beef-tea wash were aswim with bacterial life. Stewart detected common streptococci, a few snowy white forms he couldn't identify, and a number of microbes with a superficial resemblance to typhoid germs. But search as he might, Stewart could not find the real thing—not a single specimen of *Salmonella typhi*.

While the evidence wasn't quite conclusive—he still wanted those dirt samples from the privy area—Stewart was closer than ever to sharing the troubled opinion of a previous visitor to the estate, pathologist Frank Hall. The weirdly spontaneous invasion of typhoid bacilli and their strange disappearance once they'd done their mischief did suggest the methodical workings of a scientific experiment. Stewart was leaning toward the opinion that if the germs could have left a trail, it would lead straight to Doctor Hyde's office cabinet and his colonies of microbes breeding in the dark.

———————

Back in mid-December, while Hyde was on his New York trip, Doctor Stewart had managed to talk his way into Hyde's office and examine his private stock of disease bacteria. After discovering that a frightening amount of typhoid culture had been harvested from its glass container, Stewart noticed something else. Germs from the glass tube labeled "Diptheria" had been skimmed away as well and the tube was broken at the base, where a tiny ooze of gelatinous medium was visible.

The scraped typhoid culture was by far the greater cause for alarm, of course, and Stewart at the time gave little thought to the diphtheria sample. Still, something about it stuck with him. No one in the Swope family had shown the slightest sign of coming down with diphtheria. Yet it *was* a deadly disease, and Stewart no longer trusted Hyde's stated reasons for collecting laboratory germs that could kill. He decided to take another look at the contents of that broken tube.

Stewart got his chance on December 27, two days before hearing of Hyde's apparent typhoid infection. On this Monday morning, Hyde telephoned Stewart and asked the bacteriologist to drop by to discuss some County Medical Society matters. Stewart waited until afternoon, then walked the two blocks to Hyde's office where the two men talked business. Somehow, during the course of the visit, Stewart was shown the specimens of bacteria he had given to Hyde back in November. Pretending he hadn't previously noticed the break in the diphtheria tube, Stewart asked if he could take it back to his lab for a closer look. Hyde readily consented.

That consent, Hyde would soon realize, was a serious mistake.

The minute Doctor Stewart got back to his laboratory, he and his office partner, Doctor H. O. Leonard, made a slide from the tube's germ culture and slipped it under a microscope. Immediately they saw that the "diphtheria" bacteria were something else entirely. They were common pus germs, the nasty but seldom fatal microbes that swarmed throughout infected cuts and sores. The two bacteriologists were nonplused. Stewart asked his colleague to make a written record of their finding, as he had of the harvested typhoid culture Stewart had taken from Hyde's office thirteen days earlier.

It is unclear who made the connection or exactly when. In any event, the theory constructed around the mislabeled germ colony would strike a damaging blow to Clark Hyde's legal defense. It went like this:

Suppose—one of so many supposes in the Swope mystery—that on the night of December 12, when Hyde crept into Margaret Swope's sickroom ostensibly to give her a shot of camphorated oil, he had planned to inject her with something else. Suppose he had loaded his needle from the tube marked diphtheria, unaware that it contained nothing more lethal than ordinary pus germs. Suppose the shot in Margaret's left arm, designed to induce a fatal disease, produced only the fiery inflammation and grotesque swelling that tormented Margaret for weeks afterward.

It did make for a plausible scenario, didn't it?

Chapter 13

In the ninth day of his strangely benign bout with typhoid fever, Doctor Hyde hadn't a clue that Doctor Edward Stewart—the very model of concerned colleague and caregiver, a man he called a friend—was acting, in effect, as a double agent.

Hyde undoubtedly hoped the bacteriologist would conclude he was just another unfortunate victim of the pestilence that swept the Swope household. Stewart had other ideas. His laboratory research, he knew, could ultimately help unmask the Swope son-in-law as a scoundrel and a possible killer. Not to mention a deviously cunning medical faker trying to save his own skin.

Day after day he had shown up in Hyde's sickroom, tracking the patient's vital signs, monitoring his symptoms, filling more pipettes with blood. On evenings he had run and rerun his lab tests, coming up with the same negative or inconclusive results. Stewart's hypothesis that Hyde's illness was self-induced was crystallizing into a dark certainty. The mild case of fever, more quasi-typhoid than the real thing, was simply a ruse to throw his accusers off the scent.

By Thursday, January 6, Stewart could no longer keep his suspicions to himself and a handful of medical friends. After visiting Hyde in the morning—the patient appeared thinner and wore a prickly, half-grown beard—Stewart made up his mind to telephone Doctor G. T. Twyman in Independence, whom he knew to be the Swope family's physician. Twyman heard him out and promised to come to Stewart's Kansas City office the next day to learn more about the bacteriologist's findings. The small-town doctor had needed no urging. His belief in Hyde's guilt, by now, was more or less unshakable.

At the appointed hour, noon sharp, the Independence doctor arrived at the bacteriologist's office accompanied by his physician son, Elmer. Elmer hadn't been expected. Most likely he had come along simply to drive the Twyman family car, which his horse-and-buggy father was either unwilling or unable to do.

No one had planned on convening a wider, more formal meeting. It grew into one, however, when Stewart's partner, H. O. Leonard, along with two other doctors whom Stewart had consulted about the case, Franklin Murphy and Scott Child, showed up and asked to join in. By the time the session broke up an hour later, all the visitors agreed that Stewart's arguments were powerfully compelling. If the Swope typhoid outbreak had its cause in nature, why had it left no bacterial tracks at the family's home or grounds? If Hyde were truly a victim of the same fierce contagion that raged through the Swope mansion, why was *his* infection so weak that lab tests could barely detect it?

As the others slipped into their coats to leave, the senior Twyman pulled Stewart aside. He'd be much obliged, he said, if the bacteriologist could come out that evening to his Independence office, where he'd be discussing the Hyde-Swope situation with another interested party. Stewart agreed to make the trip, a ride of at least forty minutes by streetcar. What's more, he volunteered to bring along his partner, Doctor Leonard, who had been in on every step of Stewart's lab work and had come to the same troubling conclusions.

The other party at the Independence meeting was interested indeed. He was no less a player than John Paxton, the patrician Independence lawyer who was already at work crafting the case against Hyde. Stewart and Paxton had never met, but the two of them, with Twyman and Leonard, had plenty to talk about—so much that the session lasted two and a half hours. Meticulously, Stewart spelled out the damning implications of his field study at the Swope estate and his lab analyses of Hyde's blood. In turn, Paxton and Twyman filled him in on details of the horrors visited upon the

Swope family. For the first time, Stewart learned of Hyde's presumed financial motives for doing away with the old Colonel and his heirs. He learned of the vanished capsules, the nurses' rebellion, the results of the Chrisman Swope autopsy. It all seemed to dovetail with what Stewart had concluded on his own about the enigmatic Doctor Hyde and the typhoid invasion of the hilltop mansion.

Almost before he realized it, he was now a full member of the network of medical men, Swope advisers, and family members bent on seeing Hyde prosecuted for murder. Late that Friday night, by the time he reached his home trolley stop, Stewart knew he had no choice but to go after Hyde with all the energy and cunning at his command.

It wasn't until late the next morning, as Stewart returned from a house call on a sick child, that a plan of action suddenly burst across his mind. On the face of it, the idea was a shade melodramatic—you could even call it juvenile, like some caper in a dime detective novel. But when Stewart talked it over with his friend Leonard as they ate lunch, the latter agreed it just might work.

To make sure he was still on solid scientific ground, Stewart tried again that day to grow a detectable number of *Salmonella typhi* in 2 cc's of Hyde's blood mixed with sterile beef tea. Again, after warming the solution in an incubator, he found it to be germ-free—hardly what you'd expect from a patient recently stricken with the dangerously infectious disease. He was ready to move ahead with his plan.

It started with a house call Sunday morning, January 9, on the convalescent Doctor Hyde. Prepared with a notebook detailing his latest laboratory results, Stewart was greeted at 3516 Forest Avenue by a patient who scarcely seemed ill at all. Quite the reverse, Hyde was in buoyant spirits as he socialized with two visitors, a Doctor Van Eman and a lawyer named Guthrie. For a while Stewart joined their conversation in the fragrant haze of good cigars. Then the others took their leave and Stewart was alone with the man he planned to entrap.

His ostensible purpose for paying his call was to update Hyde on business matters of the Jackson County Medical Society. Among other things, he had to inform Hyde that because of a scientific pre-sentation already booked for the January meeting, Hyde's formal installation as president would have to be postponed for a month. As secretary of the society, Stewart was in charge of scheduling all programs. His reasons for using this authority to stall Hyde's inau-guration were clear enough. Hyde's accusers were still collecting evidence. No one was ready to file criminal charges. Outside the tiny circle of Stewart's close allies, no society members had an inkling of the allegations against their president-elect. Stewart was playing for time. It would be worse than embarrassing—it would be appall-ing—if the gavel were passed to a man who would shortly be under indictment for murder.

Stewart was sure that Hyde would welcome nothing more than indisputable proof—test-tube proof—that his body was teeming with potent typhoid germs. What Stewart had to report this morn-ing, however, was not what Hyde wanted to hear. There was still no visible evidence of bacteria in Hyde's bloodstream and until the germs swam into the field of Stewart's microscope, he could not certify that Hyde's typhoidlike illness was a full, fresh, virulent case. A few Widal tests had come up positive, it was true. But those results might indicate nothing more than a residue of agglutinin in Hyde's blood left over from his bout with typhoid years ago.

Stewart was not giving up, he assured his patient. The flask of beef broth mixed with Hyde's blood was still sitting in his labora-tory incubator. He'd be keeping an eye on it on the chance that the telltale bacilli might yet wriggle into view.

If Hyde was distressed by the news, he wasn't showing it. He and Frances insisted the bacteriologist stay for lunch, but Stewart told them he needed to get back to work on an overdue diphtheria report. Before he bundled up to leave, however, he made sure to drop several offhand remarks. He was working with blood from a patient of Doctor Child's, he said, which was practically seeth-ing with typhoid germs—it too was in his incubator. Doctors were forever bringing him specimens like that throughout the day or night. For their convenience, he explained, he took the minor risk of leaving his laboratory door unlocked at all hours. One could never be sure of being on hand to receive colleagues who needed his services. As a matter of fact he'd be absent from the office this very evening, he told Hyde. He had tickets to the theater.

Back in his lab, Stewart busied himself setting the trap. First he removed the flask of Hyde's blood mixture and replaced it with a twin substitute filled with a sterile mix. This he labeled "Dr. Hyde's blood" and smeared the neck with a drop of his own blood to make it appear recently handled. Then he retrieved the blood culture from Doctor Child's seriously ill patient, also identified by label. After coating both flasks with the thinnest film of oil, Stewart restored them to the incubator. Any intruder who opened the incubator door would spot them at once, side by side. Anyone who dared to dribble some of the typhoid-rich culture from Child's patient into the sterile counterfeit marked as Hyde's would leave unmistakable fingerprints on the oily glass.

Stewart's next trick—again, straight out of a pulp detective yarn—was to position a glass slide in such a way that it would fall to the floor if the incubator door were pulled open. This, too, would help establish Hyde's intrusion. Stewart might even be alert enough to hear the "clink," although he'd be concealed in the adjoining office. Finally, the bacteriologist cut a tiny spy hole high in the door between the rooms so that by standing on a box he could witness any mischief that was taking place in the dimly lit laboratory.

All these measures took time and stressful concentration, and once he'd set everything up Stewart was too tired to do much else. He tried until dark to write up some case notes, but the pages kept blurring. At around 6:45 p.m., wrapped in his overcoat, he dozed off on the office couch.

Stewart had resolved to sleep lightly, sensitive to any sound or stirring that might brush his mental trip wire. It didn't work. For nearly ten hours he lay like a dead man, insensible even to the chill of the comfortless room. If the glass slide had fallen next door he'd have heard nothing. In fact, as Stewart discovered after waking up in the dark at 5 a.m., the slide was still in place on top of the incubator. The two flasks stood where he'd set them, their oil-filmed surfaces innocent of a single print or smudge. By the time he'd finished breakfast in a downtown coffee shop and caught the streetcar home, he was bedeviled by a fierce headache.

<hr />

For ninety-six days, the remains of Thomas Hunton Swope had occupied a private catacomb within the receiving vault of Forest Hill Cemetery, a south-side burial ground for many of Kansas City's prominent early families. There the Colonel was to have lain undisturbed until his splendid permanent tomb in Swope Park was completed at the expense of a grateful public. What the planners could not have guessed was that the old man's repose would be interrupted by the exigencies of criminal investigation. Colonel Swope's date with Professor Ludvig Hektoen's autopsy team was set for Wednesday, January 12.

To avoid sensational publicity on the eve of the postmortem, attorney John Paxton had ordered that the Colonel's body be removed by dark of night for delivery to Ott's undertaking rooms on the Independence square. The job fell to Ott's junior partner, R. B. Mitchell, who had chauffeured Chrisman's body to the same autopsy room just twelve days earlier.

After presenting his removal order to the Forest Hill superintendent, a Mister Cook, Mitchell enlisted the latter's help in extricating the casket. First they hung a blanket over the iron gate to the vault's interior. This would block the frigid wind blowing from the west, as well as hide any lights that might be seen by passersby from the street. Getting the old man's remains from catacomb to mortuary wagon was no small chore. For security reasons, the coffin had been encased in a heavy stone box. Once Mitchell, Cook, and the wagon driver had wrestled the coffin into the central hall of the building, Mitchell raised the lid and proceeded to unscrew and open the copper liner that shielded the body from damp. It was awkward work in the pale kerosene light, but they managed to shift the Colonel to a body basket and load him aboard Mitchell's horse-drawn carrier. The cargo reached Independence on schedule. The postmortem could proceed the next day.

By the light of morning, however, the embalmer realized he'd have to bring a worrisome fact to the immediate attention of his partner, Henry Ott. It seemed the old gentleman in the basket was frozen—literally frozen stiff.

"I don't see how they can work on it," Mitchell said, "and they had better wire the doctor that they was expecting to put it off a little while." (The "doctor" may have been Ludvig Hektoen, newly arrived from Chicago, or Jackson County Coroner Bernard H. Zwart, who would serve as the official in charge.) Ott insisted the procedure had to take place by midafternoon. "So I lit an oil stove, a coal oil stove," Mitchell would recall in testimony, "and put it in the room to try and warm up the temperature ... and also [to see] if it would have any effect at all towards thawing out the body."

It didn't. Although hours had passed by the time the autopsy team showed up, the doctors could only stand around aimlessly while Mitchell tried to get the cadaver ready for the scalpel. The last of the group had arrived around 3:30. Those in the room, besides Hektoen and Zwart, were Doctors Twyman and Stewart (the latter agreed to take notes); the Kansas City pathologist Frank Hall; a Doctor Calvin Atkins, City Physician of Independence; and two undertaker assistants. None had come up with a better idea than Mitchell's for thawing the corpse.

After heating a kettle of water on a basement stove, he poured it over three towels arranged on the body's abdomen, then piled on a hot-water bag. He also doused the Colonel's scalp to soften it up for cutting in that area. If there were a bathtub handy, he told the impatient onlookers, this would take half the time. By around 4 p.m. the skin and flesh appeared soft enough to permit the first incisions.

As it turned out, the whole procedure was something of a mess, even by the postmortem surgery standards of 1909. Just how ineptly it was handled would be revealed months later in trial testimony. Hektoen would be forced to admit that he himself had once advised, in the strongest terms, against attempting autopsies on frozen bodies. The warning had appeared in a textbook published in 1890 and revised in 1907. Among other things, the respected pathologist had argued that examination of the frozen brain could lead to invalid findings. Yet here he was in January 1909, alongside fellow dissector Frank Hall, getting ready to saw through the skull and pull out the frozen-solid brain of Thomas Swope.

Hektoen later acknowledged that his approach "deviated somewhat from the usual way of taking the brain out." Well, yes. In an unfrozen state, the thing could be lifted intact from the skull crater with very little effort. But in this situation, once the skullcap was removed it would take potentially damaging pokes, cuts, and blind handling to do the job. Undertaker Mitchell would recall that Hektoen "kind of pried around a little" as he tried to free up the brain. Hall and others would describe the use of a long knife to dig down to the basal part of the brain—to the floor of the skull—and to slice the organ into half-inch slabs. At some point during the maneuver, a large chunk of gray matter broke off, like ice from a warming glacier (Coroner Zwart insisted later it was only ice that split off, not brain tissue). The frozen pieces were laced with cracks.

Everyone, of course, had one overriding question in mind. It was the big forensic poser: Did or did not Colonel Swope die of apoplexy, as Hyde had stated unequivocally at the time? If what killed the old man was a cerebral hemorrhage—the correct term—it would have left signs. Hektoen saw none. All the arteries were intact—no ruptured vessels, no bloodstains, only a small yellowish bit of thickened tissue along one of them. Hall saw nothing to suggest apoplexy. Neither did the coroner.

But *could* they have spotted any subtle or significant clues in that pile of icy pieces, sliced and pried and scooped from the Colonel's skull? None of the examiners was about to admit they'd botched the job. Two subsequent autopsy reports gave only brief mention to the brain's frozen state and neither indicated concern about the way it was dug out. One report, though noting that the organ had to be cut into sections while it was still in the skull, declared that this "in no wise prevented an accurate determination of the question of whether or not there was any apoplexy." No one—not Hall, not Hektoen, not Stewart, not Zwart—had any hesitation in ruling out brain hemorrhage as the cause of death.

In opening the rest of the body, Hektoen started his incision below the chin and worked downward. Once the skin and flesh were drawn back, it took only a glance for the pathologists to realize there would have to be more thawing. Again, Mitchell was summoned. This time the undertaker poured as much as four kettles of hot water straight into the body cavity. It was essential that heart, lungs, liver, stomach, and other viscera be taken out for viewing, packaging, and transfer to a laboratory for closer analysis. Some of the organs thawed a little on the surface, others did not. At least the doctors were able to pry out the vitals and examine them closely enough to allow for some conclusions.

One of their more surprising discoveries was that the liver—that of a man who had spent thousands of hours of his aging life more or less drunk—seemed to be cirrhosis free. Everything else appeared normal enough, as well. There were the small hard spots known as "clax" distributed over the aorta, but no one took them very seriously. There was the two-inch spherical tumor on the left kidney, but when Hall was asked about it later he said with confidence, "This was not a malignant growth."

When all was finished, the incisions sutured and the body buttoned back into its Prince Albert suit, the medical functionaries in Ott's back room had come to a verdict. It was unanimous. Every bit of visible evidence proclaimed that the great philanthropist had died neither of disease nor of "senile debility."

That being the case, if it was the case, then there was no escaping another question, by implication the most unsettling: What, exactly, *had* done the old gentleman in?

Chapter 14

As one story has it, the *Kansas City Star*'s Independence correspondent got wind of the Thomas Swope autopsy the next morning, Thursday, January 13, thereby enabling him to scoop all rivals with an account in that afternoon's paper. It is also said that the Independence reporter for the *Post,* when admonished for his failure to stay on top of the news, admitted he'd heard about the Colonel's postmortem but decided not to file the story out of sympathy for the Swope family—"such nice people." Whether the *Star*'s man got a bonus or the *Post*'s reporter got fired is known only to the Ghosts of Newsrooms Past.

Certainly by first thing Friday, however, it seemed that *every* newshound in the Kansas City press corps had descended on the county seat with notebooks and darting pencils in hand. All at once local physicians, city and county officials, and neighbors of the Swopes had been elevated from mere citizens into news sources whose every quote was as eagerly pursued as a rare butterfly.

About the only knowledgeable insiders who *stayed* inside, closed off from the clamoring press, were members of the Swope family. Mrs. Swope had for some time realized that her family's private nightmare would sooner or later become a public sensation. She had even engaged a night watchman to fend off nosey trespassers. Thus the *Star* reporter who climbed the hill Friday morning in hopes of an interview could hardly have been surprised to find every window shuttered and not a soul in sight. He rang the doorbell anyway, but the woman who answered, one of the nurses, was not encouraging. "I suppose you are a reporter,"

THE LATE COL. THOMAS H. SWOPE, MILLIONAIRE AND PUBLIC BENEFACTOR, WHOSE DEATH IS NOW THE SUBJECT OF AN INQUIRY TO DETERMINE ITS CAUSE.
Kansas City Times, Fri., Jan. 14, 1910, p. 1.

A HOME OF FATALITIES (THE SWOPE RESIDENCE [FROM EAST FRONT] AT INDEPENDENCE, WHERE COLONEL SWOPE DIED AND WHERE HIS KINFOLK WERE STRICKEN WITH TYPHOID FEVER).
Kansas City Times, Fri., Jan. 14, 1910, p. 1.

she said. "Mrs. Swope has given orders, positive orders, that she will see no one." In case the newsman hoped the nurse herself might have some newsy snippet to offer, she shut him off before he could ask. All he got for his trouble was a brief peek into the front hall, where he saw a pair of dark eyes, those of a teenage girl, gleaming from an inside doorway.

Undeterred, the reporter tried the more up-to-date approach—a telephone call. Mrs. Swope herself answered, thinking it was Doctor Twyman on the line. When she realized who the caller truly was, she informed him icily, "I have nothing to say. I can answer no questions. I have placed everything in the hands of Mister Paxton."

Most attempts to cover up the latest developments and rumors were, of course, more or less futile against the tide of reporters and the willingness of so many sources to tell what they knew, or thought they knew. "Independence had been waiting for weeks for something to happen," wrote the *Star*'s on-scene correspondent in Friday's paper. "Yesterday it happened, but [people] only shook their heads knowingly and talked and talked."

Among other things, they talked of poison as the dead men's possible vehicle to the hereafter. Word was out that the stomachs of the autopsied Swopes had been taken to Chicago for analysis by a Doctor Hektoen and a toxicologist at the Rush Medical College, one Professor Haines. As if that weren't enough to give readers a deliciously morbid shiver, it was also disclosed that Coroner Zwart had sworn in a coroner's jury to look into the two deaths. Everyone knew what "coroner's jury" meant. Such panels were not appointed to scrutinize the ordinary deaths of ordinary folks.

The six jurymen, good solid businessmen, had been rounded up in their workplaces and on the street by a deputy marshal named Phelps, just hours before Wednesday's autopsy. The unsettling haste of it all and the coroner's demands of absolute secrecy lent further melodrama to the jury's initial task—a visit to Ott's undertaking rooms to view the old Colonel's remains. Then there was the macabre setting. Poe himself could not have picked a more chilling site for one of his gothic fictions. Deputy Phelps recalled

the jury's descent to the mortuary basement and their single-file progress down a narrow passage. At the end was a small room described as the "morgue." There on a stretcher lay Swope's body—fresh from the autopsy—covered by a sheet except for the face and bald head. The incision had been sewn back up. Most of the jurors had seen the old man in life and had no trouble recognizing the frozen-blue features.

Anyone who thought the impaneling of a coroner's jury or the autopsy itself could be concealed from the public was deluded. The *Kansas City Post* carried its version of the story on Friday. The *Post*, a newspaper enjoyed (or deplored) for its attraction to the lurid, reported that the jurymen "staggered" as they viewed the old man's body.

From the press's numerous interviews, the voices that spoke

most damningly—or at least most tantalizingly—were those of attorney John Paxton and Doctor G. T. Twyman. Both men were careful not to make any out-and-out accusations in their statements to the press. But their comments gave off strong signals of suspicion, which neither tried to conceal.

Paxton told a *Kansas City Times* reporter it was "just possible" that some legal action might be taken *even before* the official reports were in from the scientists analyzing the dead men's viscera. "I do not know," he went on. "I have tried to work from the beginning on the theory that no one was guilty of contributing to the deaths of Colonel Swope and his nephew, but in the last forty-eight hours I have changed my mind."

He noted significantly that Thomas Swope, while weakened by age, was not at all ill on the day he died. While the death of Swope's cousin Moss Hunton had been a grievous blow to the old gentleman, the shock had not been so severe as to threaten his life. Paxton regretted that he was not at liberty to describe the scenes leading up to the Colonel's death, but he then offered something just as newsworthy: "We are certain of only one thing—we believe we are certain of it: that Colonel Swope's end was hastened by some means. Why is yet to be learned."

The attorney's remarks grew more specific as he talked on. "The nurse, an experienced woman of mature years, had given [Colonel Swope] medicine as directed only a few minutes before the beginning of the end," Paxton told his interviewer. He emphasized further that the autopsy "showed positively that Colonel Swope's brain was normal. There was no broken blood vessels [*sic*] such as accompanies apoplexy."

As for the typhoid contagion, conditions in the home precluded any possibility that the disease had its roots there, Paxton said. He was satisfied with the findings of experts—pathologist Hall and bacteriologist Stewart—whose sanitary inspections had turned up no natural breeding ground for the germs.

Unlike the family attorney's comments, the family doctor's were more revealing for what they *didn't* say. Callers at Twyman's Main Street office found him affable but initially closemouthed. He recalled a bit of homely advice he'd gotten from his old father, also a doctor, when he began his medical studies. "His first lesson was 'Doctors should never talk,'" Twyman told one reporter. "I learned this lesson. I can't discuss this matter further."

Whereupon he discussed it anyway, describing in detail the fatal illness of Chrisman Swope, right down to the typhoid germs racing through his bloodstream.

At another point Twyman resorted to a coyness that was startlingly out of character for a straight-talking rural practitioner. He had just declared that Chrisman Swope's sickness and death were "undoubtedly due to typhoid fever" when the interviewer tossed him a charged question: "Was his death due to typhoid *alone*?"

Without a blink, Twyman replied, "Rather cold outside, isn't it?"

The reporter refused to back off. When his questions grew more irksome, Twyman put a stop to them. "See here," he said, "I am not accusing anybody. I do not say there were unnatural incidents connected with the sudden epidemic of typhoid fever in the Swope family. I do not say there were not. I am simply the family physician.... I am cognizant of all the suspicions, the actions and moves made by the family. I have my own private opinion, but what that opinion is, is nobody's business."

Of course Doctor Twyman, like his friend Paxton, *was* accusing somebody, and the suspect's name would inevitably become everybody's business. Those townsfolk who kept up with local gossip must have known exactly whom the doctor and the attorney were talking about. The newsmen knew it too—they were just waiting for official confirmation before their papers displayed the name in bold-face type. No reporter worth his press card—certainly none who'd been tracking events since the first deaths in the mansion—could have failed to pick up the speculations and rumors that had been swirling for days around the courthouse square.

The subject of all the chatter, Doctor Bennett Clark Hyde, may have been relieved that none of the Swope family, so far, had identified him openly as the prime suspect. He was not, however, a naïve man. He knew who his enemies were and he had undoubtedly guessed that before long his name would be hollered to the skies by every street-corner newsboy in Greater Kansas City.

The first phone call from a reporter took Hyde by surprise. "What's that you said?" he asked the caller. "They've taken up Colonel Swope's body to examine it? Why, I didn't know a thing about it. They hadn't told me a thing about it."

When the newsman furnished details of the Colonel's autopsy, Hyde's words took on a defensive note. "Colonel Swope died of apoplexy. There is no doubt about it. It was as plain a case of apoplexy as I have ever seen. The Colonel was getting old and feeble.... The stroke of apoplexy was probably induced by the excitement and shock attending the sudden death of [Moss] Hunton, a cousin, and a very dear friend of his."

Asked about Chrisman Swope's illness, Hyde was insistent: "Chrisman Swope's death was due to typhoid fever. While I attended Mister Swope and signed the death certificate myself in his case, Doctor Twyman of Independence, the family physician, had direct charge of the typhoid fever in the family.... There was no doubt they were suffering from typhoid fever.... What it was caused by, we were not able to learn, but I have always thought it came from the milk."

Then Hyde said something he'd probably been waiting for the chance to say: "I have been sick from typhoid myself. This is only the third day I have been able to be about. In my case I am practically sure I got the fever from milk or in handling the typhoid patients at the Swopes'."

Speaking to another reporter the next day, he repeated the claim. "I was down with [typhoid] myself. It was a light attack. Doctor J. W. Perkins tested my blood and found the typhoid germ." In fact, Perkins got his positive results using the Widal blood agglutination test. There was never any indication that he'd attempted to grow typhoid bacilli in a solution of Hyde's blood and a nutrient-rich broth, as Doctor Stewart had tried and failed to do.

The one credible authority who came to Hyde's defense during the press invasion was Independence City Chemist Walter M. Cross. Doctor Cross seems to have told anyone who'd listen that he *knew* how typhoid had entered the Swope mansion and it had nothing to do with any deliberate malfeasance.

Cross had made a sanitary survey of the premises and had "personal knowledge of conditions that would account for every case of typhoid there." It had all begun the previous February, he said, when the cook's 10-year-old daughter had come down with the disease. Flies from the servants' privy had carried the germs to the household milk containers, from which, he concluded, the bacteria had reached the kitchen and the family dining table. "I believe from this information that any attempt to hold any individual responsible for the deaths and sickness from this typhoid infection would be a great injustice." Though Cross undoubtedly had in mind the person who would suffer that "great injustice," he kept the name to himself.

The patience and discretion of the Kansas City papers during this and following weeks might seem quaint from a twenty-first-century perspective. Yet all of the city's dailies, even the gaudiest of them, exercised amazing restraint as they waited to put a name on the putative villain of the drama. For whatever reasons, they decided to play it safe until there was some major break to blow the story wide open.

That break, it was assumed, would be the report by the Chicago forensic experts who were poking through the stomachs and livers of the two deceased Swopes. If their finding was death by poisoning—as everyone expected—the news would clang like a fire alarm throughout the city's newsrooms. The county prosecutor's office would have no choice but to respond by filing criminal charges. Hyde would no longer be the nameless shadow-suspect hidden in the wings, but the man at center stage with the accusers' spotlight on his face.

For now, the focus was on Chicago and the investigations of two respected scientists. Ludvig Hektoen, the impressive pathologist, and his colleague at the Rush Medical College, toxicologist Walter S. Haines, were the men of the hour. Haines especially seemed to enchant reporters who had gone to Chicago to be there for the big story. With his oddly combed white beard, his wizened features, and his habit of locking himself in his lab for all-day work marathons, he seemed almost a cartoon of the eccentric scientist in a nickelodeon picture show. Soon the two Chicago experts would be joined in their work by a nationally known chemist who'd been brought in from the University of Michigan, Doctor Victor C. Vaughan.

What they'd discovered so far, the *Post* exclaimed in a bold front-page headline on Saturday the 15th, was a suspicious white powder in Chrisman Swope's stomach. When Doctor Hektoen denied on Tuesday that he'd found any such powder, the press could have vowed to double-check the facts in future dispatches from Chicago. But journalists' instinctive urge to beat the competition at all costs got the better of them. Again and again they jumped the gun, only to find today's scoop refuted by tomorrow's top story in a rival paper.

The *Chicago Record-Herald* reported on January 17 that "it is believed that the pathological examination of the stomachs of Col. Thomas H. Swope and his nephew, Chrisman Swope, has resulted in the discovery of the evidence of the inoculation of typhus bacilli." The story not only misidentified the germ (typhus and typhoid are separate diseases) but it turned out to be a total fiction.

"Strychnine Found in Col. Swope's Stomach," the *Post* proclaimed on the 18th. Two days later the *Kansas City Journal*'s reporter on the story gave quite a different account. "Every attorney connected with the case was seen yesterday," he wrote, "and each denied that traces of poison had thus far been found."

What frustrated the press most of all were the scientists' repeated delays in releasing their findings and their vagueness in telling why. At times the forensic wizards appeared willfully tight-lipped. One reporter characterized Doctor Hektoen as a type of sophisticated source familiar to all newsmen—he could issue statements that seemed candid and informative until one stepped outside and realized that every one of them was pure air.

On Tuesday, January 18, the *Kansas City Times* told its readers that "Chicago experts hope to make a report tomorrow." Tomorrow passed—and tomorrow, and tomorrow—with not a word from the experts in their labs.

On January 20, the *Star* assured its readers that attorneys for the Swopes "will know definitely by Tuesday morning" exactly what the chemists had discovered in their laboratories. Tuesday the 25th came and went. The scientists' reports did not materialize.

Throughout much of the waiting game, two attorneys on the prosecution's A-team were ensconced in the Brevoort Hotel near the Chicago medical college, where they could monitor the scientists' progress. John Paxton had brought with him his colleague, John H. Atwood, as a fellow strategist of the Swopes' legal offensive. Tom Swope "Junior" also had come along, probably at his mother's urging, as had a lawyer from Tennessee with a personal interest in the case, W. S. Fleming. The latter's cousin, Stuart Fleming, had caught typhoid fever at the Swope mansion while carrying out his duties as a co-executor of the Colonel's estate. Stuart, a nephew of the old man and a well-liked family adviser, was still too ill to leave his sickbed in Columbus, Tennessee.

Back in Kansas City, County Prosecutor Virgil Conkling worked on plans for handling an arrest should the evidence call for such action. In Independence, the curious still clustered at the foot of the Pleasant Street hill, gazing up at the shuttered mansion on the crest. And just about everyone spent hours of their free time poring over the newspapers. Folks in Kansas City may have had more diversions than did their small-town neighbors to the east, but they were equally obsessed with the unfolding drama. Every new edition delivered from the presses would vanish almost before it hit the newsstands,

It had been a difficult time for the press. For weeks, reporters and feature writers had hustled to keep the copy flowing, despite the dearth of really big, hot-from-the-oven news. Whole pages of type were devoted to recaps of old stories, color pieces, human-interest profiles, and "backgrounders" on the Swopes and their ordeals. All the while, the real story—the Big Story—waited to be told.

And all of a sudden, it was. On Monday, January 31, eighteen days after readers had learned of Colonel Swope's autopsy, a bonanza of sensational news practically engulfed the front pages of the evening papers.

John Paxton, fresh home from Chicago, got to the heart of the matter in a statement printed in boldface by the *Star* and *Post*: "On account of the widespread interest in the investigation … into the death of Thomas H. Swope, I feel it proper for me to make public the fact that Doctor Hektoen, Doctor Haines, and Doctor Vaughan, as the result of their investigations extending over a period of several weeks, give to me their opinions that Mr. Swope died from the effects of poison."

Strychnine, the papers revealed, had showed up in several places in the Colonel's viscera. While analyses of Chrisman Swope's organs were still incomplete, according to the *Star*, "it was said that traces of strychnine were found in his liver." The *Post*, as usual, took it a step further: "The [scientists'] report said that in both Chrisman Swope's and Col. Thomas H. Swope's organs, enough strychnine had been found to indicate death from poisoning."

Just as sensational was the second big story of the day, in which Doctor Hyde came right out and acknowledged that he was the suspect, falsely and ruinously labeled as a murderer. That very morning he had brought lawsuits against John Paxton and others for alleged slander and libel. If anyone in Jackson County hadn't already guessed Hyde was the accused, there in black and white were his name and picture for a quarter-million readers to behold.

And there was more. Doctor Hyde and his wife—how lovely she was in the engraving, her head tilted just so, her eyes soft with melancholy—had given statements fiercely defending his honor and innocence.

"It has been eighteen days since I was indescribably shocked by the newspaper statements regarding the suspicions surrounding the illnesses and deaths in the Swope family," wrote the doctor. He had kept his feelings to himself "in the face of palpable insinuations." It was unthinkable "that any person of fair mind could consider me such a monster as to have even wished the death of any or all of these unfortunate people, who were near and dear to me, much less to have had a hand in any of their deaths."

Now he demanded that the county coroner conduct a searching and speedy investigation to weigh the validity of these charges

DR. B. CLARK HYDE AND MRS. HYDE.
Kansas City Star, Mon., Jan. 31, 1910, p. 1.

against him, "and we will gladly render this official all of the assistance in our power in such an inquiry."

If Doctor Hyde's tone was that of the incensed victim, Frances Hyde's tone expressed sorrow, a devoted spouse's loyalty, and a simmering bitterness toward her mother. "When my husband and I left Independence on December 18 we were both ill," she wrote. "He has since undergone a siege of typhoid fever, and unfortunately I have had no communication with my mother. I have been reliably informed that since that time she has paid out of her personal funds $5,000 to one lawyer and $10,000 to a firm of lawyers, to conduct an investigation into the cause of the deaths in our family...."

Frances lamented the fact that Mrs. Swope had never become fully reconciled to her marriage, even though nearly five years had passed since the wedding. "I have noted the cruel insinuations and rumors reflecting on my husband in connection with these deaths," she continued. "I have followed very closely all the so-called circumstances which surround our misfortunes. The most of these 'circumstances' do not exist, in point of fact, and a simple explanation, within my knowledge, exists in every instance where there is any basis of fact."

Surely, reading her words—matching them to the pensive face in the picture—only the cynical or coldhearted could be unmoved. To the very last sentence, they evoked the triumph of wifely trust over personal anguish: "My own knowledge of my husband's innocence is the only thing that has made my situation at all bearable during these awful days."

Somewhat less conspicuous in that Monday's news was a fact that testified to the aggressiveness of Hyde's enemies.

Among the defendants in the libel case was the large and influential *St. Louis Post-Dispatch*. It turned out the paper had run three stories virtually accusing Hyde of murder, and it had done so *weeks earlier,* starting with a page 1 blockbuster on January 14. The multi-deck headline of the *Post-Dispatch*'s initial story read:

Swope Poison Plot Suspect Watched by Five Detectives.
Arrest in murder for a 10 million stake anticipated.
Chemists search stomachs taken from two bodies exhumed.
Plan to kill family with typhoid germs.
Investigators who work secretly convinced of wholesale murder attempt and ability to fix blame on guilty man.

This was bolder stuff than the Kansas City papers had dared to print and it was followed by more of the same, all in the heavy-breathing prose of scandal journalism. The stories contained a few exaggerations and fact errors, but no matter. By January 16, when the paper ran a large picture of Clark Hyde, it had all but branded him as the poisoner of Swope mansion.

How the St. Louis paper got hold of the story—and got it way back on January 14—was never explained. The likeliest theory is that Paxton planted the idea with a *Post-Dispatch* editor, though he later denied it. If so, he was merely borrowing a tactic as old as propaganda itself—the use of the preemptive news offensive to win over the public before the other side could state its case. At the very least, Paxton had given the reporter some powerful quotes as to Hyde's alleged crimes.

Then, according to Hyde's lawsuit, Paxton repeated the same damning statements just a day later before a powerful group of Kansas City news executives. Among them were Charles A. Bonfils and A. B. McDonald of the *Post,* Selby Cline of the *Journal,* and Henry Haskell and George B. Longan of the *Star.*

What he reportedly told them was ripping good stuff, even if he phrased it in the stiffest of legalese English: "I believe that Col. Thomas H. Swope and Chrisman Swope were poisoned and did not die from natural causes, and I believe that Doctor Hyde poisoned or caused them to be poisoned and thereby cause[d] their deaths. And I believe that he inoculated the Swope family with typhoid fever germs and caused several members of said family, including Margaret Swope and Lucy Lee Swope, to contract typhoid fever. And that he attempted to poison said Margaret Swope and Lucy Lee Swope ... and that [he is] guilty of the crime of murder [and is] liable for capital punishment therefore, and also guilty of the crime of assault with intent to kill."

Amazing as it seems, the Kansas City editors chose not to publish the statement, or even to name the accused man, until after the strychnine report came in on January 31. To this day, questions linger: Why had they allowed their papers to be scooped so brazenly by the *St. Louis Post-Dispatch*? And why had they suppressed red-hot material that Paxton had handed to them on a plate nearly three weeks earlier?

Perhaps they held their fire in the cause of ethical, responsible journalism—a bit of a stretch, perhaps, in light of the era's free-for-all reporting standards. Perhaps they feared a libel action of the kind brought against the St. Louis paper. By late January, Hyde had engaged his own legal counsel, one of the city's smartest and most combative lawyers.

Whatever the case, the whole grim affair was out in the open now. The lines were drawn. Hyde's accusers were closing in like a hanging party. The doctor had signaled he was ready to fight.

Chapter 15

Granted, with all the accusations, gruesome details, and raw emotions on stage in the Swope-Hyde drama, anyone might have welcomed a bit of comic relief. Granted, the perfect clown came along just in time to provide it. Granted, he was a quack and a prodigious liar who profited from gulling the sick. Yet the glee with which the press stripped him down and dangled him before a guffawing public seems, in retrospect, both mean-spirited and racist. If anything, one feels a bit of sympathy for the outlandish character whose very name was an object of fun: Chasing Hatred Chase Jordan.

There was something engaging about the dark-skinned herb doctor (or "yarb doctor"), a self-styled native of Chile and specialist in treatments of the liver and gallstones. He was certainly no more a fraud than countless other potion peddlers who worked the Midwest in the early 1900s. One even gets the sense that Jordan *believed* that his homemade remedies, nostrums, and philters could cure everything from simple headaches to far more debilitating ills. Like many a mountebank before and since, he may have succeeded in bamboozling himself.

It was Jordan's reputed gallstone cure that led to his celebrity. One day eight years previous, Mrs. Logan O. Swope had traveled the considerable distance from her Independence home to his office in Kansas City, Kansas, to seek relief from that painful condition. Jordan's treatment would be her last resort before resigning herself to surgery, at the time a risky solution at best. Jordan came to the rescue, installing a curative bath in the Swope house and prescribing his own herbal remedy in the form of black-colored tablets labeled "No. 6." In no time the stones were gone, never to return.

Maggie Swope was so gratified by Jordan's results that she insisted the whole family turn to him for treatment of various aches and ailments. Her son Tom had dosed himself regularly with Jordan's compounds, as had his wife and father-in-law. The sickly Chrisman Swope had relied on the pills as well and was said to have purchased some for relief of a headache

DR. CHASSEZ HATRED CHASE JORDAN.
Kansas City Times, Tue., Feb. 1, 1910, p. 2.

only days before he was diagnosed with typhoid. The daughters were regular customers, and Jordan had mailed a supply of pills to Lucy Lee for use during her sojourn in Paris. Even the Swope servants had to swallow the yarb doctor's potions when they reported in sick. In fact, the only member of the household who seems to have evaded Jordan's therapies was, surprisingly, Uncle Thomas Swope, who disliked medicines but would grudgingly try anything that might relieve his disorders. In Maggie Swope's defense, it should be noted that the most acute maladies were still entrusted to the family's physician, Doc Twyman. Once the typhoid epidemic had a grip on the household, it appears that Jordan's cures were shelved in favor of more conventional prescriptions.

On the day word got out that poison was suspected in the Swope deaths, a detective who had heard about Jordan's association with the family raised an interesting question. Might the Chilean healer's medicines contain a smidgen of something toxic?

Say, strychnine? The detective, along with a lawyer and a reporter for the *Times,* immediately showed up at Jordan's office suite at 610 Minnesota Avenue. They found the five rooms richly furnished and presided over by an efficient full-time secretary; this was no storefront snake-oil shop set up for a fast buck and a quick get-away. Other gentlemen of the press followed that same day and the next. Their initial news reports indicated confusion about the doctor's name. Depending on which paper you read, four versions of the first name saw print—the pseudo-Hispanic "Chassez," the present-tense "Chases," the present-participle "Chasing," and the variant form "Chessing." After days of sticking with their own preferences, the editors agreed on "Chasing" or "Chessing," either one as correct a handle as any other.

In his first encounter with the fourth estate, Jordan presented a dapper if exotic appearance. Visitors noted his skin color, his whorled black hair, his mustache waxed into rococo curls at each tip, and his curly goatee. He was missing his left arm, which was amputated, he said, following a firearm accident that blew off his hand years ago. He greeted his callers in an accent that was ... what exactly? Something *like* Spanish, anyway. And he was a chatty host, seemingly eager to answer every question, including some that nobody thought to ask.

"I was born in Chile, in Valparaiso," he told the *Times*'s man. "Oh, it's a grand city. Haven't you ever read of it? The parks, the band playing, and women in pretty dresses walking down the Plaza." Jordan's eyes closed in dreamy reminiscence."Yes, I went to medical schools there. ... That is where I got my degree [as a] Doctor of Medicine and Liver and Gallstones." He had come to the States sixteen years ago, he said, and had continued his studies in American medical colleges. After living for a while in Fort Scott, Kansas, he had set up his practice at the Minnesota Avenue location.

Like a chef asked for the recipe of his celebrated Canard à L'Orange, Jordan was loath to disclose his secrets. "I make them mostly from South American herbs, which I import," he said. "They possess high curative qualities. While they act rather harshly at first, making the patient very sick, they bring about an almost certain cure and they are not dangerous to take. No one knows what they contain but myself."

Very quickly the whole town knew the contents of Jordan's headache tablets, if not his entire pharmacopoeia. Thanks to a speedy chemical analysis, the *Star* on February 1 was able to disclose the formula. It was nothing more mysterious than bicarbonate of soda and an analgesic and fever reducer known as acetanilid, used in many patent medicines at the time. (Acetanilid had some wicked side effects and its medicinal use was abandoned thirty-some years later.)

Perhaps unsettled by all the press scrutiny, Jordan made quite a show of demonstrating to a *Post* reporter that his remedies were poison-free. The newsman asked about strychnine. "That is one thing I never have used," the doctor assured him. "I never had a grain of it in my laboratory. I never use morphine or any drug. I have only yarbs and simple little things." Then he said, "Look here." As the astonished reporter watched, Jordan popped a handful of white pellets into his mouth, chewed, and swallowed. "Have some yourself," he offered. "They won't hurt you." The visitor declined.

Then the reporter decided to have some fun with his host. "They say you are of Spanish extraction, and not a Negro," he said.

"I am a native of South America," Jordan asserted.

"Tiene usted una phosphero?" asked the interviewer.

"Si, señor," Jordan replied, but made no move.

The newsman repeated, "Tiene usted una phosphero?"

"Si, señor."

"Then where is it?" demanded the visitor.

"Where is what?" Jordan said.

"The match I have been asking for all this time."

Jordan answered, with a laugh, that he had been in America so long he'd forgotten most of his native tongue.

The reporter so enjoyed his cleverness at tricking the "South American doctor" that he went on for another paragraph reiterating how he'd exposed Jordan's linguistic lie. Investigations into the yarb doctor's past became a kind of competitive lark. Rival papers had been chipping away at Jordan's persona for only three days when it broke apart like a plaster of Paris figurine.

An African-American woman named Frances Jarrett, thought by lawyers to be Jordan's sister, told the *Post* rather testily that she was no sibling to the "yaller Kansas doctor that rides 'round in a carriage." Her family in Coffey (or Coffee), Texas, had taken him in as a "stray" and raised him as one of their own. "Nobody knowed where he come from," she said. "He didn't know himself."

An elderly black resident of Fort Scott, Kansas, told the *Star* that Jordan had lived in the town twenty-five years under the name "Chasey" Jordan and was said to have married a Mexican. Reporters found that he'd worked as a painter at the Hotel Wellington in Kansas City, Kansas, and that a white housekeeper had sued him for breach of promise when he took up with the woman he now lived with. The roster of licensed physicians in the city, the *Times* revealed, showed no listing for Chasing Hatred Chase Jordan. A local doctor confirmed there was no one of that name on the rolls of the Wyandotte County (Kansas) Medical Society.

Thus undone—with pants down and wig askew, so to say—Jordan slunk offstage in a metaphoric hail of rotten tomatoes from the press gallery. He would set foot on it once again, but only briefly, his dignity fallen beyond resurrection.

Meanwhile, two vastly more dignified figures had arrived to join the dramatis personae. Master duelists in the courts of law, Frank Walsh and James A. Reed had acquired legal and political reputations far beyond the limits of Jackson County. Some of their hardest-fought cases had pitted them against each other, and their mutual dislike lent a decided edge to their rivalry. The contest over Hyde's guilt or innocence would be, for each, an epic showdown in a celebrated career.

Alike in brilliance, the Kansas City barristers could hardly have been more different in personal style or even appearance. A few days into the Hyde trial, an editorial writer for the *Post* resorted to a fanciful comparison of the two: "Reed is a gray, graceful figure whose repose of mien and manner, and whose

Frank P. Walsh, 1910–1925.
National Photo Company Collection,
Library of Congress.

James A. Reed, March 1911.
Library of Congress Prints and
Photographs Division.

proud and ornamental appearance, suggest an ivory and gray steel scabbard, sheathing a rapier of white hot attack. ... Walsh looks like one of Howard Chandler Christy's modern men had stepped from the artist's canvas, but something coarser, more virile, more charged with life and intelligence."

Reed was indeed tall and imposing, with eyes that reporters invariably described as "keen" or "piercing." Walsh was stocky, with the blunt-featured look of a fighter. It was one of those rare cases where each man's physiognomy somehow seemed to match the driving forces within.

Reed saw himself in the august role of a national leader—precisely what he would soon become. Propelled by his association with the powerful Pendergast wing of the Democratic Party (the "Goats"), he had already politicked his way from city councilor to county prosecutor to mayor, an office he served with dazzling energy and distinction. His success had laid the groundwork for a run—in this very year of 1910—for U.S. senator from Missouri (he won and stayed for three terms). It says something of Reed's nature that H. L. Mencken, the mocking iconoclast of *The American Mercury,* would later praise "the noble music" of his Senate attacks on the Volstead Act, the League of Nations, and naive reformers of every stripe.

Walsh, allied with the rival Joe Shannon faction of the Kansas City Democrats (the "Rabbits"), might have been of a separate species, philosophically. Humbly born, he was a passionate advocate for the poor, for workers, and for social welfare causes that Reed would have scorned as liberal folly. Soon Walsh would be adulated, by no less a titan than the AFL's Samuel Gompers, as the "Great Tribune" in the service of organized labor. Like Reed, he reached national prominence—in his case as co-chairman of Woodrow Wilson's Commission on Industrial Relations.

When Walsh and Reed had butted heads in court, it was usually over labor-management wrangles. Now that they were squared off in the Hyde murder case, their roles in the affair took on a predictable symmetry. Walsh, the natural ally of the persecuted, was the perfect choice to represent Hyde, who he seems honestly to have believed was a victim of injustice. Reed, a born political striver, at home in the halls of power and money, could hardly have resisted prosecuting the alleged slayer of the sainted philanthropist. On top of the prestige it would bring, the job would afford him a very respectable fee—reportedly $10,000 up front—from a grateful Mrs. Swope.

It would be two months before the famed barristers would cross swords again, in the trial of Doctor Hyde. Just now they and their legal associates were called to more routine tasks—preparing for the legal skirmishes that would precede the actual trial (if the case ever came to that). For one thing, they would have to advise their clients ahead of the coroner's inquest, which would take place in a matter of days, probably on Monday, February 7. Until the coroner's jury arrived at the probable cause of Colonel Swope's death, any move to arrest Doctor Hyde would have to wait.

Then there were the slander and libel suits brought against John Paxton and the *St. Louis Post-Dispatch,* among others. Testimony would have to be taken, showing either that Hyde was a blameless victim of defamation by Paxton and the Swopes, or that the spoken and published accusations against him merely stated the horrible facts of his guilt. James A. Reed, of course, was the leading advocate for the family.

What followed, not surprisingly, was a scramble of competing lawyers to line up anyone and everyone who could speak for their clients' interests. Out went subpoenas from Reed's office, in the stately New York Life Building, and Frank Walsh's suite in the Scarritt Building, the city's most elegant skyscraper.

A sheriff's deputy dropped by 3516 Forest Avenue to serve Doctor Hyde with a summons to sit for a deposition by Reed. Subpoenas for Nurse Pearl Kellar, John Paxton, Doctor Hall, and Doctor Stewart were issued by lawyers on Hyde's legal crew.

Counsels on both sides were eager to question Mrs. Swope, who was as hard to lure from her shuttered fortress as a bank robber from a backwoods hideout. A couple of Walsh's men and a sheriff's deputy named McCrory tried their best one morning. After parking their car on the street, they climbed the hill and knocked at the forbidding front door. The nurse who answered told them the lady of the house was not at home.

A half hour later they called again, hoping to find Nurse Kellar. This time the greeter in the doorway was W. C. Rice, the tough special officer hired to guard the house. McCrory stiffened his back and announced, "I am a deputy sheriff and demand the right to see Miss Kellar, a nurse here."

Rice was unimpressed. "Nothing doing," he said.

In some subliminal way, the mood of urgency was probably heightened by the press's habit of turning up the heat wherever it saw an opportunity. Everybody hungered for news—for something to *happen*. Reporters dogged the steps of process servers or made flying visits to wherever some key witness might be found lurking.

One morning they flocked to the home of Clark and Frances Hyde, where a lawyer, John Cleary, spoke to them on the front porch. "We think it inadvisable that they should receive visitors at this time," he said.

However, one newsman got a peek inside—perhaps through an undraped front window—and published a remarkably full description: "The living apartments on the first floor are a drawing room, a rear parlor, and a reception hall, a cheerful room, half of which is taken up by the stairway that leads to the sleeping quarters on the second floor. The drawing room is finished in dark green, with white lace curtains and valances at the windows. The furniture, consisting of several pieces, is of some dark tinted wood. On the walls are a half-dozen excellent etchings. A few books scattered about lend a suggestion of comfort."

Most of the action in this first week of February centered on the slander suit accusing Paxton of smearing Doctor Hyde's good name. Thus, the *real* Swope case—the dark struggle between an alleged murderer and the powerful enemies who wanted him hanged—would be upstaged briefly by a legal sideshow. By any measure, it was less high drama than unintended farce.

Lawyers for both camps, avid for sworn depositions from the most favorable witnesses, jockeyed for two days to take testimony from more or less the same people. Some, like Nurse Kellar, had simply vanished when process servers came to call. Others, it turned out, were subpoenaed to testify in two different places at once. Hyde had been summoned to appear Wednesday morning in Reed's office at precisely the same minute he was to present himself in Walsh's office a quarter mile away. Some witnesses must have wondered where they were supposed to show up and when. Apparently frustrated by the same crossed signals, reporters dashed from one law firm's paneled suite to the next in hopes of catching a key player's testimony.

What it really came down to was an effort by each side to question the top witnesses first and to block the rival team's attempts to do likewise. After all the legal hustling and end runs, Judge Herman Brumback finally put a stop to the whole imbroglio until he could figure out a means of assuring equal access to the witnesses by all parties. Meanwhile, Hyde tapped off some of the steam by agreeing to dismiss his individual lawsuit against Paxton (Hyde's second lawsuit, which also cited the *Post-Dispatch,* was still on the table). This maneuver spared him—for the time being—from having to face interrogation by the fearful James Reed.

A handful of witnesses did manage to give depositions that week, before the judge called a time-out. In Walsh's office, Sylvester Spangler, the late Colonel's business agent, testified about his boss's unhappy final days and his anxious desire to make a new will. In Reed's office, James E. Vincil, a former secretary of the police board, revisited the ugly subject of Hyde's police-station abuse of the black woman years before.

The most sweeping testimony, however—and maybe the most awkward, under the circumstances—was given by John Paxton in his deposition hearing before Frank Walsh. The Swope family's genteel attorney and the proletarian union lawyer were civil enough during the questioning, but the presence of another person at the oblong meeting table must have given Paxton a moment's pause. He was none other than Clark Hyde, who had dropped by Walsh's office that morning and stayed on to hear what Paxton—the man behind his prosecution for murder—had to say.

The core of Paxton's testimony was a ten-page letter he had written to his co-executor, Stuart Fleming, while the latter was recuperating from typhoid on his Tennessee farm. With Hyde seated just feet away and reporters taking notes in the background, Paxton read aloud his account of every horror visited on the Swope family since December. It was all there in coolly rendered detail: Chrisman's death, the mysterious capsules, Margaret's near-fatal convulsion, the nurses' rebellion, Lucy Lee's typhoid attack after the train ride from New York, Doctor Stewart's medical detective work—*everything.*

At times during the reading, especially when poison was mentioned, Hyde smiled broadly. All the reporters noticed it. It would add a nice touch to their front-page stories.

Chapter 16

If there had been no Winifred Black to write about the Hyde-Swope murder case, someone would have had to invent her. She was an improbable creature of gutsiness and gush, of talent and showgirl pluck. In an age when men ruled the newsroom, it was women like Winifred Black—the "sob sisters," they were called—who seduced readers with newsprint valentines of true love, heartbreak, and dark passions.

Perhaps more than any of her rivals in the press corps, Black of the *Kansas City Post* managed to capture and define the Swope drama's irresistible allure to readers everywhere. She practically *embodied* the tale's glamour. The case had it all: the patrician family, the suave suspect, the alleged poisonings (more than one story alluded to the Borgias), the Poe-esque plague within the castle walls. If anyone cherished such dime-novel fantasies—and reveled in their appearance in real life—it was surely Winifred Black.

Black had covered the lurid trial of society bad boy Harry K. Thaw, murderer of New York architect Stanford White. Her sympathetic stories about the woman in the case, Thaw's unhappy wife, earned her and her fellow newswomen the "sob sister" sobriquet (a famous member of the sob-sisterhood was the fabulous Nellie Bly of the *New York World*). Black had started out on William Randolph Hearst's racy *San Francisco Examiner*. After a wild series of scoops, publicity exploits, and investigative tours-de-force, she moved on to the *New York Journal,* and thence to the *Denver Post*. It says much about that paper's reportorial values that its co-owner and publisher, flamboyant Frederick G. Bonfils, also owned a circus.

In 1909, just in time for the Swope tragedies, Bonfils added the *Kansas City Post* to his holdings and made sure it displayed the same spice and audacity of his Denver paper. He also gave it—or rather loaned it—the services of Winifred Black, his priestess of the personality feature. She would stay in town right through Hyde's trial, filing regular stories for her Denver readers as well as new fans in the Missouri metropolis.

No doubt about it, Black knew how to grab readers with her prose style and her eye for poignant details. But she seemed also to possess a rare empathy that her subjects recognized and trusted. Sources opened up to her, and she saw in their hearts and predicaments the seeds of great melodrama. A column for the *Kansas City Post* of February 3, 1910, typifies her style and is worth revisiting in full.

"IF DR. HYDE IS A MONSTER, HOW CAN MOTHER LEAVE ME WITH HIM"

Mrs. Hyde Breaks Silence and Discusses Puzzling Swope Case With Winifred Black; Declares Husband Innocent; Deserted by Family.

(By Winifred Black)

"My husband is innocent," said Mrs. B. Clark Hyde yesterday. "I don't only think he is innocent, I know he is.

"I would go straight on knowing it if every human being in Kansas City, or in the world either, for that matter, should go into open court tomorrow and accuse him of murder."

Mrs. Hyde is not very well just now, and the strain of the last few days has been enough to completely break down any ordinary woman. But Mrs. Hyde herself didn't look a day over 22 as she lay in her bright, pretty little room in her bright, pretty, unpretentious little home and told me how it is that she knows that her husband is innocent.

She is not a pretty woman, this little wife who is standing by her husband through good and evil report without one instant's wavering—she is a beautiful woman. She would be beautiful in any company and in any dress. Her dark hair makes a soft cloud around her beautiful brow—the brow of a Minerva or a calm visaged impartial Portia. And her great, liquid eyes are as brown, and as clear, and as untroubled as a forest pool, deep in the woods, in the quiet autumn.

She has little white, delicate hands—the hands of a woman of intuition and character and decision—and a beautiful column of a throat. No, I have never seen a more beautiful woman in my life than Mrs. B. Clark Hyde, the wife of the man who has just brought suit to defend his name from a hideous slander.

She smiled gravely, not wistfully, not pitifully, not emotionally, as another woman of less heroic mold might smile at such a time, but gravely, when I asked her how she knew that her husband was innocent.

"I know my husband," said Ms. Hyde. "That would be enough, if there was nothing else.

"But there is something else. I was with my brother when he died. I held his head on my arm when he breathed his last. I was the first member of the family to get to him when he was taken sick.

"I held Moss Hunton's hands in mine when he died.

"I was in complete charge of the sickroom in both of these cases. I know all about the sickness, the symptoms, and what happened in the room, and not one of these people who have been hinting that my husband murdered my brother and my cousin and my uncle has been near me, to ask me one single question about one single case.

"Why?"

"I do not know."

"You might ask them that question."

"I have not seen any member of my family since the 17th of December when I left my home, or what used to be my home in Independence, and came here with my husband. No one has been near us, none of the family, I mean, to see how we are bearing this trouble.

"I have not heard from my mother at all.

"Yes, my mother and I were always very dear friends, more like sisters, people used to say, than mother and daughter.

"I was the eldest girl, you know, and after father died, I sort of took charge of things at home. None of my sisters ever bought a dress, or a hat, or a new piece of music without getting me to go along and help.

"I am fond of housekeeping. I like to cook and go to market, and I always did that at home, so as to take the care off from my mother's shoulders.

"My brother who died was very shy and retiring. He spent most of his time in his room. He was very good natured and gentle and always went downtown after the mail, but he took no active interest in things around the house.

"My other brother has never been very well, you see, and so of course things seemed to rest a good deal on me.

"I liked it, and I think I was a good deal of help to my mother.

"I tried to be, I know.

"We never had one word of disagreement, except about men.

"My mother never liked any man who paid any attention to me.

"It made no difference who the man was—as soon as she saw that he liked me, she took a violent dislike to him.

"It was so with Dr. Hyde. She never could bear Dr. Hyde—after she saw that I was fond of him.

"I never deceived her about him in my life. I was engaged to him for two years, and I never saw him without telling my mother that I was going to see him.

"She was very angry when we were married, and she has always disliked him bitterly ever since.

"I don't know why—just because I love him, I reckon.

"My mother is a good woman, and she has always been very good to me. I can't imagine why she doesn't come to see me."

The great, liquid eyes grew wistful for an instant, and I thought there was a look as of coming tears in their soft depth; but it passed, and Mrs. Hyde went on again, her voice as calm and measured, her words as well chosen, as if she had been telling a grave story to an audience of serious children.

"If she thinks my husband is such a monster, I wonder how she dares to leave me with him.

"Why doesn't she rush into the house and try to take me away?

"If she thinks he is innocent, why doesn't she come and tell me so?

"It is such a little ways here from Independence. I keep wondering and wondering why my mother does not come.

"My sisters—?

"No, they have not come either.

"They are young and perhaps they are afraid or something.

"My friends have all been more than good to me. They besiege the house all day and part of the night, too, sometimes with all kinds of offers of sympathy and help.

"I was brought up in Independence, you know. Born and brought up there. My uncle, Colonel Swope, lived at our house with us. We didn't know him very well. No one knew him very well. Even his own mother, so they tell me.

"And now he is gone, and my brother is dead, and my cousin Moss is dead, too, and they are trying to make me believe that my husband, the man who never spoke an unkind word to me in all his life, is to blame for it all."

Mrs. Hyde's dark eyes widened suddenly, and she laughed, the quiet laugh of a loving, trusting woman.

"It would be funny if it wasn't so terrible.

"I saw it in the newspapers first. I had to read the article over four or five times before I could believe that I really understood what it was trying to say. But now I understand—but I can't believe it—yes—I mean I can't really believe that any of it is true.

"It all seems to me like one of those awful dreams that you can only vaguely remember when you wake up.

"Some day my husband and I will wake up out of this dream and then we will laugh at it—together.

"Oh! I am weary for my dearie," somebody whistled as he passed the house.

Mrs. Hyde's soft lips set and then her tall, good looking young husband came into the room and sat down by the bed, and took her little, delicate, white hand in both of his. And we all began to talk about Harry Lauder and of the love songs he sang, the simple, sweet little Scotch love songs, so full of the old, old refrain, all about fidelity and faith and simple trust and honest love.

When I went out of the house I was crying. But Mrs. Hyde did not shed one single tear.

———•◦•———

Nothing short of war, pestilence, or a plague of locusts could have kept Winifred Black and her fellow reporters away from the Independence courthouse on Monday morning, February 7. Likewise, hundreds of townspeople would sooner have risked the Lord's wrath than have missed the day's big event. A coroner's jury of six sensible citizens—a real estate man, the president of the First National Bank, a druggist, a store owner, a bookkeeper, and a hardware dealer—would begin hearing testimony regarding the cause of Thomas Hunton Swope's death.

The inquest wasn't to begin until 10 a.m., but three women were already waiting on the front steps when janitor Joe Brown opened up. They got their front-row seats all right, at the cost of a freezing wait while Brown stirred up the coal heat. Out on the square, townsfolk were forming into chatty clusters or queuing up at the door. Monday was washday for the town's housewives and one glance at the crowd made it clear a lot of clothes would go unlaundered that day. So much of the male workforce gravitated to the courthouse that some business owners simply didn't bother to open shop.

Those at the rim of the crowd were the first to see a red car pull up and Clark Hyde step out with attorney John Cleary. Like paparazzi of a later age, onlookers surged toward them. Hyde pressed ahead as his lawyer forced a path in front. The doctor's face was slightly flushed, his lips clamped into a tight, thin line. He wore a black suit and black bowtie befitting the occasion's gravity. But he seemed to brighten up once he was inside the courtroom, where he took a seat behind his lead attorney, the stocky, wavy-haired Frank Walsh.

When a reporter asked how he was getting along, Hyde's reply was almost jaunty. "I don't know when I've seen a prettier winter morning than this," he said. "It makes me feel good all over. I only wish Mrs. Hyde were able to be out and enjoy this fine, fresh air." Regrettably, she'd been ordered by her doctor to take a day's bed rest.

The courtroom was filling fast. Apparently no one had calculated the room's capacity or guessed how many would want in. With the jurors seated and the front tables occupied by lawyers, stenographers, and the press, there were chairs for only three hundred spectators. All seats were taken a half hour before starting time and anyone who'd been let in after that had to jostle for standing room against the wall. Scores never got in at all and stood outside peering through the windows.

Finally the show got going, with Coroner B. H. Zwart and his deputy, J. E. Trogdon, as the sole examiners of witnesses. Attorneys for Hyde, Paxton, and the Swope family—there was quite a contingent of them—were entitled to observe but not cross-examine or make statements. Near them sat the dour-faced county prosecutor, Virgil Conkling.

About all the morning session had to offer was people-watching—principally Hyde-watching—and some raw meat for the morbidly inclined. R. B. Mitchell, the embalmer, gave a matter-of-factly gruesome account of his handiwork in preparing the Colonel's corpse. Among other things, he said he'd chosen a super-strength embalming fluid because of the hot weather. He also related how the frozen body was spirited from Forest Hill cemetery by dark of night.

And he described the autopsy—as Winifred Black put it—"as if [he] were talking of so much beef or mutton instead of human flesh."

Hyde himself was the star just by *being* there—the celebrity suspect who said nothing and showed nothing. To one onlooker he appeared "tired and worn, and his thin face was drawn and pinched." His expression was so blank during witnesses' testimony that the press had to make do with describing each fidget or shift in his chair.

Interest picked up in midafternoon when a limousine, its passengers invisible behind curtains, drew up on the west side of the square. Spectators craned their necks to peer out the courtroom windows. The portly woman who stepped out was as heavily veiled as a beekeeper, but no one doubted it was Mrs. Logan O. Swope, accompanied by three of the family's nurses and a lawyer. One of the nurses, Pearl Kellar, was scheduled to testify within minutes.

While Kellar was sworn in, Maggie Swope, the other nurses, and a *Times* reporter were seated in an anteroom. Someone opened the door so they could hear the testimony and scan part of the crowd. Just as Mrs. Swope murmured some complaint about people's morbid curiosity, one of the nurses interrupted: "You can see him now. There's Doctor Hyde."

The matriarch rose in her chair. Sure enough, there he was. "How would you like to be in his boots?" she asked the reporter. "He isn't quite as calm and collected as you said he was when they were taking depositions, is he?"

Then she noticed that her estranged daughter Frances was not at the doctor's side. A nurse said she'd heard Frances was home in bed, too sick to attend. All at once the fierce-eyed Maggie Swope morphed into the grieving mother. "My poor girlie, my little girlie," she said. Tears flowed behind her veil. "How my heart goes out to her. It is indeed a time of sorrow for her, my little daughter."

None of the testimony amounted to much for the rest of the day. Doctor Stewart said the Colonel's autopsy had turned up no signs of apoplexy. Sylvester Spangler said the old gentleman had stopped taking his iron-quinine-strychnine tonic about three weeks before his death. Kellar was the usual Kellar—direct, unintimidated, a little starchy. Her eyes in a *Star* sketch practically dare anyone to contradict her. She had just finished describing the Colonel's precarious health and Moss Hunton's collapse when the deputy coroner gaveled the day's hearing to a close.

At ten o'clock the next morning, Hyde and his legal squad gathered for an oddly blithe pre-session conference. At one point, a remark by attorney John H. Lucas drew a laugh. Hyde's joking reply got another one. Judging by the doctor's mood, he may have believed that—all things considered—he was in for another relatively easy day. Or maybe he was heartened by the bright sunshine that suffused the room. Or maybe it was all just a pose for the press table. Hyde had to know that Nurse Kellar would be back in

MISS PEARL KELLAR, THE NURSE WHO ATTENDED COLONEL SWOPE IN HIS LAST ILLNESS, AND WHO WAS THE CHIEF WITNESS AT THE CORONER'S INQUEST THIS MORNING. *Kansas City Star,* Tue., Feb. 8, 1910, p. 2.

the witness chair. He had to know her testimony would not play well for his claim of innocence.

It didn't. Throughout the morning, the 36-year-old nurse in her prim white shirtwaist and turban hat related the whole awful sequence of events in the Swope mansion back on that first weekend of October. She left out nothing, from Moss Hunton's death to the Colonel's sudden metamorphosis from cozy old man reading a newspaper to victim of a violent convulsion leading to death. She told of Hyde's attempt to co-opt her in his scheme to become an executor. She told of the "digestive" capsule she had given Swope, on Hyde's order, minutes before the attack. She told of her subsequent, failed search for the pink box the capsule had come in.

"Do you know anything that might have caused Colonel Swope's death other than that capsule?" Coroner Zwart asked.

Kellar replied, "I do not."

The spectators—there seemed to be more women today—were as rapt and silent as witnesses to the sinking of the *Titanic*. One woman did break into uncontrollable sobs and had to be escorted from the courtroom. Otherwise, no one so much as coughed during the highly charged testimony.

Things hardly improved for Hyde during the appearance of the next witness, Professor Ludvig Hektoen of Chicago. Speaking crisply in a clear professional tone, the pathologist read affidavits from the two chemists who had run tests on the Colonel's viscera. They had found one sixth of a grain of strychnine in about one seventh of the dead man's liver. "From which we may conclude," one of the toxicologists had written, "that the entire quantity [of the liver] contained upwards of a grain of poison. This amount is a fatal dose."

A juryman wanted to hear Hektoen's own opinion of what would constitute a fatal dose. The pathologist answered that half a grain would suffice.

An incident over the lunch recess tested Hyde's talent for displaying nonchalance in acutely awkward situations. Just as he was leaving the courthouse with Frank Walsh, he found himself face-to-face with Maggie Swope, who was standing near the door. Hyde's cheeks flushed briefly and, as the *Star*'s man put it, Mrs.

Swope's "usually kindly, motherly face became as if of flint." They didn't exchange a word before heading separate ways. Hyde then turned to Walsh with a laugh and said, "You're going to dinner with me, aren't you Frank?"

The adjective most used by reporters in describing Mrs. Swope was "motherly," followed by "kindly," "tender," and whatever else conveyed the loving nature of the selfless, caring soul. Composed on the witness chair, her hands folded, the plump-faced woman in silky black might have been sitting for a J. S. Sargent portrait. But in Clark Hyde's eyes, it's doubtful she appeared so benign.

Not that her afternoon testimony was harsh in any way. She spoke softly, rather haltingly, her voice quavering at times. Her words were restrained, lacking any accusing tone or edge. Indeed, nothing she said was half as damaging as what Kellar and Hektoen had told the jury before lunch.

She did throw out some interesting facts, if facts they were. She testified that everyone in the family—including Hyde—had known that the nieces and nephews were the big beneficiaries of the Colonel's estate. What's more, Hyde knew perfectly well that Uncle Thomas planned to change his will, diverting $1.5 million from the children to the poor of Kansas City. Hyde had *told* her as much right before or right after the Colonel's death, she said. If the rest of her testimony was unremarkable, bits and pieces must have caught the crowd's attention.

There was the family's peculiar reliance on medicines—the mansion was a virtual warehouse of pills, powders, laxatives, and tonics, some purchased from "yarb" doctor Jordan, others from Pendleton & Gentry's drugstore in town. Mrs. Swope knew that some of the potions contained strychnine. They had lain around for years and when Colonel Swope died she had dumped the whole hoarded heap into the trash.

There was the witness's account of the Colonel's crotchets and unpleasant habits. For anyone who still revered him as the sainted benefactor, the friend of underprivileged children and mistreated animals, it must have been a letdown to learn he had thoroughly disliked the children of his sister-in-law, or at least had found their company intolerable.

And there was Maggie Swope's three-word response to a question from Trogdon. "Did you, Mrs. Swope, have any feelings against Doctor Hyde?" the deputy coroner asked.

She replied, "I did not." Which must have raised a few eyebrows among close friends of the witness, who knew her true feelings toward Hyde, which had curdled within her for years.

Maybe it was the mother-in-law's location in the courtroom Wednesday morning—she sat only eight feet from Hyde—that stole whatever jolliness he'd been able to summon on previous days. Winifred Black, at her purple best, compared his glittering eyes and pallor to those of "a man deep with a wasting fever." His face, she wrote, showed "a wonderful iron resolve that he wears to defy the closest scrutiny, like a mask of polished steel." She concluded that Hyde expected the worst from the coroner's jury but was hell-bent on hiding his fear.

Hyde was slated to testify at around 11:30, an anticipated treat that probably kept spectators from walking out during the boring, repetitious testimony of two preceding witnesses. Hyde's turn on the stand was bound to liven things up.

Things livened up all right, but for quite the opposite reason. Barely had Coroner Zwart called Hyde's name when Frank Walsh rose to his feet and announced, "The attorneys for Doctor Hyde have advised him not to testify."

It took an instant for Zwart to grasp what the attorney had said. Walsh said it again: "We do not care for him to testify here, and therefore, at our suggestion, he must decline to be sworn."

Zwart was aghast. The county prosecutor was irate. Waving a rolled-up, week-old newspaper, Virgil Conkling declared that it contained Hyde's promise that he'd welcome a full investigation and would gladly tell everything he knew. The argument got nowhere. Lawyers bustled about in whispered conference or shouted their objections.

A few minutes later Conkling had to acknowledge he'd lost the match. The law was the law. If a witness preferred not to answer questions, he could refuse to do so "under the well known shield of constitutional rights." In other words, Hyde was taking the Fifth.

At 12:57 p.m., just short of an hour after the jurymen had begun deliberations, they filed from the cramped jury room and foreman Samuel H. Woodson handed a sheet of paper to the coroner. Zwart asked if they had agreed on a verdict. Woodson said they had and Zwart instructed the foreman to read it.

Stripped of its ornate formalities, the document was simple enough: "We, the coroner's jury … find that said deceased came to his death by strychnine poisoning, and from the evidence we believe that the said strychnine was administered in a capsule at about 8:30 a.m. on the day he died by the direction of Dr. Bennett Clark Hyde, whether with felonious intent, we, the jury, are unable to decide."

Hyde bit his lips and jerked forward involuntarily. It took him a moment to collect himself before he spoke a few words with his attorneys, both visibly bitter. Frank Walsh's only comment to a reporter repeated what his face had already telegraphed: "We didn't have a fair show." Then the three of them stepped out to a waiting car and rode off to Walsh's Kansas City office for a lengthy counsel of war.

———•—•——

While the coroner's jury labored to solve the dreadful conundrums of death, poisoning, and felonious intent, members of the Jackson County Medical Society had a less dire problem to confront. Tuesday night's regular meeting at Kansas City's General Hospital was to be devoted to the installation of officers for the ensuing twelve months. A sizeable faction of the society, however, was determined to block Bennett Clark Hyde's ascension to the group's highest office. He'd been voted president-elect two months earlier, before his life and reputation had tumbled into a free fall. Hyde's friends continued to back his presidency, but did they have enough heft to prevail in a revote? How many in each camp would attend the meeting? Would *Hyde* attend the meeting?

He or a stand-in apparently did, but only to pass a letter into the hands of Doctor Franklin Murphy, the presiding officer. It read, in part: "On account of the unfortunate litigation, with which you are all, no doubt, familiar, I feel that in justice to our society, the best interest of which I have deeply at heart, I ought not to qualify. I therefore formally resign as president-elect of the society."

The level of relief among the sixty members present may be gauged by the absence of any objection—not even a peep—to Hyde's move. In fact, there was no discussion of it whatsoever.

Chapter 17

In the annals of criminal justice, it seems doubtful that any arrest has been handled with more cordiality than that of Bennett Clark Hyde on Thursday, February 10. An artist's sketch in the *Kansas City Times* depicts the occasion. It could easily pass for an affectionate reunion of old friends rather than a solemn legal action. Joel Mayes, the county marshal, radiating joviality from every feature including his walrus mustache, clasps the extended hand of Frank Walsh. To the attorney's left stands Hyde with the expectant look—is that a half-smile?—of a man about to be introduced at a social event. Only the reporters' serious, intent expressions belie the cheery atmosphere.

Not shown in the picture are Virgil Conkling and John Paxton, parties for the prosecution. Conkling had drawn up the arrest warrant that morning, on a sworn complaint by the Swopes' family attorney. Now counselors for both sides faced each other in the marshal's office in the Criminal Court Building, a substantial brick and stone structure in downtown Kansas City that also housed the county jail.

"Mister Mayes," said Walsh, "this is Doctor Hyde."

No one noticed any awkwardness as the two shook hands, though a reporter did sense a hint of apology in Mayes's voice. "I suppose you know, Doctor Hyde, that I have a warrant for you," he said.

Hyde answered, "Yes, I know."

As the attorneys retired to another room, a visitor in the outer office strolled over to offer Hyde a bit of cheering-up. He turned out to be an old classmate from William Jewell College. For a few minutes as they spoke, Hyde revisited the giddy days of Phi Gamma Delta and the playing field. He'd been on the football team himself. Who could forget that glorious play when a team-mate ran seventy yards to score!

Just then Walsh and another defense lawyer approached, and Hyde's face sobered. The prospect of spending the night in jail was much on his mind. That morning, before he caught the streetcar downtown, he had told his wife: "I'll be home for dinner, dear. Don't you worry a bit. I don't look worried, do I?" But worried he was, and his tight, pale features were starting to show it.

It wasn't until two hours later, at the bond hearing in the Independence courthouse, that Hyde got some welcome relief. With no objections from either side, bond was set for $50,000 by Justice of the Peace W. S. Loar. Friends of Hyde's were at the courthouse to post the amount and he was free to go. As he left the courtroom, he asked a small favor of the affable county marshal: "Call up Mrs. Hyde, please, and tell her I'll be home to dinner."

In its basic function, the grand jury is a body of citizens appointed to determine whether the evidence against an alleged criminal is sufficient to bring the suspect to trial. Jurors examine witnesses presented by the prosecuting attorney, then make up their minds whether to indict—that is, to issue a formal charge against the accused—or to pronounce the State's case too weak to pursue in court. The idea, since the earliest days of English common law, has been to protect citizens from unjust or malicious prosecution.

However, legal critics have argued that in practice the grand jury system often favors not the accused but the accusers. Defendants who testify cannot be represented by their attorneys and may not call witnesses of their own. All proceedings are secret, the testimony closed to everyone outside the locked hearing room, including counsel for the defense, reporters, and of course the public. Modern-day refinements have much improved the fairness of the system, while many jurisdictions have scrapped it altogether. Still, grand juries by their nature enable the prosecution—free of outside scrutiny—to gather, develop, and conceal its own cache of evidence.

On the Thursday of Hyde's arrest, Criminal Court Judge Ralph S. Latshaw met briefly with Prosecutor Conkling and Hyde's attorneys, then ordered an immediate grand jury investigation. He wanted no dillydallying. Jury members were to be selected promptly and sworn in no later than Saturday, February 12.

His insistence on haste was a matter of fairness, Latshaw explained to a reporter for the *Post*. "The whole city and county is interested in the Swope case," he said. "The coroner's jury has cast a shadow of doubt over Dr. B. C. Hyde. If he is innocent, it ought to be known. If he is guilty, that too ought to be known as soon as possible."

Hyde's lawyers certainly knew that the secret hearings put them at a disadvantage. But an unusual development in the Swope case handed them a rare opportunity to even the odds.

On January 31, Hyde had brought a libel suit against his chief accuser, John Paxton, charging him with defaming his good name in statements to the press and in a letter to Paxton's fellow executor, Stuart Fleming. Hyde dropped the civil suit before his chief attorney, Frank Walsh, had taken more than a handful of depositions from witnesses. However, the lawsuit had since been reopened, and Walsh again was entitled to subpoena and question anyone who might support his client's libel claim.

The benefits to Walsh were obvious. Though he was barred from hearing testimony in the grand jury room, he could grill the very same witnesses, quite openly, in his own office. By extracting their statements under oath, Walsh could gain at least some idea of the prosecution's key evidence.

This did not go unnoticed by John Paxton. Back in Walsh's office to continue giving his own deposition in the libel case, Paxton was asked a question he didn't like. Walsh wanted to know whether the Chicago chemists had found traces of poison in any other material sent for analysis. Red-faced, his voice rising, Paxton stated his blunt opinion that the libel suit was brought not in good faith but as a scheme by the defense to spy out the prosecution's confidential findings.

"I am associated with Mister Conkling in the investigation of one of the greatest crimes in the history of the country," Paxton argued, "and I will refuse to answer any questions which tend to give our evidence to the defendant's attorneys. We have much information which at the present time we are keeping secret."

Walsh jumped to his feet. "We don't wish to embarrass justice in the least," he said, "but we are prosecuting a suit for libel filed by a man who is accused of a crime of which he is innocent." Paxton, he asserted, had no legal excuse to avoid answering.

The squabble may have been sharpened by personal dislike. It's hard to imagine that the big-city labor lawyer and champion of the proletariat would have felt much kinship toward the gentleman offspring of a Confederate general. After a few moments the shouting receded, and Walsh's right to question the grand jury's witnesses was acknowledged. One of Walsh's tactics, however, did cause some indignant grumbling by the other side. On Monday morning the 14th, as the grand jury was about to question its first witnesses, Walsh sent an assistant, James Aylward, to station himself a few feet outside the hearing-room door. As prosecution witnesses arrived to testify, they had no choice but to walk past Aylward, who handed them Walsh's subpoenas as brazenly as a street-corner anarchist passing out tracts.

The dozen grand jurymen were a diverse bunch—farmers, bankers, real estate dealers (four of these, for some reason), a hardware merchant, an engineer, and a retired haberdasher. They would have a busy time of it for the next three weeks, excluding Sundays when the Lord's work trumped the cause of justice.

With the exception of Clark and Frances Hyde, who were legally exempt from testifying before the grand jury, just about everyone else connected with the murder case would have his or her turn on the witness stand. Day after day they appeared in sober attire, their comings and goings recorded by reporters, photographers, and sketch artists. Most of them refused comments to the reporters clustered in the hall and what they had to say to the grand jury was, of course, strictly confidential. But once they showed up in Walsh's office to provide their depositions, all secrecy fell away. Walsh got

CHICAGO SCIENTISTS IN THE
OFFICE OF THE PROSECUTOR
THIS MORNING. DR.
LUDVIG HEKTOEN, THE
PATHOLOGIST, AND DR.
WALTER S. HAINES, CHEMIST,
LOOKING OVER ONE OF THE
REPORTS IN THE SWOPE CASE
IN MR. CONKLING'S OFFICE,
JUST BEFORE DOCTOR
HAINES WENT BEFORE THE
GRAND JURY.
Kansas City Star, Sat., Feb. 19,
1910, p. 1.

DR. VICTOR C. VAUGHAN,
THE THIRD OF THE SWOPE
SCIENTISTS, WHO ARRIVED
IN KANSAS CITY AT NOON
YESTERDAY AND APPEARED
BEFORE THE GRAND JURY
YESTERDAY AFTERNOON.
Kansas City Star, Sun., Feb. 20,
1910, p. 2.

179

along with news people and readily invited them to listen in on the testimony. Thus, whatever any witness told Walsh, under oath, became snack food for the hungry press.

In point of fact, most of what came out under Walsh's questioning was not particularly new or newsworthy. A lot of it had been revealed by enterprising reporters as far back as mid-January. Other details of the Swope mystery had come to light a week before during the coroner's inquest.

Heeding an old newsroom dictum, "You gotta go with what you got," reporters dutifully recorded practically everything they hoped might grab *somebody's* attention. Their rambling stories mostly ploughed over old ground, though occasionally they turned up something fresh or intriguingly odd. In the latter category were the latest statements of "Doctor" Chasing Hatred Chase Jordan, most of which seemed inflated if not preposterous. One of his improbable claims was that the Swope family had paid him between $10,000 and $20,000 for medicinal products over the years.

Meanwhile, the prosecution's men kept trying every tactic they could think of to stop Walsh from co-opting their grand jury witnesses. One of their few successes was the discovery of a long-forgotten statute that allowed two of the forensic scientists, Hektoen and Haines, to dash home to Chicago before Walsh could get his hands on them. Otherwise, most of what the grand jury heard in secret reached Walsh's (and the public's) ears soon enough.

Everyone's favorite witness, it seemed, was Mrs. Logan O. Swope. She had so much to say that the grand jury called her back seven times after her initial questioning, and Walsh had her in on three consecutive days. No wonder. She'd been right in the midst of almost every horror inflicted upon the Swope household. She had vehement opinions about everything and no fears at all about speaking them. At times her vinegary remarks must have made her discreet lawyers wince. And she displayed an arresting personality—the Dixie belle in dowager's black silks, the tragic heroine with a touch of the flirty ingénue.

For her first round of testimony before Walsh, she arrived with a retinue of advisers and confidants—Paxton; her brother, Judge

MRS. L. O. SWOPE ON THE WITNESS STAND.
Kansas City Times, Wed., Feb. 9, 1910, p. 1.

Lee Chrisman; and attorney T. A. J. Mastin. Along with Walsh and his aides, the number of men around the table came to a half-dozen, leaving Maggie Swope a minority of one. Her status as the sole female seemed to agree with her. She laid on the charm: a pretty smile here, a tiny impertinence there ("Well, if you're going to make me tell the truth …"). She thanked "Mister Stenographer" warmly for his patience.

Walsh's questions about Colonel Swope's personal crotchets let her indulge a fondness for relating anecdotes. There was the time Mrs. Paxton, with her husband, came by the house to thank the old man for a gift to the YWCA. "I went up to his room and asked him to come down," Mrs. Swope recalled, "and I was never so surprised in my life when he came down to the library. The Colonel was afraid of women." She laughed. "He didn't mind going anywhere to talk to men, but if he heard a woman was around, you couldn't get him to come."

When asked what, exactly, Uncle Thomas would yell during his bedroom temper tantrums, she played the scandalized Victorian prude: "Now see here, Mister Walsh, I'm not going to repeat all those profane words here." It got another laugh. Turning to the other grinning observers she added, with a chuckle, "I guess you know what he said, all right."

Maggie Swope could, as easily, vent her bitterness and fury. During another day's questioning in Walsh's office, she let loose on her detested son-in-law. With voice trembling and tears flowing, she repeated her charge that Hyde had married her daughter only to get his hands on the Swope money. Her attorneys tried to shut her off. She wouldn't stop. "Distressful as this may be to my feelings," she cried, "I must tell it all. I must tell you why I feel toward Doctor Hyde as I do. I must tell you everything, whether I ought to or not."

When she got around to the broken relationship with her beloved eldest daughter Frances, Mrs. Swope came close to screaming. "She is a dear, pure girl. I have never said anything against her.... I defy anyone to name a thing I have said against her. I defy them to. I defy them to. Why, if I heard anyone saying I had said anything disparaging about Frances I would smack them in the mouth. I just couldn't help it."

———•◦•———

To no one's particular surprise, the members of the grand jury, on Saturday evening, March 5, filed into Judge Ralph Latshaw's criminal courtroom and handed him eleven indictments against Bennett Clark Hyde. As listed in boldface in the *Sunday Star,* the charges were:

> **First Degree Murder—For the death of Col. Thomas H. Swope, October 3.**
>
> **First Degree Murder—For the death of Chrisman Swope, December 6.**
>
> **Manslaughter—For negligently killing Col. Moss Hunton by bleeding him to death.**

Poisoning—Three counts in one indictment, charging that three attempts were made on the life of Margaret Swope; first, by the use of typhoid germs, November 25; second, by hypodermic injections, December 12; and third, by use of strychnine, December 18.

Poisoning With Typhoid Germs—Lucy Lee Swope, November 25.

Poisoning With Typhoid Germs—Mildred Fox, daughter of S. Walter Fox, 3816 Troost Avenue, a visitor in the Swope home, on or about November 25.

Poisoning With Typhoid Germs—Sarah Swope, November 25.

Poisoning With Typhoid Germs—Stella Swope, November 25.

Poisoning With Typhoid Germs—Georgie Compton, seamstress in the Swope home, November 25.

Poisoning With Typhoid Germs—Nora Belle Dickson, seamstress in the Swope home, November 25.

Poisoning With Typhoid Germs—Leonora Copridge, negro servant in Swope home, November 25.

Either the grand jury or the *Star* was inexplicably careless about the facts. Lucy Lee could not have been poisoned by Hyde on November 25, almost three weeks before her return from France. Miss Compton's name was Georgia, not Georgie. Nora Belle Dickson's identification as a seamstress was an affront to her social rank; she was *family,* as well as a onetime governess for the children.

The jury's reason for sparing Hyde a twelfth indictment, charging him with infecting Cousin Stuart Fleming with typhoid fever, was not explained.

———•◦•———

For a man indicted on two counts of murder in the first degree and nine other felony charges, Bennett Clark Hyde was remarkably tranquil. Over dinner at home the previous evening he had told his guests, Frank Walsh and two other attorneys, that he was confident of vindication by any fair-minded jury. Hyde's mood of well-being stayed with him throughout the next day—Monday, March 7—and into a night that might have brought terror and despair to other men facing the same ordeal.

Shortly before noon he arrived with his lawyers at the Criminal Court building at Fourth and Oak Streets and headed up to the courtroom on the second floor. Judge Latshaw took his seat on the bench at one o'clock. Already at the prosecution table were Virgil Conkling, officially in charge of the state's case, and James A. Reed, who'd been engaged by Conkling and the Swope family to spearhead the effort to send Hyde to the gallows. Hyde had to have known Reed by reputation—everyone did. For the doctor to have sat there unblinking before the inquisitorial eyes of this fearsome adversary must have required an almost Zen-like self-control.

Hyde's lawyers waived the formality of arraignment and both sides agreed on a trial date of April 11. Then they disagreed on the question of bail—whether the $50,000 bond posted for Hyde after his initial arrest in February was still enough to keep him out of jail. Conkling wanted to raise the sum considerably. After all, the man was charged with murder—*two* murders. A hearing to settle the matter was scheduled for the next morning. In the meantime, Doctor Hyde had no choice but to resign himself to a night's lodging at the county's expense.

He had guessed this would happen and had dressed handsomely, in black suit, fine black coat, and black derby, as if determined to execute a dignified surrender. Frances had packed a suitcase with his nightclothes, toilet articles, a change of linens, and several magazines to help ward off boredom.

County Marshal Mayes, with the thoughtfulness of an attentive hotelier, did his best to assure the prisoner's comfort. Instead of confining the doctor in a common cell, Mayes assigned him to the empty jail hospital, a large room with cots the width of double beds and an adjoining lavatory and bath. Brand new sheets and pillows were furnished by a guard. It wasn't the most inviting guest room, with its high ceiling, hanging lights, and barred door, but it afforded Hyde a chance to enjoy some welcome solitude or to visit in private with friends.

As suppertime approached, a deputy marshal, James Gilwee, asked Hyde if he would like his evening meal sent up. Hyde explained that it wasn't necessary—one of his attorneys had already made arrangements. "Somebody must have been knocking our soup," Gilwee said, and both men laughed. Shortly, John Cleary arrived with two hampers packed with a picnic supper of omelet, chicken salad, club sandwiches, apple pie, cheese, white bread, and a large pot of coffee. The lawyer and client dined together. Then Hyde was left alone with his magazines and his thoughts.

At 11:30 the next morning, after conferring with the various attorneys, Judge Latshaw set bond at $100,000. Hyde could not have been more grateful—to the six moneyed supporters who posted bail, to the well-wisher who'd brought him a hearty breakfast, to the jailers who'd made his stay as pleasant as one could ask, all things considered. Before leaving for home, he stopped by the marshal's office and the guardroom to shake hands all around.

For Hyde's anxious wife, alone except for a maid and a nurse in the house on Forest Avenue, the day had begun much less agreeably. With no idea whether Clark would be freed that morning or held for another night, she telephoned one of her husband's attorneys at nine o'clock and told him firmly, "If they don't let him out before night, I shall go to the jail, demand admittance, and stay with my husband as long as he is in confinement."

It was then—just when she least needed more trouble—that a limousine drew up at the curb and her mother, whom she hadn't spoken with in months, slowly emerged. Another passenger, her brother Tom, stayed in the car with the chauffeur while Mrs. Swope climbed the steps to the porch and rang the doorbell. The maid answered.

"I want to see Mrs. Hyde," she said.

"She is not well this morning. I will call her nurse," the servant answered.

Mrs. Swope's lips were trembling as the nurse appeared and told her, "I am very sorry. Mrs. Hyde is receiving no one this morning."

"But you know who I am," the visitor said. "I am Mrs. Hyde's mother. Won't you go up and ask Mrs. Hyde if she won't see her mother?"

The nurse complied reluctantly and let her in. For a few minutes the older woman was alone in the front hall. Then she heard a footstep on the stairway and looked up, smiling, apparently thinking it was her daughter. It was the nurse again, whose message this time was more blunt: "Mrs. Hyde says she does not care to receive Mrs. Swope."

Maggie Swope pleaded, "Please go back to Mrs. Hyde and ask her to see me. Please, please do all you can—use your influence to get her to see me." Again the nurse went upstairs, then returned with the final word: "Mrs. Hyde will not receive Mrs. Swope."

Who knew why the matriarch had come? Maybe she had wished only to speak a few tender words, to break the cruel silence. She would never have shown up—just like that—if she hadn't known Clark was still at the jailhouse awaiting release. Or maybe she hoped to use this time alone with Frances to talk sense to her. To beg this headstrong young woman to abandon her marriage to a homicidal fiend.

In either case, it was a hopeless errand. Two minutes after the nurse ushered her out the door, Maggie Swope was back in her limousine, watching forlornly through a window as her daughter's house receded into the streetscape of bare trees.

As dismal as the morning had been for Frances, what happened shortly after noon changed everything. She heard a quick step on the porch, recognized her husband's tread, and ran to the door to greet him. The happy homecoming was described by a reporter for the *Kansas City Post,* in distinctively *Post* style:

"In a moment she was clasped in his arms and was telling him, as only a woman can, how glad she was to have him at home with her again."

———•◦•———

And on that note of wifely ardor and loyalty, the news of Doctor Hyde and the Swope mysteries more or less slipped off the front pages. The tales of ghastly death, poisons, and murder indictments had been told and retold. The trial would not begin for weeks. What few stories did make the papers—mostly Walsh's endless deposing of witnesses—didn't have much zing.

Happily, for fans of the lurid and scandalous, an incident on Saturday, March 6, filled the gap while the Swope drama was in temporary limbo. Like the Swope affair, the story would survive in local legend, though all it amounted to was a droll footnote to the city's gilded past. It too involved the rich and wellborn. The male principals were John P. Cudahy, of the Chicago meatpacking Cudahys, and Jere S. Lillis, president of the Western Exchange Bank. Cudahy, who had run the family's business interests in Kansas City, had quit to devote himself to more pleasant pastimes such as hunting and high-style horsemanship. Lillis, a dashing bachelor who fancied fast automobiles, also fancied Edna Cudahy, the ravishing wife of John P. It was believed that she fancied him back.

Cudahy, afire with jealousy, could endure the situation no longer. And so he took steps. Informing Edna that he'd be out of town for the weekend, he holed up in the Baltimore Hotel downtown and waited for his trap to be sprung. He had instructed his burly chauffeur to lie in ambush in the Cudahy mansion at Thirty-sixth and Walnut Streets. If Lillis showed up with obvious designs on Mrs. Cudahy's virtue, the chauffeur was to seize and bind him, and then telephone the husband, who would dash home.

It worked like a well-oiled revolver. Jere Lillis had taken Edna Cudahy on a joyride in his Packard runabout, then returned with her for recreation, presumably, of another kind. Out sprang the chauffeur, and in no time Lillis was on the floor, immobilized, with John Cudahy looming over him, knife in hand.

In describing the scene, the papers showed utmost tact. They reported that a policeman, summoned by a hysterical maid, had found Lillis drenched in blood with severe gashes on his face, arms, and bare legs. Lillis was screaming, "Please, Jack, please don't do it." Not one adult reader could have mistaken what Lillis meant by "it."

The follow-up stories could be described as serial farce. Lillis, of course, was blamed for everything, while his assailant got away with a $100 fine. A reporter at Lillis's bedside was shown proof, in the flesh, that Cudahy had not accomplished what he'd set out to do to his amatory rival. Lillis, as the certified scoundrel, was cashiered from the Kansas City Country Club, while Cudahy did the gentleman's thing and resigned. Lillis slunk off to Europe, where his name and shame were unknown. And weeping Edna, denying all guilt even after her marriage collapsed, was offered a spot in the chorus of *Hello, People,* a road show on stage in a downtown theater.

Chapter 18

They were still snickering about the Lillis-Cudahy affair when the story Kansas City was *really* waiting for—the upcoming murder trial of Bennett Clark Hyde—again upstaged every other news event in town. The trial date was dead ahead—April 11. Already the jury commissioner, L. M. M'Clure, had been photographed turning the jury wheel, which revolved like a giant ice-cream freezer and yielded the names of 150 white, male, tax-paying citizens.

The case that twelve of these worthy gentlemen would try, however, was not quite the one originally planned. Though Hyde had been indicted on eleven charges, the prosecution team had decided their best strategy was to try him on one count only—the murder of Colonel Swope. That was not only the easiest charge to prove, they reasoned, but if Hyde were found guilty on that one—it was, after all, a hanging offense—who needed convictions on the other ten?

And so it came to pass, at nine o'clock on a rainy Monday morning, that the most publicized trial in the region's history—breathlessly awaited by readers throughout Missouri, Kansas, and states beyond—began with the monotony and tedium of an eight-hour probate hearing. Only worse. And far longer.

For the next five days, from morning to mid-evening, the reporters seated before and behind the judge's bench had essentially two subjects to write about. The first was the voir dire, the trudging, one-by-one examination of the ninety-five men who had answered the call to civic duty. The potential jurors knew they were in for a bad time. Those who weren't excused would spend at least a night in the nearby Ashland Hotel, where the final dozen would be sequestered for God knew how long.

The predictable result was a recital of alibis, dodges, and falsehoods worthy of a party of frat boys rounded up in a brothel raid. Reasonable excuses such as bias, illness, deafness, and distrust of medical experts got the lucky ones out the door before some quibbling attorney could call them back. Others in the jury pool cited moral opposition to the death penalty. That issue appeared to become moot on Tuesday morning when the prosecutors accepted one opponent of capital punishment, then another. To Hyde's undoubted relief, it seemed the State had abandoned its plan to march him to the gallows.

The second source of material for the press was the array of characters in the case. Most of the players were already well known to everyone who had read the newspapers in the last three months. But here they were, larger than the front-page pictures, larger than life. Here was Judge Latshaw, his gentle face and patient eyes in total contrast to the gargoyle features of the stereotypical hanging judge. Here were the great barristers—Frank Walsh, his face jutting like a

THE CRIMINAL COURT ROOM

COURT ROOM

THE [CRIMINAL COURT BUILDING AND] **COUNTY JAIL (FACING PAGE), THE CRIMINAL COURT BUILDING** [COURT ROOM] **(TOP), PLAN OF COURT ROOM (ABOVE). WHERE DR. BENNET[T] CLARK HYDE WILL FACE A JURY OF HIS PEERS BEGINNING TOMORROW MORNING.**
Kansas City Star, Sun., April 10, 1910, p. 2A.

boxer's on his way to the ring; James A. Reed, the tall, almost languidly confident avenger for the Swope family and the State.

Here was the loyal wife, Frances Hyde, the most poignant figure in the room, scrutinized for every hint of feeling revealed by face or gesture. Now in her fifth month of pregnancy, she had put on some plumpness but still had those lovely eyes and pensive mouth. Under swaths of dark fabric, her pregnant state showed clearly. But in case it didn't show clearly enough, her husband's attorney had provided extra padding, later ridiculed as a "Walsh pillow," to wear around her abdomen. Or so it was rumored among the prosecution's men.

Frances's bitter standoff with her mother had been noticed during the coroner's inquest, and here in Criminal Court the two were seated even closer to each other, separated by a rail. At times they nearly brushed shoulders on the way to their chairs. Frances avoided eye contact, but her mother's eyes never seemed to leave the daughter's face. The *Post*'s Winifred Black was watching closely, as usual. "A little lock of Mrs. Hyde's hair escaped from the pins during the morning," she wrote, "and I thought Mrs. Swope was going to step over and arrange it for her."

Mrs. Swope sat beside her imposing brother, Judge George Lee Chrisman. Frances had brought a schoolteacher friend, Mary Flaven, for support and comfort. And then there was Hyde, pressed in close to his wife, smiling and whispering to her and appearing not the least like a man under threat of lifelong imprisonment and disgrace.

With much to see but little to report, the news people yielded to their literary ambitions. No American newsroom was without its would-be Twains, Zolas, and Flauberts, eager to show the world their talents. Covering this trial would give a writer a chance to *write*... whether the effort was well advised or not.

A *Star* reporter's commentary on Frances Hyde's wifely devotion was typically over the top:

"Out from a mother's roof she went to wed Clark Hyde, and only when forgiveness came to him did she return to it. She accepted none that was not his also. Again when he was driven forth, hounded by suspicion and the dogging shadow of guilt, she followed, a faithful wife. With him she lived through months of innuendo and evil report when a new whisper of a new and more fearful crime was a daily portion. Then came the charges. Murder and again murder. And then arrest and now trial. But for better or worse, until death do them part."

To be fair, some feature stories showed skill and insight. James E. Craig, writing for the *Post,* offered this observant cameo of the man on trial:

"His face is somewhat long, with a heavy, aggressive chin, closely set lips, rather a prominent nose, and good eyes veiled behind gold-rimmed spectacles. Ten years ago he probably looked as old as he does now. Ten years hence he probably will look as young. His face will always be youthful but it will never be boyish. It is hard to tell whether it is a scientist's face or a gambler's face."

At eight o'clock Friday evening, when everyone was almost too exhausted to care, the jury selection finally was over. Those who had made the cut were a respectable but hardly blue-ribbon panel: William W. Castle, fresco painter; W. C. Crone, medicine salesman; Cyrus W. Whitehead, abstractor; William Beebee, watchmaker; George C. Feldt, drapery salesman; Byron C. Lillard, Pullman conductor; William W. Curran, clerk; John A. Pilant, boarding house keeper; Samuel R. Johnson, farmer; Frank Claypool, cattle speculator; Frank P. Hedges, bookkeeper; and Eli Rivers, also a bookkeeper.

A few minutes before they were to be sworn in, however, Prosecutor Virgil Conkling announced some bad news—potentially very bad for the prosecution side. One of the State's most important witnesses, Doctor George T. Twyman, had been taken to the University Hospital a half hour previously with abdominal pains. Conkling had been informed in a phone call from John Paxton that the Swope family doctor could face surgery the next day.

On Saturday it was reported that the operation for acute diverticulitis had gone well and Twyman had rallied encouragingly. Assuming that the patient would be well enough to testify before too long, Judge Latshaw ruled that the trial proper would begin on Monday morning, April 18.

THE REV. GEORGE W. HYDE AND MRS. HYDE OF LEXINGTON, MO., FATHER AND STEP-MOTHER OF DOCTOR HYDE. *Kansas City Star,* Mon., April 18, 1910, p. 1.

Begin it did, with crowds and gawking and a hustle of reporters that hadn't been seen around the Criminal Court building in memory. The day had started off gloomy and near freezing, and the steam heat inside the courtroom, along with the body heat from spectators, made the air stuffy. The usual cast filled the usual seats, though Hyde was now surrounded by more of his kin, most conspicuously his father, the Rev. George Washington Hyde of Lexington, Missouri. With his flowing beard and gaunt features, the retired Baptist divine might have passed for an Old Testament prophet.

Looking back, one has to wonder whether anyone in the courtroom—at least anyone outside the lawyers—could have guessed that the first action that day would turn out to be the most consequential in the entire trial.

James A. Reed, the prosecution counsel selected to make the opening statement, locked eyes with the jury and got straight to the point: "In this trial, the State will endeavor to present such an

194

array of facts that will demonstrate that this crime was planned and carried out in such a way that it could have been done [by] no other than a skilled physician. The State will endeavor to prove that the plan was a general one, that it was one with its motive and mainspring a desire to gain great wealth, and that from the first the conception was in [Hyde's] brain, and the plan was formed, to exterminate the entire Swope family. We shall endeavor to prove...."

Instantly, defense attorneys Walsh and John H. Lucas jumped up and objected that Reed was trying to prejudice the jury. Hyde was on trial for one alleged crime, the murder of Colonel Swope. What was all this about some outlandish plot to kill the whole family?

The judge broke in: "The court believes that nothing except the essential facts should be allowed to enter. However, there are exceptions, and when other crimes are so intimately connected to show a scheme relatively dependent upon it, I believe that the entire matter is admissible."

Translated from the legalese, the judge's ruling meant that *all* the State's allegations against Hyde—not just his purported role in the Colonel's death—were now on the table.

Latshaw had handed the prosecution a sizeable advantage. To exploit it, the State had only to make the case that every evil act charged against Hyde was part of a single, murderous, premeditated design. Thus, testimony concerning the whole range of damning circumstances—Moss Hunton's bloodletting, the typhoid outbreak, the violent seizures of Chrisman and Margaret Swope, the hypos and capsules and germ cultures—could be admitted into evidence.

Reed was free to describe for the jury each one of those alleged misdeeds which the State promised to prove and the defense hoped to suppress. His statement ran well into the afternoon—lucid, thorough, coolly focused. Hyde's attorneys kept objecting, and Judge Latshaw kept overruling, and Reed kept pressing the theory of a diabolical master plan.

Though he used his mellifluous voice to good effect, Reed's performance was rather restrained for a lawyer admired for his dazzling oratory. Reed knew his audience, the common man in the jury box. One test of a speaker is the gift for reducing the complex to the simple, and Reed kept his remarks plain and direct. They were simple to the point of quaintness at one point when he took pains to explain what a germ was—"this little microscopic creature" that caused "many of the ills from which men suffer." The press reported that some spectators were mildly disappointed—and the Hydes visibly pleased—that Reed's opener wasn't as fierce as they had anticipated. Many had believed he would reopen the State's demand for the death penalty. Reed finished his statement without ever mentioning it.

Frank Walsh got his shots in the next day, holding the jury's close attention for two hours and five minutes without once using notes. The blocky defense counsel had obviously done his homework. If Reed intended to broaden the fight to include all those extra accusations against Hyde, Walsh was ready to return fire.

The evidence, he declared, would topple every one of the State's charges. It would show that Moss Hunton was nearly dead before Hyde reached the mansion. That Colonel Swope had dosed himself with strychnine for months and was afflicted by deadly uremic poisoning. That Hyde had known nothing of the old man's will or any plan to change it. That Mrs. Swope had held a deep animosity toward the defendant. That the typhoid could have spread from several likely sources. That the pathologist, Hektoen, "had violated every rule of science in his autopsy."

Walsh's opening remarks had more punch than Reed's, largely because he didn't allow verbal niceties to get in his way. His mockery of the State's scientific experts was almost jeering, his denunciation of John Paxton rich with disdain. Describing the day of Colonel Swope's death, Walsh wheeled around to face the Swope lawyer and nearly shouted: "The vampire of this case, John G. Paxton ... was called into this house where a dying man lay, to pounce upon the Swope will the minute the breath of life left the sick man's body."

Thus the shots continued until 2 p.m., when Walsh left the floor. Whether Hyde read the *Kansas City Post* that evening is

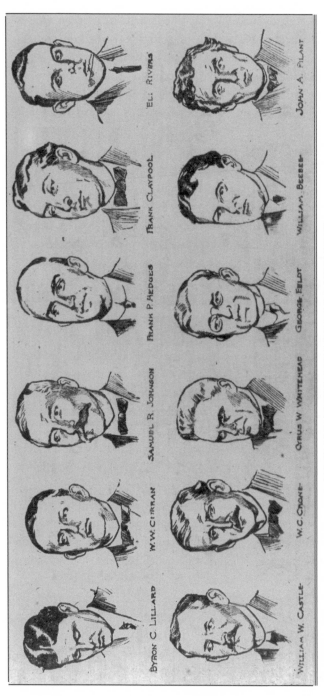

THESE MEN DECIDE THE FATE OF DOCTOR HYDE.
Kansas City Star, Fri., May 13, 1910, p. 1.

unknown. If he did so he'd have spotted a piece of front-page news that the *Star,* unaccountably, had failed to report. The item quoted a statement by Prosecutor Virgil Conkling: "When the proper time arrives for me to do it, I shall ask the jury to assess the death penalty."

The news would not have been conducive to a good night's sleep.

Perhaps it happens in most major trials, perhaps not. In *Hyde vs. State of Missouri,* crises and disruptions dogged both sides of the contest before a word of testimony had been spoken. There was the battle over admissibility—whether all of Hyde's alleged atrocities could be deployed against a man charged with only a single murder. The defense's protests would keep popping up like gas bubbles in a dark pond.

The next blow was to the prosecution. The witness whose testimony might have packed more weight than anyone else's for the State had died on Sunday night. Doctor G. T. Twyman had been close—closer than most—to nearly all the grim happenings in the Swope house. He was also a trusted professional whom people liked. Even Frank Walsh, who would have cross-examined Twyman mercilessly if the doctor had lived to testify, spoke sadly of the deceased as a valued friend. The *Times* reported that Doc Twyman had succumbed to "a poisoned condition of the blood caused by paralysis of the liver." The surgery had been too much.

The third crisis was the discovery that the grand jury notes had gone missing. The secret documents spelled out every detail and tactic of the State's case. If Walsh had somehow gotten hold of them, it would amount to a priceless windfall for Hyde's defense. Rumors started to circulate that the notes had been stolen in an act of espionage.

Latshaw had no choice but to ask Walsh if he knew their whereabouts, and when the defense attorney responded, "I refuse to answer," the judge reddened with fury. To soothe the court's anger, Walsh acknowledged that he had the notes, "but they are the property of my client and I refuse to give them up."

The ensuing brouhaha was more like a cockfight than a gentlemen's dispute in a court of law. Shouted threats and accusations filled the air like feathers, and someone even demanded that Hyde's bond be revoked and the defendant slapped in jail. At length things calmed down enough for the State to explain what had happened. It was almost too embarrassing to admit.

The previous Saturday, one Ruby Garrett, an attorney in Reed's firm who'd been working with the notes, had left work with the documents stuffed in an overcoat pocket. Rather than head straight home, he detoured toward the city market to buy some vegetables. Somewhere the notes fell out. Later they were found by a black man named Finney, who had taken them home and asked his wife to run a classified ad. Luckily for Walsh it was one of his people, not one of Reed's, who had spotted the ad and commandeered the notes. The fate of the hapless Ruby Garrett was not disclosed.

Seeking to resolve the matter fairly, Judge Latshaw soon arrived at a Solomonic solution. The grand jury notes would be made available to everyone in both camps. They would even be given to the *Kansas City Star,* which eight days later would publish an edited transcript for all the public to read.

Chapter 19

In one of her rapturous columns for the *Post,* Winifred Black predicted that the trial would come down to a "battle of the women": Frances Hyde, "as pale as any magnolia that ever flowered under Southern skies"; the vengeful mother-in-law, Mrs. Logan O. Swope; and Nurse Pearl Kellar. It remained to be seen whether the testimony of Frances and Mrs. Swope would be as powerful as Black anticipated. But none would ever dispute Kellar's impressive showing as the State's first major witness.

In eight hours on the stand, April 20 and 21, Kellar stood fast before a constant barrage of objections and hectoring challenges from Walsh. He hammered away at every edge and angle of her story as she recounted her experiences in the Swope mansion. She stuck with every detail she had sworn to before—of convulsions, deaths, and disease, of unfound capsules and Hyde's words, and her own growing suspicions. There were no surprises, nothing added or left out. The very phrasing of certain statements could have been lifted verbatim from previous testimony she had given before the grand jury and coroner's jury.

Kellar's deportment on the stand was noted by the press with something approaching awe. George Creel of the *Post* found her "easily one of the best, coolest, most resourceful witnesses that ever figured in a murder trial. ... Nothing ruffles her, no attack destroys her poise or takes away from the cool, watchful calculation of her black eyes." A *Times* reporter wondered, "How many women—or men either, for that matter—could answer correctly for three hours the questions of an expert cross-examiner trained in all the tricks of lawyers to tangle a witness? Substantially that is what Miss Pearl Kellar, a nurse, did yesterday afternoon."

If Kellar was the star witness for the prosecution, the nurse who followed her to the stand, Anna Houlehan, was a capable supporting player. Her role was to fill in key episodes of the Swope mystery that happened in Kellar's absence. Those were Chrisman Swope's terrible death, the torments of his sister Margaret, and a smaller incident, whose telling caught the instant attention of every listener in the room.

Houlehan, a pretty, oval-faced woman in a big flowered hat, was asked by J. A. Reed if she remembered a box of candy given by Hyde to anyone in the Swope family.

"Yes, Doctor Hyde gave Stella Swope a box of candy," she answered.

"Did she become ill afterwards?"

"Yes."

"When?"

MISS ANNA HOULEHAN UNDER CROSS-EXAMINATION BY MR. WALSH THIS MORNING.
Kansas City Star, Sat., April 23, 1910, p. 1.

"Just seven days afterwards she became ill enough for bed from typhoid."

The whole exchange took just thirty seconds, and although Houlehan later admitted that she hadn't actually seen Stella eat any of the sweets, the damage was done. Hyde had been depicted as the sort of beast who would give candy laced with deadly germs *to a 15-year-old child*.

Houlehan turned out to be nearly as hard to intimidate as Kellar had been. Walsh had a way of planting his heavy frame before the witness, pushing his face in close, and barking each question with a jerk of his head. Several times he was admonished by the judge to show more respect. Except for a misstated fact or two and some moments of confused memory, the nurse got through the cross-examination with reasonable aplomb.

It was just as well that Margaret Swope, who testified the following Monday, was not subjected to one of Walsh's more robust

MISS MARGARET SWOPE ON THE WITNESS STAND. *Kansas City Times,* Tue., April 26, 1910, p. 1.

grillings. The third oldest of the Swope daughters was articulate enough in recounting experiences such as Hyde's creepy visit to her room to give that agonizing shot. She was not, however, a comfortable witness.

A sketch in the *Times* captures her insecurity and plainness—the downcast eyes, the drab hairstyle, the fleshy figure clad in a dreary suit. She tended to answer Reed's and Walsh's questions in short sentences with long pauses. Often her voice dropped so low she had to be urged to speak up. Wisely—and perhaps out of sincere pity—Walsh was courteous and gentle the whole way.

It would be inaccurate, and unfair, to depict Frank Walsh as some kind of raging bull in the courtroom. He could apply finesse as well as toughness, and his nature was anything but unkind. By all accounts he was a bighearted, affable man, with warm friends in all walks of life.

For this trial, however, he needed every polemic weapon in his arsenal. The prosecution's top strategists had handed him a formidable challenge. The case they had fashioned, though not airtight, was impressive in its thoroughness. No fewer than forty-four witnesses (forty-five if Doctor Twyman had lived) had been enlisted to testify for the State. These comprised both frontline players—doctors, scientists, members of the family—and lesser figures to fill in minor chinks in the evidence,

Sometimes the lesser witnesses put on the best show. On April 25, an Independence druggist named O. H. Gentry was called to testify about the elixir of iron, quinine, and strychnine that Colonel Swope had purchased from his shop. As soon as Gentry was seated, Virgil Conkling handed him a bottle of the tonic to verify it was the same medicine. Whereupon the witness raised the bottle to his mouth and took a swig. To the astonished prosecutor, Gentry explained he was suffering a heart palpitation and needed an emergency dose. Walsh objected that it was all an act intended to prejudice the jury. But minutes later Gentry cried for "a drink of water quick!" and Latshaw sent a marshal scampering after the drink. Gentry recovered and resumed his testimony.

Tuesday the 26th might have been called Ladies Day in the

starkly masculine courtroom. A reporter noted that women filled every available seat, looking "more like an Easter congregation, with the variation of bright colored dresses and hats, than the audience of a murder trial." Others—scores of them—waited out in the corridor, hoping space would open up in the afternoon.

Obviously word had gotten out that Lucy Lee Swope, the most glamorous of the daughters, would be on the stand that day. She was known from stories and pictures in the press. She was rich and reasonably good-looking—more so than Margaret anyway. She had been in Europe—Paris!—at the time people started dying in the family mansion. Like a fairy-tale princess, she'd been given an evil potion by a wicked man, or so it was believed by those already convinced of Hyde's guilt. And no one could help noticing, as she hurried into the courtroom, that she was more confident by half than her doleful younger sister.

While her mother smiled with approval, Lucy Lee told of the cup of water from Hyde's hands that she had drunk aboard the train. The story wasn't new. But the jurymen really perked up when she revealed the date she had drunk the water and the day of her subsequent collapse with typhoid fever. They'd been informed about the incubation time of the typhoid bacillus, and they knew how to count. None missed the significance of that seven-day interval.

If the courtroom drama had its classical characters—the central figures of Good and Evil—it also had its chorus. The Swope nurses, taken together, had observed, touched, treated, and smelled every horrible case of sickness within the mansion walls. No one of them had been present during each and every incident that had set the nurses against Hyde. But one after the other, through the last week of April, they interwove their separate tales of grievance and suspicion.

Elizabeth Gordon recalled Hyde's use of dirty water in preparing an injection for Chrisman; she could not protest because "it was an ironbound rule that a nurse must not criticize anything a doctor does." Mae Pierce told of Chrisman's wrenching cries of terror and despair: "'I want my mother,' he kept calling, 'I'm going to die and I want my mother.'" Rose Churchill revealed that Doctor Twyman, alarmed by Margaret's convulsion, had ordered the nurses to burn all their medicines and obtain new ones, in case Hyde had contaminated them. Lou Van Nuys said she had prudently hidden her drugs in her shirtwaist whenever Hyde came around.

In that same last week of April, the State's case shifted focus. It was now less on the family's sufferings than on the sinister science of the alleged murderer. On a single day, April 27, a cascade of hostile testimony poured from the witness stand. The soberly handsome Doctor Edward Stewart related his accounts of deadly germ cultures and his troubling bacteriological survey of the Swope estate. Druggist Hugo Brecklein confirmed Hyde's purchases of cyanide "to kill some dogs," and described his own uneasiness in selling the stuff. Nurse Van Nuys, stiff-backed and spectacled, told of smelling the odor of bitter almonds on Tom Swope's hands the night he picked up Hyde's capsules in the snow. Capsules filled with cyanide and strychnine, a tube of pus germs, a bottle marked "Poison," and lab vessels for growing germ colonies were lined up on the evidence table.

It just kept getting worse. Coroner B. H. Zwart testified that Colonel Swope had not died from natural causes—the autopsy had proved it. He insisted the postmortem examination had been handled faultlessly, even as Walsh tried to refute the claim during cross-examination. Walsh's questions were reasoned and erudite—he was well informed on the reliability of autopsies on frozen corpses and the condition of brains cut from the skull in broken chunks. Walsh may have been too erudite. One reporter suggested that all the scientific terms probably went right past the jurors' heads.

From the press's standpoint, it was easily the most interesting session since the trial began. And then, unexpectedly, moments before adjournment, it got a lot more interesting. As spectators began to stir and lawyers collected their scattered papers, the voice of Judge Latshaw broke through the murmuring crowd sounds. Heads swiveled toward the bench. The judge had an announcement: "In view of the testimony thus far given in this trial the court is constrained to say that it amounts to a presumption that, under the law, deprives the defendant of the right to bond. He is hereby, and for that reason, remanded to the custody of the marshal."

He added, "Mister Marshal, take charge of the prisoner."

Hyde's head jerked upward, as if he'd been startled. At the words "deprives the defendant," Frances Hyde threw her arms around her husband's neck and her head fell to his shoulders. She began to sob. Several friends rushed to the table where the Hydes were sitting and pressed around them consolingly.

Frances was heard speaking to her husband: "Let me go too. Let me go too, dear. I've nothing else to do, nothing else, no one to live for except you."

A few feet away, Mrs. Swope stood along with her cigar-chewing brother and two of her daughters. It was hard to read the mother's expression. Some interpreted it as righteous satisfaction, but when she glanced toward the weeping Frances, her eyes filled.

The defense, of course, objected. Attorney John Lucas argued that locking up the defendant for the duration of the trial would prejudice the jury, leading them to believe him guilty. Walsh started to argue, too, but got out only five words—"If it please the court…"—before Judge Latshaw shook his head, raised his hands palms outward, and said, "It is no use, Mister Walsh." Hyde spent the night in cell number seven, with no special comforts or privileges except the right to enjoy home-cooked meals brought in by his wife or friends.

Winifred Black had just been handed her next column, as it were, by the Muse of Melodrama. As Hyde left his cell the next day, she wrote, he was followed by "the acrid, unmistakable odor of a prison." His face was "as white as a bleaching bone," his "cold eyes still gleam and sparkle, but his glittering smile is gone." His wife "sat close, close beside him—so close that every breath she drew must have stirred the garments of the man who took her from her mother's house and promised to love, cherish, and protect her not many laughing years ago."

Black was equally breathless—but more on point—when she changed the subject to Hyde's chief attorney. Walsh was no longer "the ruddy, smiling Frank Walsh, who stepped so debonairly into the case a week or so ago." He was "a man with a heavy face, heavily marked with deep lines, almost like scars. A man who shows his teeth, not as they are shown in laughter, but as a fighting dog shows them when he is ready to fight."

Walsh was ready, all right. The next witnesses were the scientific experts the State relied on to drive in the last nails for their case. Walsh had either prepped himself mercilessly for taking on these scientists or been coached by a skilled and knowledgeable tutor. Whatever the case, it was obvious the defense counsel was an awesomely fast learner.

After the lanky pathologist, Doctor Frank Hall, told the jury he could only conclude that the Colonel had died of poisoning, Walsh put him through a grilling as fierce as any oral exam faced by a class of trembling med students. He got the doctor to admit that Swope's kidneys were badly atrophied, that this condition could have led to fatal uremic poisoning, and that Hall had previously told him (Walsh) that if he had filled out the death certificate, he would have listed "senile disability" as the cause.

Cool, clear-eyed Ludvig Hektoen, by his demeanor alone, seemed just the unflappable man of science to affirm the facts once and for all. He was *the* State's authority on death and all its riddles, a man of national eminence. From the moment Hektoen took the stand on Saturday, April 30, the press and spectators were quite certain he would stand up admirably to Walsh's interrogation.

Hektoen was confident—it wasn't just his words but the way he spoke them—that Colonel Swope had not died from apoplexy nor Chrisman Swope from meningitis. The witness had overseen both autopsies. Step by anatomical step, he described every organ taken from the elder Swope's body and explained that not one of them showed signs of fatal disease. The brain was frozen solid, to be sure, but he had removed it himself in neat slices quite suitable for close examination. In his opinion, both Swopes had died from the effects of "some convulsive and paralyzing poison."

No sooner had Walsh begun his cross-examination than he made it clear he was anything but overawed by Hektoen's reputation. Early on, he implied that the pathologist was a "professional expert witness" with a profitable link to the Chicago coroner's

office. Hektoen denied it. Walsh suggested that Hektoen's much-vaunted studies at European universities had been less extensive than he'd let people think—his terms abroad had mostly been for a few weeks only. "Nosiree!" Hektoen protested, but further questioning extracted the truth.

On the same day, Walsh used his hastily acquired medical knowledge to catch Hektoen in a serious error. Didn't a certain membrane on Chrisman's brain show a condition suggesting meningitis? The witness had to admit it was true, thereby throwing doubt on the poison theory.

It wasn't until the morning after the Sunday recess, however, that Walsh got in his most decisive—and humiliating—blows against the State's top medical witness. He was cross-examining Hektoen on aspects of the Swope autopsies when he asked whether the witness was familiar with a book called *Peterson and Haines on Legal Medicine and Toxicology.* Hektoen was—in fact he had contributed a chapter. Walsh reminded him that the book recommended certain rules for using scientific evidence. Hektoen said he was aware of them.

One of the rules, Walsh noted, was that experts hired by the opposing sides should make a point of sharing their evidence and conclusions, in order to prevent any suspicions of error or impropriety. Hektoen began to look uneasy. He knew what was coming, and it did. Walsh forced him to admit that he and his Chicago colleagues had used every kind of trick to keep the defense experts from examining—or even finding—the viscera collected from the autopsies. Walsh must have savored the moment.

After challenging Hektoen on several lesser points, Walsh got around to the question he'd been waiting to ask all day: "The body of Thomas Swope was frozen, wasn't it, and when you went to remove the brain you cracked it in a dozen places?"

Hektoen replied, "Well, I don't remember just how many places were cracked."

Walsh read a section of Hektoen's own chapter in the book setting out the proper way to remove the brain. "Is that the correct way?" he asked.

"It is the ideally correct way," came the answer.

"But when you came to remove this brain, you cracked it. Was that because it was frozen?"

Hektoen tried to divert Walsh's line of questioning by tossing out a few lame denials and excuses. The witness's discomfort was almost palpable.

Finally Walsh quoted a few warnings from Hektoen's chapter concerning autopsy procedures. An autopsy on a frozen body, Hektoen had cautioned, was not advised. The use of hot water to thaw a frozen corpse was not advised. Organs could not be removed from a frozen body without compromising the accuracy of tests. The frozen brain could not be removed without ruinous damage.

For a distinguished man of science, under fire from a hostile lawyer who kept scoring direct hits, only one thing worse could happen—and it did: The crowd laughed.

Two more days of prosecution testimony remained, but most of the action seemed anticlimactic after the fascinating parade of witnesses that had come before.

The few left to testify included the toxicologists recruited by Hektoen—Doctor Walter S. Haines of Chicago, with his forked beard and pedantic manner, and Doctor Victor C. Vaughan of the University of Michigan, whom Winifred Black described as a "cherub in a cemetery." Walsh kept up the pressure on them with his usual tenacity and command of the facts. But the two scientists acquitted themselves with such skill that Walsh made little headway against them or their stubborn insistence that poisons were found in significant quantities.

Maggie Swope was chosen to testify last, ending the prosecution's case on a note of high emotion. Her scheduled appearance drew such a throng of women that they packed the halls, jammed

DR. WALTER C. HAINES ON THE STAND TESTIFYING TO THE FINDING OF CYANIDE.
Kansas City Star, Tue., May 3, 1910, p. 1.

the circular stairway, and spilled into the street, where a vendor peddled sandwiches, soda pop, and chewing gum. Those lucky enough to find seats were undoubtedly moved by her familiar saga—retold how many times?—of the events that had plagued her family since the previous October.

None of it was new, including the witness's tears. They glistened on her plump cheeks as she recounted one especially heartbreaking moment with her tortured elder son, Chrisman. He was delirious from the fever and terrified that Hyde might operate on him. "I put my hand over his eyes," Mrs. Swope said. "They stared so, I couldn't bear to see them." She recalled the promise she'd made to the dying man: "I won't let anyone hurt you, Chrisman, or deceive you."

James A. Reed and the prosecution team couldn't have scripted a more heart-tugging finale.

The witness stepped down. The State rested its case.

Chapter 20

I f ever a pompous medical expert was faithful to stereotype,
it was Doctor Frederick W. Froehling of Kansas City, the first
scientific witness for Hyde's defense. German-born, German-
schooled (Berlin, Bonn, and Leipzig), he had a pedantic way of
answering questions—even simple ones—in lengthy perorations
that no one seemed able to shut off. That he also spoke in a stiff
Teutonic accent, and rebuked lawyers for asking him to give short
answers, made him seem all the more puffed up and superior.

When a questioner *could* get him to reply in a one-word affir-
mative, it would almost always be "Sure," rather than "Yes." Froehling answered "Sure" so frequently that it seemed a kind of verbal
tic. During cross-examination on Thursday, May 5, the audience
began to giggle every time he said "Sure" and Judge Latshaw had to
warn them this was a court of law, not a vaudeville show.

The unfunny truth about this long-winded physician, however,
was that he was a masterful witness—perhaps the most broadly
knowledgeable medical expert (in 1910 terms) to appear so far.
He'd made a name for himself as an excellent practitioner—his
field was internal medicine—and he was well informed on the latest research.

For the better part of the morning, defense attorney R. R.
Brewster steered the doctor from one piece of State's evidence
to the next. On cue, Froehling then deflated each one with his
impressive arsenal of facts, medical doctrine, and clinical observations—all of it, presumably, state of the art for that era.

He knew of cases where typhoid fever triggered convulsions

identical to those caused by poisoning.

He described one form of meningitis that could not be detected through examination of the victim's brain, even with a microscope.

He testified that nearly all modern doctors in Germany—and many in America—used injections of camphorated oil as a heart stimulant, even though the shots were painful and (significantly) could induce long-term soreness and swelling.

He declared that the atrophied state of Colonel Swope's kidneys could have led to uremic poisoning, convulsion, and death. That the sclerotic condition of the great aorta could have weakened the Colonel's heart and sped him to the grave. That Chrisman Swope's 107.8-degree fever could very well have been what killed him.

James A. Reed's cross-examination of the witness after lunch was a contest marked by notable lapses in civility. After one of Froehling's wordy replies, the irritated Reed snapped, "Here, we don't want a long speech." Froehling retorted that it wasn't nearly as long as Reed's rambling question. As the subject turned to cyanide, the witness refused indignantly to answer what he called "a catch question" with a simple yes or no. The attorney intimated surprise that the doctor didn't know one feature of cyanide poisoning. Froehling responded sarcastically that he knew at least as much about it as Reed did.

In the end, Reed failed to get what he wanted—Froehling's agreement that cyanide and strychnine, blended in one deadly pill, could mask each other's symptoms, delay death, and confuse efforts to pinpoint which poison, if any, was the killer. The theory was at the heart of the State's case. Reed needed expert confirmation in order to show the jury that only a doctor of demonic genius could have plotted these crimes. Froehling's stubborn refusal to endorse the idea did not sit well with the increasingly frustrated Reed.

Listening from her press table, Winifred Black found herself a little alarmed by Reed's change from urbane champion of the law to fierce combatant. "The mellifluent voice he has used all through the trial," she wrote, had taken on "a brazen note that sounded like the trump of doom."

The strength of Hyde's scientific defense was due mainly to the skills of one man, whom Walsh had recruited at Fordham University's medical school. Doctor Ernest Ellsworth Smith, a Yale-trained professor of physiological chemistry, knew poisons the way a three-star chef knows fine herbs. When Walsh needed a mastermind to orchestrate the testimony of experts, Smith was the ideal choice. Days before the trial, Walsh had had him writing sample questions, coaching the witnesses, and—it turned out—drilling Walsh himself on the fundamentals of toxicology and forensic pathology.

It was also Smith who helped select the seven physicians and chemists who were signed on to dispute everything the State's scientists had to say. They included an aged country doctor named Allen, who swore that a tiny pinch of cyanide was a good cough remedy (but "if anybody takes a fair dose, he'll die like a shot"); City Chemist Walter Cross, who had examined the Swope mansion and found the dumbwaiter unsanitary; and Hyde's personal physician and former office partner, John Perkins, who said it was not unusual for up-to-date doctors to possess and experiment with germ cultures.

On May 6, Smith himself delivered a droning critique of the State's chemical evidence that was so arcane it lost even the most attentive jurymen. An astute reporter for the *Star* saw it as a psychological turning point in the trial. The jurors were weary with their long confinement and mental strain, he wrote, but above all they'd had it with scientific testimony. "As the trial develops," he continued, "it appears more and more as if the jury may weigh the stories told by Miss Kellar and the other nurses against the testimony to be given by Doctor and Mrs. Hyde, and from this make up their verdict."

If the *Star* writer had it right, the morning and afternoon sessions of Monday, May 9, would get the trial back to the basics—people, words, and passions the jury could relate to. Frances Hyde would testify first in her husband's defense, then the man she hoped to rescue would follow her to the witness stand. Cold science would give way to the imponderables of human motive and behavior.

On the day before he faced the jury, Hyde was treated to a Sunday dinner prepared by an elderly family retainer known as

Aunt Becky. The *Post,* which tended to treat black people as either amusing or dangerous, devoted a story and an editorial to the occasion. Aunt Becky had prepared a jailhouse dinner "as only an old-time Southern Negro cook can prepare," it reported. "And with the customary prodigality of the 'Aunt Becky' school of cooking, there was enough of it not only for Dr. Hyde but to provide a dinner for every other prisoner on the third floor of the jail."

The weather on Monday was auspicious—sunny and fresh, at last, after weeks of chill and dampness. Frances did not look confident, however, as she stepped heavily to her chair. Winifred Black described her attire—a black silk dress decorated with a gold locket and her husband's college fraternity pin. The *Post* writer thought she detected traces of recent tears.

Still, Frances kept her poise throughout five hours on the stand, and her testimony was remarkable for one reason only, having nothing to do with high drama. What struck everyone in the courtroom was her resolute, unbreakable, unwavering denial of virtually everything used in evidence by the prosecution. It was almost as if she were speaking from a parallel universe in which all concepts of reality were precisely reversed.

All of it, by her account, was a skein of untruths: Kellar's description of the bleeding of Moss Hunton. Kellar's story of Hyde's actions the morning of the Colonel's seizure. The nurses' testimony of Hyde's cruel injection of Margaret's arm. The linking of the children's typhoid to a box of candy. Her own mother's claim to have strongly opposed sending Hyde to meet Lucy Lee's ship in New York.

And the most treacherous falsehood of all, she indicated, was Tom Swope's tale of leaving the house the night of December 18 and watching Hyde throw capsules into the snow. It did not happen, Frances told the jury. It could not have happened. She had been with Tom the entire evening, right there in the sitting room. He had never once left her sight.

As Winifred Black summarized it, Frances "contradicted, word by word, and almost syllable for syllable, nearly every possible bit of evidence which had been introduced by the State against

her husband since the trial began." The witness spoke with quiet composure, painting Hyde as "a persecuted martyr and plaything of an ironic and vengeful fate, the helpless victim of idle gossip and cruel and relentless slander."

In his heart, attorney James A. Reed probably wished he could drop the gentle approach toward this sympathetic young wife—*a wife with child!*—and blast her testimony with all the fury and dark arts at his command. He was stuck in a delicate situation, however, and his cross-examination essentially let the witness off easy.

Hyde's turn before the jury, starting Monday afternoon, gave every indication that he had been extremely well prepped. He strode toward the witness chair with an air of complete self-possession, facing the jurors and smiling slightly as he took his seat.

In fact, he had nothing to fear for the first two hours or so. Frank Walsh's direct examination was about as challenging as an open-book quiz, the questions so clearly and unambiguously stated that many could be answered with a "yes" or a "no."

The defendant was careful not to sound overly coached, however. Replying to Walsh's questions, Hyde preceded each statement with a short, thoughtful pause. Thus, with the confidence of a man invincibly shielded by the truth, he laid out his version of each horror in the Swope household and each action he'd taken as family protector and concerned healer. Hyde's testimony, like his wife's, left no hostile evidence uncontradicted. He and Frances might have been reading from the same script.

But on Tuesday morning he came under the power of Virgil Conkling and everything changed. Why the county prosecutor took charge of the cross-examination, rather than the formidable James A. Reed, is not known. It's doubtful that Reed could have done a more bruising job of it, though. Conkling's insolent mouth and bullet head lent him the appearance of a monk-inquisitor during the *auto-da-fé*. His interrogation style also was unlike Reed's—it was punchier, less polished. By the end of the day Hyde was wiping his forehead with a handkerchief and speaking in a small, weary monotone.

Conkling started off blandly enough, his early questions non-threatening. Hyde's answers were calm and direct—perhaps the prosecutor's initial tone had put him off-guard. When Conkling turned the inquiry to Hyde's purchases of cyanide, however, the attack was on.

Hyde said he had used the poison for eight or ten years to remove stains of silver nitrate—a commonly used disinfectant—from his fingers. It sounded plausible until Conkling asked Hyde where he'd bought the stuff over all these years and the doctor could recall only one supplier, Brecklein's drugstore. The prosecutor repeated and rephrased the question over and over. He asked, "Can you tell any day in your whole life when you bought cyanide before?" Hyde was starting to bristle. "That is so many days I cannot tell you," he shot back.

Conkling struck again. "If you used cyanide every day, as you say, and you bought only four capsules September 13, why was it you bought none from that date to December 4?" Hyde had no explanation. December 4 had been a dark day in the Swope mansion: Chrisman Swope was ill with typhoid fever and would die two days later after the second of two convulsions.

Hyde, who had once said he needed the cyanide to destroy some pesky dogs, now testified that his target was a more humble creature—the cockroach. The bugs had been attracted to his office by piles of used towels stained with blood and pus. The use of cyanide to eliminate the pests had been recommended in a medical pamphlet sent to him in the mail, he said.

Unfortunately, when Conkling asked the name of the pamphlet and who published it, Hyde found himself at a loss. Conkling demanded, "What kind of a pamphlet?" Hyde showed a hint of the sarcasm that would intensify—and play badly for the jury—as the day went on. "It was a pamphlet made of paper comprising something about ten inches long and six inches wide and composed of about eight or ten leaves."

Conkling kept grinding away at the pamphlet issue, as if Hyde's inability to recall where it came from were the most damning evidence of his guilt. As both men grew more heated, their exchange took on a kind of Kafkaesque absurdity

Q: Doctor, there was no pamphlet issued by anybody recommending the use of this for cockroaches, was there?

A: I don't think the pamphlet description was entirely limited, but one of the means as to the cyanide of potassium in there was that. It was an incidental suggestion.

Q: How is that?

A: If I remember, this suggestion was more incidental; the pamphlet contained other things.

Q: You don't tell this jury, do you, that any pamphlet or any medical work recommended the use of cyanide of potassium to kill cockroaches?

A: I don't know. There might be.

Q: You never saw it yourself?

A: I never saw it in anything except this pamphlet.

Q: You never saw it mentioned, you never read of it in any other work except this pamphlet?

A: No, sir.

Q: Anybody ever recommend cyanide of potassium to kill cockroaches, to you?

A: Not except this pamphlet.

Q: And are you quite sure you read it in the pamphlet?

Conkling kept up his Gatling-gun interrogation almost without letup, turning his attention next to Hyde's stockpiling of germ cultures. The prosecutor brought out a sinister prop, the very same tube of typhoid culture taken from Hyde's laboratory. After handing the item to the defendant, he asked whether Hyde had scraped away any of the germs from the culture medium. Hyde thought deeply, looking at the ceiling with brows drawn together, and said, "I don't really remember." Then he admitted he had taken some of the bacilli to make "smears" and to use in Widal tests.

Conkling pressed him on specifics—what patients had he tested? Hyde was starting to seem rattled. He could remember only one, a Mister Brent.

Q: There have been enough typhoid germs taken from this tube to make one hundred Widal tests, haven't there?

A: No, I don't know.

Q: Now, doctor, look at this. Hasn't there been enough bacteria removed to make two hundred Widal tests? (*Conkling had risen to his feet and raised his voice to a shout.*)

A: It might have all been used in one Widal test.

Q: Doctor, isn't it a fact that five hundred Widal tests can be made from one healthy tube of culture?

Hyde protested: "Now see here, either you don't understand me, or I don't you." It was useless and his next line of defense was worse. Hyde's tendency to strike back with sarcasm was one of his self-damaging traits. When Conkling linked his purchase of germ-culture tubes to the illness of two nieces a week later, the defendant couldn't stop himself: "I think the week after I bought them there was an earthquake down in the West Indies."

The judge rapped on his desk for order and admonished him to "answer the questions and not to make any remarks."

So it went for five hours, "as merciless an inquisition as one is likely to hear in a courtroom," the *Kansas City Times* wrote. "It bristled with 'Why, why, why?' and 'Cyanide' and 'Poison' and 'Typhoid cultures.'" *Post* reporter Elizabeth Kelly described Hyde as "nervous, at times irritable, and plainly belligerent." A colleague on the same paper, James Craig, observed, "It was a new Doctor Hyde. It was a Doctor Hyde who was plainly self-conscious, who was plainly distressed. It was a nervous man who clutched frequently at his collar, as if it hurt him."

———•◦•———

In an era when oratory was public entertainment—when local theaters rang with the Bard's soliloquys and any sermon under an hour and a half long was felt to be superficial—the closing arguments in the Hyde trial were awaited with enthusiasm. Never mind that there would be seven of them—four for the State, three for the defense—delivered over two and a half days. So much the better! By now the attorneys who would address the jury had become celebrities of a kind, two of them were undisputed stars, and it hardly took a clairvoyant to see that every chair in the room would become a coveted prize.

The polemics would begin late Wednesday, May 11, directly after Judge Latshaw gave his instructions to the jury. His remarks were both circumspect and scrupulously fair. The jury must either convict Doctor Hyde of first-degree murder or acquit him—there would be no halfway choice. There was no direct evidence of Hyde's guilt—it was all circumstantial. Such evidence must be considered cautiously and it was not sufficient to warrant conviction unless it left in the juror's mind no reasonable doubt. If the jury found that Hyde had willfully, feloniously, deliberately, premeditatedly, on purpose, and with malice aforethought taken the life of Thomas Hunton Swope, it must assess his punishment at death by hanging or imprisonment for life in the state penitentiary.

In the manner of rock concerts a century later, the debate started with an opening act to warm things up. Henry Jost, first assistant prosecutor, laid out the State's accusations in chronological sequence, aiming for clarity rather than high eloquence. He made an efficient job of it, with a few pithy lines tossed in: Hyde had walked from the mansion on the critical night of December 18, he said, "with poisons in his pockets and murder in his heart."

Jost's speech for the prosecution had the jury thinking. Frank Walsh's speech for the defense, the next day, had them weeping.

Four jurors and dozens in the audience were seen wiping their eyes within the first hour of Walsh's peroration. Though his rebuttal of the State's evidence was almost surgically meticulous and shrewd, what seemed to grip the jurors most was Walsh's manipulation of emotions. His strategy was clear. From the first, he directed their sympathies to the lovely, anxious wife seated just behind the defendant. Simply by *being* there, Frances Hyde was a visual extension of Walsh's theme—the victimization of a piteous innocent through the unjust prosecution of her husband.

By inference and agile argument, the attorney laid the true guilt to the wife's own family, eight of whom sat in the front row. Hyde was the hapless martyr to old hostilities, to suspicions based on faulty memories, and to "the imaginings of a group of nurses." And there sat Frances, "a good, true, virtuous woman," the second victim of the Swopes' injustice.

Walsh had begun with a cool, deliberate tone, but he erupted with passion when the time came to give the jury a jolt. Recalling Hyde's defiance and anger under Virgil Conkling's cross-examination, he said: "Did you see the other day how he rebuked the prosecutor, who sat clothed with all the mighty power of the State, with the backing of limitless wealth? This man, whom the prosecutor says is facing a death on the scaffold, who faces being choked to death like a dog, or, worse than that, being sent to the penitentiary for life, disgraced, dishonored, no longer a man among men, faced the prosecutor and rebuked him as only an honest man could have done."

Frances sobbed at the words "choked to death like a dog." Walsh had made his point.

If only for their mastery of rhetoric, the remaining speakers were a credit to legal training of the era. Listening to John Atwood, R. R. Brewster, Virgil Conkling, and John Lucas must have been like hearing a concert of world-class rival tenors. They tried every tune in the trial lawyer's songbook, including anthems to the fairness and judgment of the plain, commonsense Missouri juror.

The great virtuoso everyone was waiting for was, of course, James A. Reed. Among the public and attorneys alike, he was possibly the biggest draw in the city's history of criminal justice. An article in the *Kansas City Times* captured the scene on Friday morning: "Thousands almost fought for admission to hear the closing argument for the State. They struggled in the hallways and fell upon the stairs. They stood for hours to hear the final words and see the final acts in a trial that has lasted five weeks. They tore each other's clothing and they resisted the officers of the court."

Reed's performance was, to put it mildly, worth the fuss. Even accounting for journalistic hyperbole, one senses that the newspaper stories got it right. When Reed finished his two-hour oration, wrote Winifred Black, the jurors "drew a long breath as if they came out of some trance at the call of some familiar voice, looked about them like men dazed by a sudden light, and filed quietly and almost awestruck into the jury room."

It was, the *Post* writer added, "without any question of doubt, the most convincing, the most eloquent, the most masterful speech I ever heard in any courtroom in any city in any country in the world."

Reading the speech a century later, along with the press reports, leaves the impression that Reed's final argument was somehow greater than the sum of its parts. In language, structure, and critical logic, it was impressive. It contained memorable lines:

"The typhoid followed that man [Hyde] like sharks follow a ship laden with dead." But on top of all that, holding it together, was the artistry of a born tragedian, or perhaps a first-class conjurer.

James Craig, also of the *Post*, may have captured the essence of Reed's magic. "Reed was more than a logician, more than an orator. He was a wonderful actor in the highest meaning of that word. The expressions of his face, the gestures of his hands, his bearing, his pauses, and the modulations of his voice were those of a man trained by years and years of histrionic labors."

At one point near the end of the address, Craig reported, an unrelated incident sent a chill through the rows of spectators. Reed had just painted a verbal picture of Hyde standing under a streetlight on the night of the jettisoned capsules, an evil smile on his lips. At that moment a silvery pealing of bells floated into the courtroom from a church in the nearby Italian district. "It made one think of that terrible scene in *The Bells*," Craig wrote, "[when] the murderer in his hour of remorse hears the jangling of sleighbells, such as the victim's horse wore the night of the slaying."

———•—•———

The jury was out for three nights and two days, during which there were almost more rumors than people drifting through the courtroom. The telephone company had set up a long bank of phones and assigned a crew of operators to meet the human wave of reporters that would surge to them the instant the verdict came. The effort was premature. Throughout Saturday and Sunday, the only news for the press corps to phone in to "re-write" was non-news: Word had it (from somewhere) that seven to five jurors favored conviction. Actually, it was eight to four. No, it was ten to two.

The jury walked over from the Ashland Hotel each morning and left their sanctum in the Criminal Court Building each evening. A reporter sneaked a look at them at supper. They appeared "as solemn as pallbearers" and were barely touching their food.

As rain drummed incessantly on the windows (the *Star* predicted the wettest May on record), the Hydes holed up in an anteroom where the doctor chain-smoked cigars and his lawyers dropped by to offer encouragement and talk strategy. Should the trial end in acquittal, it was assumed the State would retry Hyde immediately on the charge of murdering Chrisman. Again, Walsh would undertake his defense. Or if the vote was for conviction, Walsh assured his client, an appeal for a new trial was nearly ready to send. In the meantime Hyde needn't fear imminent transfer to the State Penitentiary in Jefferson City. Until the appeal was resolved one way or the other, he'd be right here in the county jail, his wife and friends only a streetcar ride away.

Reporters passed the time with the Hydes as well. A *Star* man quoted the doctor's reminiscence about the old tycoon he was charged with murdering. "Why, I used to spend hours with that old man—the Swopes know that," he said. "True, he was morose and crabbed and hard to get along with, and he was against most men and believed most men were against him. But after he had delivered himself of his harsh opinions he was a delightful old fellow, an educated man, a Yale graduate, a reader of good books, and, until near the end of his life, possessed of a remarkable memory."

On Monday morning, Frances brought her husband a stack of letters from home and the two of them sat in the anteroom with a huddle of friends waiting for something to happen. At 10:15, something did. A marshal entered and asked the doctor to take a place in the courtroom. "At last," Hyde said. He stood. "Come, dearie, let us hear it and have it over. Be brave now, be brave." They walked to the seats they had occupied since April 11. Frances was white and wide-eyed; her husband appeared calm.

The red door leading from the judge's chamber swung open, and Judge Latshaw emerged and settled into his high seat. Next, the jurors appeared, led by Deputy Marshal Charles Kemper. As was customary, they formed a row near the press table instead of filing to the jury box.

"Gentlemen, have you decided upon a verdict," Latshaw asked.

"We have, your honor," said the foreman, Frank Claypool. He handed a bit of paper to Clerk of Court William McClanahan, who was asked by the judge to read the words. It was written neatly in longhand: "We the jury find the defendant B. Clark Hyde guilty of

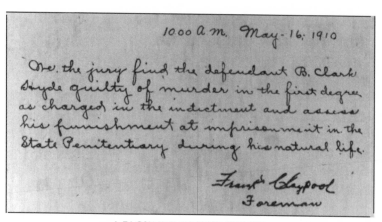

A FACSIMILE OF THE VERDICT.
Kansas City Star, Mon., May 16, 1910, p. 1.

murder in the first degree as charged in the indictment and assess his punishment at imprisonment in the State Penitentiary during his natural life."

Frances managed not to collapse. She threw her arms half around Hyde's neck, laid her head on one of his shoulders, and sobbed and moaned. Hyde remained stoical as, one after the other, the jurors repeated, "This is my verdict." He stared at them until the last one had spoken. Then he turned to Frances and said, "Come." They could have a few minutes together in the ante-room. As Hyde opened the door, he paused and told the hovering reporters, "I have not lost hope. I am innocent of this crime and the others charged against me. I am the victim of a set of terrible circumstances, some of them hard to explain. Other men have suffered this way for nothing. But I have not lost hope. No sir."

Frances's friends saw that she was driven home and provided with sympathetic companionship for the rest of the day.

At 1:00 Hyde was observed back in cell number seven, reading a pamphlet with apparent interest.

At 1:15 he abandoned his reading and was deep in a game of pitch with fellow prisoners.

At 1:30 he quit the card game and sent word through a guard that he wanted lunch.

At 2:30 he was playing pitch again. He stayed at it for another half hour, then took to his cot for a nap.

Reporters who caught up with jurors before they left for home were told it was cyanide that had poisoned Hyde's case, so to say. Even jurymen who had argued for acquittal were finally brought around by Hyde's inability to name any drugstore besides Brecklein's—*not one*—where he had purchased the poison over the ten years he claimed to have used it.

This rationale for the jury's verdict was no doubt too simple, but it would do for readers of the afternoon editions.

Mrs. Swope, according to the *Star,* had stayed home that morning and missed the climactic moment. She was reached by telephone just minutes after the verdict was read, however. She asked the caller, "What is it?" and after a moment she exclaimed, "Oh!" and hung up. To a group of family members gathered in another room, she announced, "Doctor Hyde has been convicted."

Not surprisingly, the *Post* had a livelier take on the scene. Its reporter wrote that the matriarch issued a loud scream upon hearing the news, then dropped the receiver and fainted.

Winifred Black's column that day showed none of the veiled fascination toward Hyde that had crept into previous stories from time to time. Her tone was self-righteous and pitiless: "And B. Clark Hyde, the man whose cold eyes and sardonic smile have made a hateful picture to the eye of all who looked upon him in the courtroom, has gone back to his cell—convicted under the wise and just and honest laws of the wise and just and honest state of Missouri, of murder in the first degree."

Chapter 21

Though dormant for the time being, the Hyde-Swope case was so embedded in the public consciousness that it stayed on the front pages for weeks after Hyde went to jail. Occasionally real news came along, especially as Hyde's appeal for a retrial worked its way through the legal system. But most of all, readers still craved the human stuff—the emotional leftovers of the ghastly drama and trial. The press was glad to provide it.

The *Times,* May 17: Frances Hyde issues a statement denouncing the State's counsel for alleged legal improprieties. Clark writes a letter to his wife and plays poker with five kitchen trusties until lights-out. From the cells of black prisoners two tiers below, the strains of "Nearer My God to Thee" float upward to Hyde's cell.

The *Star,* May 17: Reprinted newspaper stories from around the country comment on the case. *The New York World* ranks it with "the most celebrated poison cases of history." *The Chicago Tribune* observes mordantly: "Doctor Hyde can put away his overcoat." *The Chicago Daily News* writes that "Doctor Hyde as a scientific poisoner made the mistake of living some centuries too late."

The *Post,* May 18: Hyde's father, the elderly Baptist preacher, tells an interviewer that "Clark was as kind and loving a little chap as ever lived. I remember once how he nursed a dog back to life that had been cut with a scythe."

The *Star,* May 19: A mystery figure known as the "Woman in Black," who had attended the trial daily for many weeks, attempts to deliver a bunch of American Beauty roses to Hyde's cell. She is turned away by the superintendent after Hyde says he's never heard of the lady. She is a Mrs. Adkins, a compulsive trial-goer who lives in the East.

The *Star,* May 21: Chemist Walter M. Cross claims Mrs. Swope had once told him she was at fault for the typhoid outbreak. Cross quotes her as saying, "It's all my fault. I was the one who had the outhouse moved, and I am to blame for everything."

The *Star,* May 22: A man named Elmer Swope of Martinsburg, West Virginia, claims (once again) that he is a son of the late Colonel Swope and should therefore inherit the old man's estate. No family connection has been found.

The *Star,* May 28: Hyde's wife finds him dripping with sweat after completing a five-mile walk in the jail corridor. He shows a reporter his reading matter—medical books, two Bibles, and a prayerbook.

The *Post,* May 31: Three of the Swope nurses, Misses Pierce, Gordon, and Churchill, say they've been boycotted by local physicians for having raised questions against the doctor (Hyde) whom they were duty-bound to serve. All plan to seek work in another city. Winifred Black writes: "For shame, gentlemen of the medical profession. For shame."

The *Star,* June 7: Life in jail palls for Hyde, who complains that his attorneys have spent too little time and effort on his case. While he languishes in his cell, Hyde says, the lawyers have been enjoying themselves on vacation trips.

The *Star,* June 19: Hyde is heard shouting angrily at his wife during a visit, accusing her of neglecting him. Frances is heard shouting back. Word circulates that the marriage is breaking up.

———•◦•———

The formal sentencing was to take place as soon as Judge Latshaw had ruled on Hyde's motion for a retrial. Frank Walsh and his defense team had compiled seventeen arguable grounds for a new trial and they weren't about to see Hyde put on the train to the State Penitentiary until the judge had decided the merits of each one.

The first of their claims was that Latshaw had prejudiced the jury by revealing his own bias against Hyde. According to the defense lawyers, the judge had telegraphed his prejudice in various ways, from his order to clap the defendant into jail midway through the trial to his comments from the bench, his facial expressions during testimony, and even his body language.

This complaint may have insulted the judge's integrity and wounded his feelings, but Latshaw had a much more complex issue to deal with in the defense's second allegation of error. The Walsh team argued that testimony entirely unrelated to the single charge—that Hyde had killed Colonel Swope by poisoning—had been wrongfully admitted into evidence.

After a two-day hearing, with a phalanx of lawyers arguing both sides and the Hydes in attendance, Latshaw announced his ruling. Though it took him an hour to read it, his opinion boiled down to two simple points: Hyde had received a fair trial, and the evidence justified the verdict.

The doctor took the bad news impassively, as if the judge were declaring someone else's—a stranger's—fate. He set his watch by the big clock on the courtroom wall, then rose to escort his wife to the anteroom for a brief visit before he was returned to his cell. He would be back in court the following Tuesday to hear himself sentenced to incarceration for life. On the same day, July 5, 1910, Frank Walsh, would dispatch Hyde's appeal to the Missouri Supreme Court.

In some respects, Clark Hyde's stay behind bars was a far cry from the durance vile experienced by common criminals. Frances came often, bearing home-cooked meals and reading matter. Attorneys kept him informed on the progress of his appeal and friends called frequently. Still, he was not a cheerful prisoner. His temper was inclined to flare. According to a deputy marshal, James Gilwee, Hyde's conduct in jail "was more than once of an unpleasant and ungentlemanly nature." One day he flew into a rage when two young people from a touring student group approached his cell, drew aside the privacy curtain hung across the bars, and peeked in. Hyde flung "a missile of some kind" at them, then "dashed a glass of water in their faces," Gilwee reported. On another occasion, the prisoner spat in the faces of visitors.

The worst of his ordeals in jail—one that would have crushed almost any man—took place overnight on August 31 and September 1. It caused Hyde such anguish that years later, in a handwritten family history, he made no effort to hide his bitterness.

In the final weeks of Frances's pregnancy, Hyde wrote, he had been assured by Judge Latshaw and the jailor, Marshal Mayes, that he'd be granted an overnight leave in order to attend the childbirth. Frances was overjoyed by the arrangement, and as soon as labor began, her physician, Doctor James, notified the two officials.

Hyde's account continues: "To the dismay of Doctor James, they both repudiated their promises. Labor in this case began about 10 o'clock p.m., and for hours Doctor James pleaded with those two beasts, Latshaw and Mayes, to make good their promises, reminding them of their solemn vows, and telling them that the lives of the mother and infant were at stake. These brutal officials both declined to make their word good. In the kindness of his heart, Doctor James concealed from the suffering young mother the fact that the two brutes … had broken their pledges. … She repeatedly asked Doctor James when her husband would come, and he as often answered her that [he] was on his way and would appear at any minute." Finally James had no choice but to tell her the truth.

Three hours after Frances gave birth, Hyde at last was brought to her bedside and allowed to see his infant son. At first the baby had shown all signs of normal health. By the time Hyde arrived, however, the newborn was suffering severe breathing difficulties—apnea—from which he died two hours later. Long afterward, Hyde wrote, "This apnea was not to be explained on any other theory than that the shock and collapse of the mother had been communicated to the child."

The dark uncertainty of Hyde's legal status finally cleared away on April 11, 1911. For 280 days—more than nine months—the justices of the state's highest court had pored over the evidence, reviewed case law, and weighed the soundness (or lack of it) of the case against him. Their written opinion makes heavy reading, but it was the final eight words that Hyde yearned to hear: "The judgment is reversed and the cause remanded."

Hyde would get his new trial. In the meantime his attorneys were seeking his immediate release on $50,000 bond. It was so ordered, and on April 27, 1911, Hyde walked out the jail door to the motorcar that would take him home.

That evening, an estimated one hundred friends, neighbors, attorneys, and loyal patients showed up to celebrate at the stone house at 3516 Forest Avenue. Frances laid out refreshments. Speeches and toasts were made. Clark was jubilant. One after another, people who had trusted him as their friend and healer swore they would never abandon him.

The Supreme Court cited numerous grounds for throwing out the verdict, but lawyers to this day agree that the most interesting concerned the old matter of admissibility. On the very first day of Hyde's trial, his attorneys had invoked an old rule: During a defendant's trial on a specific charge, evidence of other crimes imputed to him was generally inadmissible. Exceptions were allowed only when the State could show that the crime charged was linked to the other crimes by motive, intent, and other key similarities. In this case, the justices ruled that certain issues introduced by the State, such as the death of Moss Hunton and the invasion of typhoid fever, did not meet the test. The parallels were dubious, the evidence weak or non-existent. In the Supreme Court's opinion, "The testimony of other alleged crimes should never have been given to the jury, and having been admitted, should have been withdrawn."

Next time around—and the next time would arrive soon—the prosecution would have to narrow its attack.

The second trial began on October 23, 1911, before a new judge, Edward Porterfield (in effect, Latshaw had been recused). It was cut short on December 11 by an incident more akin to slapstick farce than to solemn courtroom drama. One of the jurymen, a milkman named Harry W. Waldron, had squeezed over a transom in the jury quarters at the Centropolis Hotel and wandered on foot for two days before turning himself in. His escape had apparently been driven by loneliness for his wife, to whom he had sent a note in a milk bottle. Judge Porterfield ruled that Waldron was "mentally unsound" and declared a mistrial.

Hyde faced a jury for the third time on January 28, 1913, with Reed and Walsh again dueling over his guilt or innocence. It ran until March 17, ending as inconclusively as the previous two trials. After eighty-six hours of deliberation, the jury members lined up before the judge and admitted they were hopelessly deadlocked. Nine had voted for acquittal and three held out for conviction. The judge thanked them for their services and sent them home with their accumulated pay of $2 per diem, plus mileage.

And that was the end of it. The case might have run on for years to a just and decisive finale, but the State and the Swope family had already paid a total of $250,000 to seek the elusive guilty verdict and neither was ready to spend more. Most likely the State had paid the greater share. Yet the Swopes had hardly gotten off lightly, having covered the handsome fees of James A. Reed and his law partners, plus the costs of the scientific investigations by Hektoen and his team of forensic experts. The case had simply burned itself out.

After some speculation of a fourth trial, the court dismissed the case on January 13, 1914, exempting Hyde from any further prosecution on the charges. The doctor had his freedom.

If any thoughtful person could call it that.

On that night two years earlier when Hyde celebrated his homecoming from jail, he'd been promised by the guests at the party that they would never let him down. What sort of person could abandon an innocent man? Once this nasty business was cleared up, life would go back to normal—he'd have as many friends and patients as ever.

What Hyde and his well-wishers hadn't reckoned on at the time was the corrosive effect that two further trials and two more years of demonizing newspaper stories would have on his reputation and career.

Dismissal of the case in 1914 was all very well, but it wasn't the same as *acquittal*. There would always be ... questions. Though Hyde lived respectably on Forest Avenue with his wife and small children—Bennett Clark Jr. and Frances—he was no longer the esteemed professional man. His practice was rapidly dwindling. In 1919 he was expelled from the Jackson County Medical Society after writing a scathing letter to a fellow member. The doctor had never overcome his habit of lashing out at anyone he believed—or imagined—had offended him.

Frances's piece of the Swope estate, though much reduced by the cost of Clark's legal defense, continued to pay the bills. But the doctor's idleness and loss of pride must have been horrible for both of them. He was growing sullen and verbally abusive. In 1920 Frances filed for divorce, charging that on numerous occasions Clark had threatened her life and those of her children. She demanded custody and sought an injunction to restrain him from coming near the house or visiting the children.

During the divorce hearing, Hyde's attorney pressed Frances for any concealed motive behind her desire to end the marriage. "Mrs. Hyde, the doctor wants to ask one question, and in the kindest way I want to ask it," he said. "Was your action in this matter because you believed or had any suspicion of him being guilty of the crimes charged against him?"

"Absolutely not," she answered quickly. "I stand just as I always stood."

"You said that you not only believed, but you knew he was innocent?" the lawyer asked.

"I absolutely believe him to be innocent," she replied.

A few days later, the former Mrs. Bennett Clark Hyde and her mother, Maggie Swope, were reunited in forgiveness and harmony.

Doctor Hyde's activities over the following months are not fully recorded. A ruined man, socially and financially, he struggled to make a living, at one point taking work as a truck driver and mechanic. He returned to his boyhood home of Lexington, Missouri, a charming town known for its antebellum courthouse and for the Wentworth Military Academy, Hyde's secondary alma mater. A sister, Mrs. E. N. Hopkins, still lived in the community and presumably helped him fit back in.

With borrowed money, Hyde took a course in ear, nose, and throat surgery in New York and eventually resumed his medical practice in rooms overlooking the courthouse. Lexington had welcomed him back. He attracted enough patients to afford him a decent if austere living in rooms above his office. Again he taught Sunday school in the Baptist Church where his father had preached the gospel.

In August of 1929, Hyde was interviewed by a senior writer for the *Kansas City Star,* A. B. MacDonald. The reporter found Hyde's appearance little changed over the last fifteen years, though he was graying and a bit heavier. His office was filled with books, as many literary classics, it seemed, as medical volumes. These were his solace, Hyde explained. As he spoke of the ruined years of humiliation, jail, and divorce, he paused occasionally to recite pertinent passages from Kipling, Goldsmith, and Shakespeare.

Former friends had once advised him to exile himself in China or Africa, Hyde said. At one time he had even considered suicide, though the act was forbidden by his Christian faith. Sensing that MacDonald was about to offer his sympathies, Hyde objected: "Don't pity me. Whatever you do, don't pity me.... I have been crucified, yes. I have suffered as no other man has ever suffered.... I have never whined nor played for sympathy. I do not ask nor seek it now. I ask only for justice, simple justice."

Shortly before midnight on August 8, 1934, the 62-year-old surgeon strolled to the office of a Lexington newspaper to check the returns from an election held the previous day. As he walked around the front counter he suddenly stopped, swayed dizzily, and fell to the floor dead. A physician said he'd been struck down by a brain hemorrhage.

Hyde was buried in the family plot in Lexington's shady old

Machpelah Cemetery. The grave itself is unmarked.

Once the murder case finally receded into old news, the Swope family saga faded accordingly as a popular topic. The papers still printed occasional feature stories about the celebrated mystery. But news of the family itself gradually dwindled into a sparse record of decline and obscurity.

There were marriages, a death, human-interest tidbits on back pages. Several of the younger Swopes gravitated to the West Coast, others of the family stayed behind, their destinies as diverse as any clan's. What was plain to everyone who kept up with the once-privileged people on the hill was that the Swope fortune was not what it had been. Not by a very long way.

Perhaps the dreariest fate among the heirs was that of the Colonel's nephew and namesake, Tom Swope Junior. Once the manager of the family dairy farm with its fine stone residence and outbuildings, he managed to lose the property and most of his inheritance during the Great Depression. To support his family he was reduced to working a $70-a-month job as a night watchman at Swope Park. The irony was not lost on a witty columnist for the *Star*, who reported—with some relish—that Tom's wife had once owned jewelry worth $50,000.

Frances Swope Hyde came out far better. Apparently through superior skills at money management—or perhaps through good advice—she maintained a comfortable lifestyle throughout the lean times. After the divorce she moved from the Forest Avenue address to a spacious if unassuming house at 3838 Charlotte Street, where she continued to rear her two children. A newspaper photograph showed her at the opening of a new skyscraper, the Professional Building, on one of the old Swope lots. Frances never remarried.

The first of the Colonel's legatees to die in the aftermath of the murder case was Sarah Swope, who had been in her early teens during the months of horror and disease. Predictably, Sarah's death at age 20 raised suspicions—never justified—that her health had been permanently weakened by her own bout with typhoid.

In August 1911—even before the second trial—Lucy Lee Swope piled further distress on her mother by eloping with the man who would become her first husband. One can only imagine the scene when Mrs. Swope learned of Lucy's conjugal choice. He was a traveling shoe salesman called "Handsome Billy" Byrne, who had once owned a shop on Petticoat Lane. Byrne was no doubt as handsome as the nickname suggested, but Lucy grew disenchanted with him. In 1922 she filed for divorce on grounds of cruelty because he had criticized her cooking. She remarried, and with her second husband lived in Los Angeles.

Tom Swope Junior also spent the rest of his days in California, as did his sister Margaret, who had married in 1912. The second youngest of the Swope children, Stella, married and settled in Westchester County, New York.

Mrs. Swope, her fortune much reduced, seems to have spent less and less time in the mansion. She had always enjoyed California and almost certainly paid long visits to her children and grandchildren in the West. For a time the great house in Independence was occupied only by a caretaker and his wife. Perhaps it held too many ghosts for anyone's comfort, but more likely it was the cost of maintaining the mansion that forced Mrs. Swope to sell it in 1923 to the Reorganized Church of Jesus Christ of Latter Day Saints for use as a school.

Maggie Swope's *place,* as class-conscious Missourians might have said, was in the halls of wealth and prestige, even if she possessed neither. In her waning years, she did find a home that carried reminders of the grandeur she had once enjoyed. The thirty-one-room Vaile mansion is a radically opulent Victorian showplace on the east side of Independence, and Mrs. Swope must have visited it often when she—and it—were in palmier circumstances. It was eventually turned into a "sanitarium" for the elderly, a perfect home for Mrs. Swope during her declining years. On January 21, 1942, she died there at the age of 87.

Her estate had been whittled away by long-ago legal costs, the loss of properties such as the family farm, and perhaps by unwise extravagances. When the will was filed, newspaper readers were amazed to learn she'd left assets of only $3,000, to be shared among her five surviving children. It came to $600 each.

Fortunes might dissipate, prominence crumble, but like the rich of all civilizations, the Swopes left monuments to remember them by. Not that their graves (with one exception) are grand in the least: The Swope resting places in Mount Washington Cemetery are marked only by stone tablets flush to the turf, while Frances Hyde and her children lie under modest, low-lying stones in nearby Elmwood Cemetery. The memorial to Uncle Thomas Swope, however, is quite another matter. Alone, it assures that the family name will be exalted as long as Kansas Citians visit the park he founded.

Situated on a bluff toward the east end of the park, it is a graceful structure of Doric columns flanking a bronze tablet, on which the old gent's left profile appears in bas-relief. The inscription below—not the Latin epitaph Swope himself had written—is simple and dignified: "His wisdom conceived, his generosity gave to the people of Kansas City this expanse of field and forest for their perpetual enjoyment." The Colonel lies beneath the granite floor.

In remembrance of her elder son, Chrisman, Mrs. Swope gave his old college, Westminster, a large, handsome gothic chapel that stood on the Fulton, Missouri, campus from 1919 to 1967 (it was razed after structural problems were found).

What might have served as the truest memorial of all—the most telling monument to the family's fate and the transience of privilege—was the residence on the crest of the Swope hill. The mansion was built as solidly as any citadel and was surely as conspicuous, especially in winter when the trees were bare and the walls of reddish-brown masonry thrust above the snowy lawn.

Following the closure of the church school during the Depression, the house for a time was occupied only by a caretaker. It was then reopened as a sewing center for church ladies selling clothes and quilts to benefit the poor. The interior remained undamaged, although the mansion for years had been a venue for Halloween parties by the children of Independence. Even the stained-glass windows in the dining room were not so much as chipped.

After the sewing center shut down, the place began to attract trespassers and vandals. Church leaders decided the land the house stood on would have greater utility than the building itself, and in 1960, a time of little reverence for historic architecture, the demolition crews arrived. Down crumbled the walls, porches, stately rooms, and lordly tower. For a time, the bricks were for sale.

Most passersby today would never know a mansion had ever stood there. The property is now an RV park and recreational facility for visiting Latter-Day Saints paying homage to the Missouri town once considered the site of the Mormon Zion.

Before the Swope house was knocked down, however, it got a final nod from the press. The *Kansas City Star* in July 1960 published an article describing the fall of the House of Swope. Among other details, writer Joe Lastelic reported a curious discovery by workers as they were clearing a roomful of trash. What they'd come across was a quaint, turn-of-the-century stethoscope, a foot long, with a wooden bell to be placed over the heart and two rubber tubes connected to ivory earpieces.

Could anyone be blamed for imagining—for *wanting to believe*— that the artifact had once lain coiled in the leather valise of Bennett Clark Hyde, MD?

Chapter 22

From the first day of research, the author writing a book about the Hyde-Swope case faces a queue of questions that seems to stretch on forever, and he aspires (absurdly) to answer each and every one of them—especially, of course, the big one: Did Bennett Clark Hyde murder Thomas Hunton Swope on October 3, 1909? That would be a daunting challenge if the case had happened last month. From the distance of a century, any hope of exposing the whole truth about the affair is about as futile as trying to locate the True Cross. Not that one cannot learn a lot from thousands of pages of testimony, sworn statements, letters and memoirs, autopsy reports, laboratory notes, nurses' logs, maps, and period newspaper stories. But what this author wouldn't give for three days of face-to-face interviews with the dead!

This may be why no factual, book-length chronicle of the case has been published until now. Articles by the score, yes. One good chapter in a midcentury book of local history and at least one hilariously embellished account in a "true crime" magazine of the '40s. The story has been approached as fiction, cited in legal texts, even performed on stage as a discussion piece for lawyers and law students at the University of Missouri–Kansas City. In these tellings, the lack of a definitive verdict is no real loss. It merely heightens the tale's creepy allure.

But the reader seems to deserve more from a book that tries to lay out the facts more fully and reliably than previous accounts have been able to do. And still, even with more details to feed more speculations and debates, no one will ever know for certain whether Hyde murdered Swope. Or indeed whether there was any murder at all.

Throughout the research for this book, it became a habit to ask myself how I might have viewed the testimony if I had been on the jury. One overall impression is that the State mounted a much more compelling case—in every respect but one. That one exception might have led to a different verdict had the trial taken place in a more sophisticated era of forensic science.

The State's experts in pathology and chemistry were a mixed crew. Toxicologists Walter Haines and Victor Vaughan come off as conscientious and competent by the standards of the day. But their leader, Doctor Hektoen, for all his charismatic braininess and confidence, fell into such a humiliating trap—under questioning about autopsies on frozen corpses—that in retrospect you wonder why he didn't pull the State's entire scientific case down with him.

By contrast, Hyde's attorney Frank Walsh did a superb job of throwing the prosecution's experts off balance. Walsh's strategy of hiring a first-rate medical researcher from Fordham University to orchestrate the defense's scientific counterattack—which included giving Walsh himself an intensive short course in pathology—should have paid off decisively for his client. In fact it got Hyde's case practically nowhere. As often as not, the jury appeared to be bewildered or simply bored by all the technical fencing and medical jargon.

What really got to the jurors was the human factor, the personal tales of evil and accusation told by witnesses they could understand, who inhabited the rooms where those dreadful things happened. These included the nurses, especially the estimable Pearl Kellar, who simply could not be shaken from her testimony pointing to Hyde's guilt. If I had been on the jury I might have felt as I did a century later while reading the nurses' statements—that these devoted caregivers often revealed more compassion, good sense, and even clinical proficiency, than did the doctors they worked for.

Another effective witness was the bacteriologist E. L. Stewart, whose testimony linking Hyde to the typhoid outbreak was meticulous and damning. To this day, Stewart's detailed observations are hard to dismiss and they leave open the real possibility that Hyde did indeed sneak those germs into the household. Hyde's overeager attempts to convince everyone he was just another victim of the epidemic are laughable. Stewart obviously was convinced that Hyde inoculated himself with typhoid bacilli to dodge further suspicion. It's very hard to disagree.

Of the family members brought to the stand, Mrs. Swope was both the most forcible and the most moving. No wonder the State saved her for last. Her storytelling skills, enriched by deep, genuine passions, yielded a performance worthy of a Barrymore.

While the prosecution fielded more than enough strong witnesses, the defense based much of its case on the hope that two people—two figures at the dark core of the mystery—could move the jury toward acquittal. Those two were Clark and Frances Hyde.

It is mystifying why a defendant of such brains and innate charm should have had such trouble suppressing his worst traits during the most crucial test of his life. Hyde might have won over the jury with an earnest show of openness and respect for his questioners. Instead, he fell back on a prickly defensiveness that could only have cost him sympathy among the jurors. The more harshly he was cross-examined by the relentless Virgil Conkling, the more flustered and defiant Hyde became. No one knows to what extent this behavior influenced the verdict, but it surely had an impact.

Walsh took a risk in calling the intensely loyal Frances to the witness chair. She yearned to defend her husband and no witness could have done so more ardently. Her very presence before the jury was as engaging and poignant as Walsh could have hoped. But the flip side of this lovely wife's devotion—her rotelike support of every claim and denial Hyde made in his defense—dashed her credibility. In her stand-by-your-man role, she was simply too good to be true.

The verdict may have been inevitable in the environment of the first trial. The months of lurid news, the players' celebrity status, the power of human passions over objective science, virtually demanded the crowning of a certified villain. The final trial three years later took place in a much calmer atmosphere and was fairer by far. Which doesn't mean, of course, that the ultimate freeing of Doctor Hyde was any closer to real justice than his original conviction.

The discomfort of never knowing is what weighs on the writer. There ought to be a better ending. I avoid the word "conclusion," because there is nothing conclusive about this strange case.

To help provide one, I prevailed upon the kindness of a widely respected toxicologist, Doctor Edward M. Bottei. As medical director of the Iowa Statewide Poison Control Center, Bottei oversees a system that responds to many thousands of emergency calls each year and distributes up-to-date information on a wide range of poison hazards.

Doctor Bottei agreed to discuss aspects of the Swope case as long as his views were accompanied by a large caveat: the understanding that any opinions were strictly conjectural and were based on incomplete and very dated materials. The latter consisted of autopsy and laboratory reports, testimony concerning events surrounding Colonel Swope's death, and accounts of the dying man's symptoms.

As a preface to Bottei's remarks, it may help to revisit the events of October 3, 1909. Certain details were strongly disputed by Hyde. The times are approximate.

8:00 a.m.: Hyde orders Nurse Kellar to give Swope a white "digestive" capsule, which he hands to her from a small box. The old man balks at taking the medicine.

8:30 a.m.: Swope finally takes the capsule and lies back to read his newspapers.

8:50 a.m.: "Blowing sounds" are heard from the Colonel, who suddenly is seized by a violent convulsion. His head is thrown back, his stiffened body quivers, his limbs shake uncontrollably. Guttural noises rise from his throat, as if he were trying to speak. His mouth emits a thick, white substance.

8:55 a.m.: Hyde tells Kellar the patient is suffering from apoplexy (a stroke). Kellar has doubts. In her experience, apoplectic seizures, of the kind that struck Moss Hunton two nights earlier, are much less violent than this attack.

9:00 a.m.: The convulsion ends and Swope sinks into a general collapse. He is semiconscious. His pulse shoots up to a rapid 140. He retches dryly and urinates.

9:05 a.m.: Swope appears to rally and speaks several lucid sentences, among them: "Oh my God, I wish I were dead. I wish I had not taken that medicine."

9:15 a.m.: Hyde asks Kellar to inject one-sixtieth of a grain of strychnine as a heart stimulant. She is surprised by the order, given the fact that Swope's pulse is already running quite high.

9:40 a.m.: Kellar administers a second strychnine shot, as directed.

10:00 a.m.: Kellar gives a third strychnine injection, which she claims was her last. Hyde later testifies, however, that four or five such injections were given throughout the morning and afternoon.

2:00–2:30 p.m.: Swope is still unconscious. His calves turn a dark purple and his knees contract one at a time. Kellar tests his eyes for brain activity but perceives none.

3:30 p.m.: Kellar notices a slight movement of one eyelid and thinks Swope may be emerging from his coma. He remains comatose and his breathing grows shallower.

7:05 p.m.: Clark and Frances Hyde remain at the Colonel's bedside while Kellar is at dinner. The old man's breathing is almost inaudible, the breaths coming at half-minute intervals.

7:15 p.m.: Colonel Swope dies.

Doctor Bottei cautioned that any speculation regarding Swope's death had to take into account the Colonel's age and frailty. His fainting episodes could suggest he had suffered previous strokes, preludes to the one that may have killed him. If the latter had been an embolic stroke—undetectable in the brain except with a microscope—that could explain why pathologists found no blood indicating a brain hemorrhage.

What the autopsy did turn up, however, was a suspicious amount of strychnine in the Colonel's liver (54 milligrams per one kilogram of tissue). Even if Swope had excreted some poison from his system during the hours after the seizure, the remaining concentration in the liver "was definitely within the lethal range" found in the organs of deceased strychnine victims, Bottei said.

Then there was the convulsion itself. While it could have been stroke-induced, Bottei said, it seemed to him more suggestive of a seizure triggered by poisoning. For one thing, the victim's alertness almost immediately after the attack is common in poison cases, whereas stroke victims usually take longer, several minutes to hours, to struggle back to consciousness.

Strychnine kills by causing muscles throughout the body to contract in severe spasms. Eventually the muscles become so weakened that the victim is unable to breathe and dies from asphyxiation. The time between ingestion of a fatal dose and death depends on many variables, Bottei said, but an estimate—if the lethal dose were given all at once—would be from minutes to less than an hour.

"Given the data that I've been presented," the toxicologist said, "it is very possible that Colonel Swope died of strychnine poisoning."

During the trial it was argued that the old man might have taken in traceable amounts of the poison through his long use of a tonic containing strychnine. That theory was challenged by testimony that he'd quit taking the elixir many days before he died. So the question remained—how did Swope's body collect so much strychnine?

The State tried repeatedly to sell its unsubstantiated theory that cyanide had been mixed with strychnine in the fatal pill. If Doctor Bottei's premise is correct, cyanide had nothing to do with it. In fact a dose of that poison, blended with strychnine or not, would probably have killed the Colonel within minutes.

Bottei proposed a scenario—never before advanced, to my knowledge—that suggests in detail how death might have come to Colonel Swope. He was careful to note that the scenario was "plausible, not perfect." Nevertheless, it seems to me a more cohesive deduction than previous ones and definitely more chilling. For the Bennett Clark Hyde it depicts (if real) is a more cunning, cruelly methodical murderer than his accusers imagined.

How Hyde could have murdered the Colonel:

Hyde gives Colonel Swope the capsule, in which he has put a measure of strychnine. The amount is a *sublethal* dose, however—much less than the capsule's 5-grain capacity. The old man is not to die swiftly but to fail by slow degrees. Witnesses must believe that a stroke did him in, not some rapid-acting poison.

After Swope's convulsion subsides, Hyde directs Nurse Kellar to give shots of strychnine at intervals of fifteen to twenty minutes. Kellar and Hyde later dispute the number of injections Swope received. She testifies it was only three; he claims that "about five hypodermics of strychnine" were given throughout the day.

Hyde insists the shots are needed to boost the Colonel's pulse, which he repeatedly describes as weak. Just as often, Kellar finds it high or normal. In fact, Swope's heart rate is irrelevant to Hyde's true purpose.

In sublethal strychnine poisoning, the fierce muscular contractions would be expected to cease in time and the victim to recover. By giving "booster" shots, however, Hyde assures that the poison's ravages will continue hour after punishing hour, never abating, not quite killing. By evening, of course, the Colonel's exhausted muscles can work no longer and breathing stops. "Apoplexy" takes another member of the family.

Regardless of her honesty, Nurse Kellar's version of events—indicating that the last injection came at around 10 a.m.—carries no guarantee of the whole truth. However, Hyde had plenty of minutes alone with the patient to give a shot or two (or three or more) on his own. Also, should any household snoop or doctor have suspected that poison was Colonel Swope's vehicle to the grave, Hyde could readily have asserted that it was Kellar, not he, who filled and wielded that needle. Could the conscientious nurse have made some ghastly mistake?

Doctor Bottei would be the last to suggest that his hypothesis trumps all others put forward over the years. Lacking the luxury of time travel, he will never touch a slice of Swope's liver or get a peek at that frozen brain. If Hyde left a written confession, it has never come to light in some newly discovered secret drawer.

In fact, as much as his enemies proclaimed Hyde's guilt, it's likely even they had doubts. John Paxton, the Swope family attorney, wavered privately. In a memoir composed many years later, his daughter Mary wrote: "This is the only criminal case that I can recall my father's association with. He did not have that insensitivity of spirit required for a criminal lawyer. He told me later, 'In the day time I would be absolutely certain that Doctor Hyde was guilty, but I would lie awake at night and wonder if I were trying to hang an innocent man.'"

The goal of this book is not to hang an innocent man. While I come down pretty solidly on the side of Hyde's accusers, I'm still not entirely comfortable there. Which leaves only the hope that this version of the truth—flawed, incomplete, contradictory—will pass muster among the ghosts.

— THE END —

Sources

James A. Reed Papers, Western Historical Manuscript Collection, Kansas City

"James Alexander Reed (1861–1944) Papers" [introduction]. Updated 22 August 2003.

Autopsy reports (2). Unsigned, undated notes on T. H. Swope autopsy of 12 January 1910.

Certificate of Death, James Moss Hunton, 1 October 1909.

Certificate of Death, Thomas Hunton Swope, 4 October 1909.

Churchill, Rose, RN. [First] Statement, 9 February 1910; Second Statement, undated.

Clements, Annie. Complaint against B. C. Hyde before Kansas City Board of Police Commissioners, 12 February 1910.

Columbus Laboratories, Chicago. "Cyanide Symptoms in Col. Thomas Swope's Case" and "Cyanide Symptoms in Chrisman Swope's Case." Reports to James A. Reed, 25 October 1911.

Copridge, Ida. Statement before J. Paxton, F. Hall, undated.

Firman, J. M. Detective report of E. C. Hyde's activities in New York, 14–16 December [1909]. Dated 8 March 1910.

Gilwee, James P. Affidavits. 9 and 11 Oct. 1911.

Gordon, Elizabeth, RN. [First] Statement, 9 February 1910. Second Statement, undated.

Grand Jury Indictment of B. C. Hyde. 5 March 1910.

Hall, Frank J., MD. Statement to Virgil Conkling, undated.

Houlehan, Anna, RN. Memorandum, Statement, Supplemental Statement, undated.

Hyde Indictment. Jackson County Criminal Court. January 1910.

Kellar, Pearl Virginia, RN. Statement before Paxton, Atwood, Mastin, et al. Independence, MO, 15 January 1910. Supplemental Statement, undated.

Patient Logs of Nurses Churchill, Gordon, Houlehan. 4, 6, 8, 13, 18 December 1909.

Paxton, John Gallatin. Deposition before F. Walsh, undated.

Perkins, John W., MD. "Cases of Typhoid at Mrs. Logan Swope's—Independence." 2 January 1910.

Perkins, John W., MD. Statement, undated.

"Protocol in Swope Case." Author unknown, undated.

Reed, James A. Analysis of bequests in Thomas H. Swope will, undated.

———. Case chronologies and other notes, 1909-10.

———. "Digest testimony of Bennett Clark Hyde." Undated.

———. Notes on interviews with Stuart S. Fleming, undated.

Spangler, Sylvester. Deposition before Frank Walsh, undated.

Stewart, Edward L., MD. Statement, undated.

Swope, Maggie C. Statement, Independence, MO, 21 January 1910.

Twyman, G. T., MD. Statement, Independence, MO, 22 January 1910.

Van Nuys, Lou E., RN. Statement, 9 February 1910. Second Statement, undated.

Vaughn, Victor C., MD. Report of toxicological examination. Department of Medicine and Surgery, University of Michigan. Ann Arbor, 4 February 1910.

"Were Swopes Poisoned?" Editorial. *Fulton* (MO) *Gazette*, 21 January 1910.

Jackson County Historical Society Archives

Hyde, Bennett Clark. Biographical and genealogical notebooks. Unpublished, undated.

Hyde, Frances Swope. Unpublished memoir, undated.

"Path of Dr. Hyde on His Way ... to see Dr. Twyman for a 'Consultation.' " Map, undated.

Trial Transcripts, *State vs. Hyde,* Criminal District Court, Kansas City, MO, April 11–May 16, 1910. Microfilm, Vols. 1–7, pp. 623–4229.

Patrick Kelly Papers (private collection)

Digest of Decision of Missouri Supreme Court in *State vs. Hyde,* 1911. Undated.

Kelly, Patrick. Summaries of trial testimony. Kansas City, MO, undated.

Minor, Eleanor. Unpublished memoir, undated.

Missouri Supreme Court. Decision in *State vs. Hyde.* 11 April 1911.

Paxton, Mary. Unpublished memoir, undated.

Other Primary Sources

Maps of Kansas City area, 1909–1910. Missouri Valley Special Collections, Kansas City Public Library.

Mencken, H. L. "James A. Reed of Missouri." *American Mercury,* April 1929.

Michaels, William C. "The Local Bar Forty Years Ago." *Kansas City Bar Bulletin* 14, no. 1 (1938).

Papers and photographs, Swope mansion, 1923–1950s. Community of Christ World Headquarters, Independence, Missouri.

Reed, James A. "The Pestilence of Fanaticism." *American Mercury,* May 1925.

"Swope Death Mystery." Editorial. *Kansas City Journal,* 23 January 1910.

"The Grand Jury Testimony." Edited verbatim testimony of Jackson County, MO. Grand Jury hearings, 12 Feb.–5 March. *Kansas City Star,* 24 April 1909, pp. 1–8.

U.S. Bureau of the Census. Census Report, 1910.

Newspapers

Kansas City Journal. Selected articles, 1909–1911.

Kansas City Post. All issues, 4 December 1909–26 June 1910.

Kansas City Star and *Times.* All issues, 2 October 1909–29 June 1910.

Kansas City Star and *Times, Kansas City Journal, Kansas City Post.* Wide assortment of news and feature articles, 1911–1986.

Kansas City Star and *Times.* Retail display ads. 1, 3 October 1909.

MacDonald, A. B. "Profile of B. C. Hyde." *Kansas City Star,* 28 July 1929.

Interviews

Bernauer, Barbara (Assistant Archivist, Community of Christ), interview with Giles Fowler, 2006.

Bottei, Edward M. (Medical Director, Iowa Statewide Poison Control Center), interview with Giles Fowler, November 2008.

Crick, Bill (former restoration carpenter at Swope mansion), interview with Giles Fowler, 2007.

Kelly, Patrick (Dean Emeritus, School of Law, University of Missouri–Kansas City), interviews with Giles Fowler, 2006.

McFerrin, Anne (Kansas City Parks Archivist), interview with Giles Fowler, 2007.

Background Information/Secondary Sources

American Bar Association. "Frequently Asked Questions about the Grand Jury System." Online at http://www.abanet.org/media/faqjury.html.

Balentine, Jerry, DO, FACEP. "Typhoid Fever." MedicineNet.com. Online at http://www.medicinenet.com/typhoid_fever/article.htm.

Coleman, Richard P. *The Kansas City Establishment: Leadership through Two Centuries in a Midwestern Metropolis.* Manhattan, KS: KS Publishing, 2007.

"Facts about Strychnine." Centers for Disease Control and Prevention, Emergency Preparedness and Response. Online at http://emergency.cdc.gov/agent/strychnine/basics/facts.asp. Updated February 22, 2006; May 14, 2003.

"Frank Walsh." Institute for Labor Studies, University of Missouri–Kansas City. Online at http://www.umkc.edu/labor-ed/history3.htm.

"Frederick Gilmer Bonfils." *Encyclopaedia Britannica,* 2009. Britannica Online Encyclopedia, http://www.britannica.com/EBchecked/topic/73007/Frederick-Gilmer-Bonfils.

Garwood, Darrell. *Crossroads of America: The Story of Kansas City.* New York: W. W. Norton, 1948.

Gilday, John P. "Memorial to Frank P. Walsh." *Kansas City Bar Bulletin* 15, no. 7 (1939): 3–6.

Haskell, Harry. *Boss Busters and Sin Hounds: Kansas City and Its Star.* Columbia: University of Missouri Press, 2007.

Keeley, Mary Paxton. "Moss Hunton's Gifts to Children More Than Money." *Jackson County Historical Society* Winter 1970: 11.

"Typhoid Fever." In *CDC Health Information for International Travel,* 2008, edited by Paul M. Arquin, Phyllis E. Kozarsky, and Christie Reed. Philadelphia: Elsevier Mosby, 2007. Online at http://wwwn.cdc.gov/travel/yellowBookCh4-Typhoid.aspx.

"Winifred Sweet Black." *Encyclopaedia Britannica,* 2008. Britannica Online Encyclopedia, http://www.britannica.com/EBchecked/topic/67469/Winifred-Sweet-Black.

About the Author

Born in Kansas City in 1934, Giles Fowler joined the city's prominent newspaper, the *Kansas City Star,* after graduating from Westminster College and the Columbia University Graduate School of Journalism. During his twenty-four years at the *Star,* Fowler worked as a reporter, film and theater critic, and editor of the paper's Sunday magazine, and also spent a year writing for *The Times* of London. He transferred this considerable background in journalism to teaching in 1981 and held positions at Kansas State University and Iowa State University's Greenlee School of Journalism and Communication, from which he retired in 2002. While at Iowa State, Fowler pursued his interest in factual writing as a literary form, creating two courses in that area. He has lectured for national and state writing seminars and became a Teaching Fellow at the Poynter Institute, which offers resources to journalism students, teachers, and practitioners. Fowler has contributed academic articles to *Journalism History, Journalism Educator,* and *Journalism Quarterly* and a chapter on John Steinbeck to *A Sourcebook of American Literary Journalism,* as well as short fiction to the *Sewanee Review.* He currently resides in Ames, Iowa.